QUEEN
VICTORIA

QUEEN
VICTORIA

Juliet Gardiner

C&B

COLLINS & BROWN

First published in Great Britain in 1997
by Collins & Brown Limited
London House
Great Eastern Wharf
Parkgate Road
London SW11 4NQ

British Library Cataloguing-in-Publication Data:
A catalogue record for this book is available from the British Library.

ISBN 1 85585 414 7 (hb)
ISBN 1 85585 469 4 (pb)

1 3 5 7 9 8 6 4 2

Conceived, designed and edited by Collins & Brown Limited

Editorial Director: Sarah Hoggett
Editors: Katie Bent and Emma Shackleton
Picture Research: Philippa Lewis
Art Director: Roger Bristow
Designer: Helen Collins
Assistant Designer: Debbie Marshall

Reproduction by Centre Media, London
Printed and bound in Great Britain by Bath Colour Books

FRONT COVER:
Queen Victoria by Franz Xaver Winterhalter, 1845.
(The Royal Collection © 1997 Her Majesty The Queen.)

TITLE PAGE:
State portrait of Queen Victoria by Franz Xaver Winterhalter, 1859.
(The Royal Collection © 1997 Her Majesty The Queen.)

BACK COVER:
*Selection of scrapbook ephemera produced to celebrate Victoria's
Jubilees in 1887 and 1897.*
(Amoret Tanner Collection.)

CONTENTS

INTRODUCTION   6

'I AM VERY YOUNG ...'   10

VIVAT VICTORIA REGINA!   28

THE ROYAL CONNECTION   42

'MY BELOVED ALBERT ...'   58

ROYAL CONSTRUCTIONS   78

'AN INCONSOLABLE LOSS'   98

'DIZZY & THE GRAND OLD MAN'   118

A GLORIOUS REIGN   134

ENDNOTES   154

FURTHER READING   157

INDEX   158

ACKNOWLEDGEMENTS AND
PICTURE CREDITS   160

INTRODUCTION

'DEAR QUEEN', WROTE NINE-YEAR-OLD Catherine Smith from Dumfries in Scotland to Queen Victoria in September 1896, 'I write to say how glad I am you have reigned so long, and I hope you may live for many more years.' When she read this tribute from a loyal subject, the Queen was seventy-seven years old and the next year was to be her Diamond Jubilee, celebrating her sixty-year reign. It was an unprecedented event for Victoria was the longest-reigning sovereign in British history. On the twenty-third of that month she had noted with quiet satisfaction in her journal that in the royal longevity stakes she had overtaken George III. Ten years previously her Golden Jubilee had celebrated Victoria's fifty years on the throne, and the fact that she had notched up another decade was, of course, a cause for celebration and admiration, but also for perplexity. What was the anniversary to be designated? The Home Secretary certainly 'did not personally care for "Diamond Jubilee"' and explained why:

> 'Jubilee' has got its meaning from the old Jewish law, and is certainly inseparably connected with a notion of fifty years. 'Diamond' is understood because it is used to mark the completion of sixty years of married life – Silver twenty-five, Golden fifty, Diamond sixty (at least I fancy this is so). 'Diamond Jubilee' is a combination and though not strictly correct, yet

RIGHT *'The First of May, 1851' by Franz Xaver Winterhalter. On his 82nd birthday, the Duke of Wellington proffers a gift to his godson and namesake, Prince Arthur, on the occasion of his first birthday. Prince Albert holds the plans of the Crystal Palace which can be seen in the background.*

intelligible. Somebody has suggested 'Jubilissimee'. This would not, I think, take on.[1]

But recognising that he was no wordsmith, Sir Matthew Ridley conceded 'it is not for me to raise objection if the Queen has a fancy for it. And apparently it is likely to catch on'. Which it did.

The Jubilee fell on 20 June 1897, a Sunday, so official celebrations were postponed until the Tuesday. On Monday the Queen left Windsor by train for London, where she was welcomed by a number of dignitaries at Paddington Station. She then 'proceeded at a slow trot, with a Sovereign's escort of the 1st Life Guards' to Buckingham Palace. It was a hot day but 'dense crowds' lined the route and on the way the royal coach, in which sat the diminutive and rather frail Queen – dressed in the customary black that she had worn since the death of her 'beloved angel', Prince Albert, the Prince Consort, thirty-five years earlier – passed 'under a lovely arch, bearing the motto, "Our Hearts thy Throne".'

Victoria was also so regally aware that her long tenure of the throne gave her a plurality of meanings of which 'Queen of the People's Hearts' was only one. Her official titles were Queen of Great Britain and Ireland, and Empress of India. Though the latter was supposed to be only for communication east of Suez, the royal signature invariably read 'Victoria R.I.' – Victoria Regina et Imperatrix. She could also add 'Grandmother of Europe' to her credentials, for by the time of her Diamond Jubilee Victoria had seven surviving children from a family of nine, all of whom save one had married into European royal houses, tightening the web of dynastic connection and influence by producing heirs to the thrones of Germany, Russia, Greece, Romania, Norway and Spain.

Both the Jubilees – the Golden in 1887 and the Diamond ten years later – were occasions to demonstrate and reinforce her domains. The 1887 celebrations had seen the pageant of majesty when the crowned heads of Europe, from the Royal Highnesses of nation states to the Serene Highnesses of tiny principalities, had flocked to pay homage to the longest-serving member of their confederacy. The streets of London dazzled with the retinues of royalty, including the thirty-two princes who were directly related to Victoria. Even those who had no wish to partake in the celebrations, like the radical pianoforte salesman of George Gissing's novel *In the Year of the Jubilee* (1894), were inclined to take 'a walk in the evening … to see the people and the illuminations'.

In 1897, Imperial Britain was to be represented: the 'Empire on which the sun never sets' of more than three hundred million people. The Colonial Secretary, Joseph Chamberlain, was determined that British Imperial hegemony should be paraded at a time when European expansionism was threatening that position. So this time it was 'men from every part of the world … Sikhs from India, the Hong-Kong

ABOVE *The commodification of a Queen. Advertisements for cooking stoves and pneumatic tyres produced to celebrate the Diamond Jubilee. The 'Patent Cooking Stove' shows Victoria receiving tributes from her subjects. The connection may seem tangential, but both monarch and vulcanised rubber were renowned for their survival factor – and the Queen had, on occasions, bowled along on a bicycle when younger.*

BELOW *A commemorative plate produced for the Golden Jubilee in 1887.*

THE STATE CARRIAGE.

Drawn by CYNICUS from a design by J. TIMEWELL, 141 Gower Street, London, W.C.

ABOVE *'The State Carriage', a cartoon of 1895 depicting the state as a vast juggernaut with spiked wheels grinding the populous down through taxation and rent, whilst holding out a selection of carrots to urge on the toilers. At the rear, meagre charity is distributed as the destitute pile into the workhouse. Queen Victoria sits atop the monstrous edifice.*

police from China, and the Houssas from West Africa ...' who came to London. The Prime Minister, Lord Salisbury, was satisfied that the celebrations had been 'a splendid success' and predicted that they would 'live in history as a unique and unequalled demonstration of the attachment which has grown more and more in intensity between the Sovereign of a vast Empire and her subjects of every clime.'[2]

By any reckoning Victoria's had been an extraordinary reign – and one that was to continue into the next century. From an eighteen-year-old girl, raised in a hothouse of intrigue and distrust, to a rotund matriarch whose image was reproduced on mugs, plates, soup bowls, tea towels, advertisements for beverages, sewing machines and bicycles, the monarchy had undergone a remarkable transformation in the person of Victoria.

Victoria's reign had not always run smoothly: her partisanship towards the Whigs, her youthful determination to keep them in and the Tories out of office, her view of foreign policy as a family affair, her bellicose support of British power overseas, her personal likes and sustained dislikes and, finally, her withdrawal from public life after the death of Albert, had all ensured that there could be no complacency that the stock of the monarchy had risen.

But with the help of the managerial skills and constitutional intelligence of Prince Albert, the monarchy had slowly metamorphosed into a paradoxical but sustainable model. The royal couple – and then the lone Queen – were exemplars of middle-class probity and ordinariness, whilst at the same time being symbols of majesty and the power that that suggests. Victoria and Albert seemed as far distant from Victoria's 'disgraceful uncles' as it was possible to be, and ever since her youthful accession everything conspired to keep it that way. Through example and display Victoria managed to create a genealogy that leap-frogged backwards, missing her immediate forebears and re-establishing the dignity of monarchy that had been lost since the eighteenth century, and at the same time epitomising values of family and hearth that might have been thought distinctly unregal. 'A family on the throne, is an interesting idea', wrote Walter Bagehot in 1867. 'It brings down the pride of sovereignty to the level of petty life ... But no feeling could be more like human nature than it is, and it is likely to be. The women ... care fifty times more for a marriage than a ministry.'[3]

It was a strategem that might have been in danger of 'letting the daylight in on magic' in Bagehot's phrase, but it proved a source of strength. So enshrined were those contradictory impressions, of the symbolic and the ordinary, that they were a legacy into the 1980s. On the one hand George V was so embedded in this mode that the nation mourned for 'dear old Dad' on his death in 1936, whilst on the other his granddaughter, Elizabeth II, went to her coronation dressed much as Victoria had to hers and riding in a similar gold-and-glass coach and horses through the streets of London.

There were other contradictions: as Victoria celebrated her Imperial role in 1897 there was a bitter war in the Transvaal, and her kingdom was rent asunder by the demand for Irish Home Rule. The Golden Jubilee hymn, with music by Arthur Sullivan, trumpeted:

> O royal Heart, with wide embrace
> For all her children yearning!
> O happy realm, such mother-grace
> With loyal love returning!
> Where England's flag flies wide unfurled,
> All tyrant's wrongs repelling

whereas a writer in *Vanity Fair* pointed out that: 'Although in these fifty years we have waged only one European war ... we have waged a great number of wars in Africa and Asia; wars for the most part unjust, waged without due cause, and without Declaration of War.'[4] As Victoria rejoiced at Britain's commanding position in Europe, rivalries over empire-building would erupt in the Great War only thirteen years after her death, when the protagonist would be her own grandson. In Britain, the 1890s was a decade of economic downturn with labour unrest and union activity. Many of Victoria's loyal subjects were living in poverty and whilst she involved herself in philanthropic projects she certainly saw no role for the state in alleviating hardship.

However, during her sixty-four years on the throne Victoria had learned well what her uncle Leopold had commended to her as 'the [very difficult] trade of a constitutional Sovereign'. The goodwill was kept in the family and handed down the generations pretty well intact for nearly a hundred years.

BELOW *A chart showing the comparative reigns from William the Conqueror to Queen Victoria, produced by Max Lindeman for the Diamond Jubilee in 1897 and now hanging in the pages' waiting-room at Osborne House. The column representing Victoria's reign (1837–1901) inches over that of George III (1760–1820) and is crowned with a triumphal urn, whilst the column of the decapitated Charles I stands broken and shrouded.*

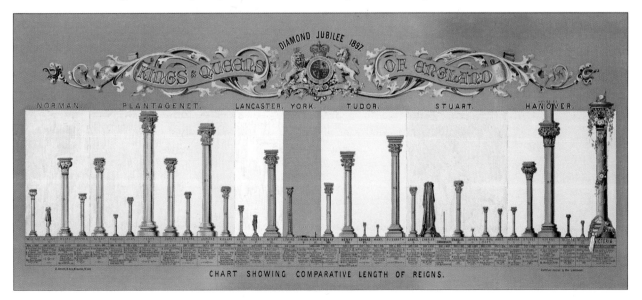

CHART SHOWING COMPARATIVE LENGTH OF REIGNS.

CHAPTER ONE

'I AM VERY YOUNG ...'

AT A QUARTER PAST FOUR in the morning of Monday 24 May 1819, 'a pretty little Princess, as plump as a partridge' was born at Kensington Palace, a large, recently refurbished redbrick building to the west of London. The infant's father, who 'had never quitted [her mother] for a moment the whole night ... had the satisfaction [after a labour that lasted six hours and a quarter] of witnessing the prosperous result of all our anxieties'. But these 'anxieties' were of greater moment than the usual concerns of an expectant father, for, in an adjacent, room were present 'the Archbishop of Canterbury, the Bishop of London, the Duke of Wellington and Lord Bathurst, Mr Vansittart, Mr Canning, besides the Duke of Sussex and Lord Lansdowne who were there as private friends'.[1]

The parents were the Duke and Duchess of Kent and the 'most perfect female child' would, it was hoped, be heir to the throne of England. But this destiny was by no means assured and the numerous intrigues and uncertainties that attended the 'race to the throne' were to colour the childhood of Victoria as they had dramatised the activities of the House of Hanover for the previous few years.

Victoria was the first – and indeed was to be the only – child of the Duke and Duchess of Kent. They had not long been married and they had married precisely for the purpose of begetting a royal heir – at least that had been the Duke's intention. For Edward, Duke of Kent, was the fourth son of the present king, George III. Under normal circumstances, on the death of George III the throne would have passed first to his oldest son, George, Prince of Wales, the Prince Regent, and then to his heir. But this was the rub. Charlotte, the only daughter of the disastrous and tempestuous marriage of the Prince Regent and his estranged wife, Caroline of Brunswick, had died in childbirth, aged twenty-one, in November 1817. Her son was stillborn. And none of George III's other offspring – he had fifteen children in all of whom twelve were still living in 1817 – had a legitimate heir between them.

At the time of Charlotte's death, her grandfather George III was himself infirm, blind and once more insane. Her premature demise thus signalled a desperate and unseemly contest between the royal sons to produce an heir to occupy the throne. This dynastic struggle seemed to epitomise the low esteem into which the royal family had fallen after the reign of the three Georges, 'an imbecile, a profligate and a buffoon'. In the year Victoria was born the poet Shelley wrote:

> An old, mad, blind, despised and dying King,
> Princes, the dregs of their dull race, who flow
> Through public scorn – mud from a muddy spring
> Rulers who neither see nor feel nor know,
> But leech-like to their fainting country cling.[2]

LEFT *Princess Victoria, aged four in 1823, from a portrait by Stephen Poyntz Denning.*

BELOW *Princess Charlotte, daughter of the future George IV and her husband, Prince Leopold of Saxe-Coburg. In May 1816 the 'capricious, self-willed and obstinate' princess married Leopold, who 'made me happy and a good woman'. Eighteen months later she died in childbirth.*

When Charlotte died, the Prince Regent, 'Prinny', was still married, though acrimoniously separated; he was fifty-five, grossly fat – when younger he had been mocked as the 'Prince of Whales' – and often drunk. The chances of him contracting a suitable marriage and producing an heir seemed remote.

The second son, Frederick, Duke of York, was hardly more propitious. His infidelities were legion and broadcast, and he was surrounded by a miasma of scandal. Baron Stockmar, a physician from Coburg, who had accompanied Prince Leopold to England as his private secretary when Leopold married Princess Charlotte, described him as being 'very bald and [having] a not very intelligent face: one can see that eating and drinking are everything to him'.[3] Frederick's wife, Princess Frederica of Prussia was 'odd', with eccentric habits and a menagerie of animals, including at least forty dogs, a collection of parrots and monkeys, but no children.

The third son, William, Duke of Clarence, on the other hand had ten children – all illegitimate. For twenty years he had lived with the actress, Mrs Jordan, but by 1811, despite the fact that she had worked throughout most of their common-law marriage and had contributed to the household expenses, William's debts had risen to such proportions that he had decided to abandon his helpmeet and solve his financial problems the only way he could think of: by making an advantageous marriage. He had paid off Mrs Jordan with a somewhat derisory settlement, but by the death of his niece he had not yet managed to achieve the marital state he had resolved upon. Finally the twenty-five-year-old Princess Adelaide of Saxe-Meiningen accepted the fifty-two-year-old Duke's offer and agreed to be his wife and stepmother to his much-loved ten children.

The fourth son, Edward, Duke of Kent, also had a long-standing unsanctioned 'marriage'. His mistress of twenty-seven years was a French woman who styled herself Julie de St Laurent and, like his older brother, the level of his debts had led the Duke of Kent to set off on the marital trail – unknown to Mme St Laurent.

The fifth son, Ernest, Duke of Cumberland, was the third husband of Princess Frederica of Mecklenburg-Strelitz, a woman who, it was rumoured, had killed off at least one husband. His mother had advised Ernest, who was universally loathed and described as 'hideous ... with one eye turned out of its place' and a vicious scar received at the Battle of Tournai in 1794, to stay out of England, and Parliament refused to grant him the customary marriage allowance. In 1817 there were no progeny of this union.

The sixth son, Augustus Frederick, Duke of Sussex, was regarded as a 'sincere and true-hearted creature with a great deal of good sense'.[4] However, his marriage in 1793 to Lady Augusta Murray had not received the sovereign's consent and thus it violated the Royal Marriages Act; the children were considered to be illegitimate and not in line for the succession. This marriage ended in 1801 and the Duke became enamoured of Lady Cecilia Buggin, a widow and daughter of the second Earl of Arran, with whom he lived until his first wife died, when they married. Again, however, this union was unsanctioned and any children would be regarded as illegitimate.

The seventh son, Adolphus, the Duke of Cambridge, was unmarried. He spent many hours conducting scientific experiments, was adept at the violin, sang, and wore a blond wig. But he did not keep a mistress and, perhaps as a consequence, was unhampered by debt. He may, or may not, in these circumstances, have been regarded as the most likely to be in a position, and of an inclination, to provide a legitimate heir. He was, in fact, the first to marry: a little over a week after the death of Princess Charlotte he despatched a proposal to Augusta, Princess of Hesse Cassel, and she accepted.

Thus Victoria's 'disreputable uncles', as she was to refer to them, and her not entirely reputable father.

Some five months after the death of Princess Charlotte the business of the succession was officially declared open. On 13 April 1818 the Prince Regent, on behalf of his brothers, petitioned Parliament to grant funds to enable him 'to make the necessary arrangements for this important purpose'. The debate in Parliament over the marriage grants – though they were only intentions at this stage – were heated and demeaning to 'the splendour and dignity' of the supplicants. 'By God!' thundered the Duke of Wellington,

> They [the princes] are the damnedest millstone around the necks of any Government that can be imagined. They have insulted – personally insulted – two thirds of the gentlemen of England and how can it be wondered at that they take their revenge upon them when they get them in the House of Commons? It is their opportunity, and I think by God! they are quite right to use it.[5]

The Duke of Kent had started out on the matrimonial stakes some time before and had already considered the sister of the Tsarina of Russia in 1815, but had not found her to his taste at all. The next year he proposed to the Dowager Princess of Leiningen, Princess Victoire, a thirty-year-old widow with two children, who was the sister of Charlotte's husband. Victoire, who had already married one much older man and was now rather enjoying her independence and was mindful of the succession of her son for whom she was Regent, turned him down. Princess Charlotte's death gave the Duke of Kent's quest a new urgency – and a personal poignancy. On 7 November 1817, the day after Charlotte's death the *Morning Chronicle* reminded the royal princes of their duty: it was now 'the earnest prayer of the nation, that an early alliance of one of the unmarried Princes may forthwith be settled'. The newspaper referred to the rumours circulating 'some time ago' of an impending marriage between the Duke of Kent and 'one of the sisters of Prince Leopold', a union that England 'would hail with rapturous delight'.

At the time the Duke and Julie de St Laurent were living in extremely straitened circumstances in Brussels; she was still unaware of her paramour's machinations. The Duke described the moment of revelation to the politician and diarist Thomas Creevey:

> You saw, no doubt, that unfortunate paragraph in the *Morning Chronicle* which appeared within a day or two after the Princess Charlotte's death; and in which my marrying was alluded to. Upon receiving the paper containing the article at the same time with my private papers, I did as was my constant practice, I threw the newspaper across the table to Madame St Laurent and began to open and read my letters.[6]

The Duke was alerted to the news in the paper by the cries of his mistress as she writhed on the floor with convulsions brought on by the shock. Stalling, he reminded the unfortunate Mme St Laurent that it was most likely that his brother the Duke of Clarence would now marry, and that the same news might well act as a spur to the Prince Regent to 'carry thro' his plan of Divorce'.

Julie de St Laurent left Brussels for Paris and a courtesy title granted by Louis XVIII. The Duke of Kent paid her a pension – which was soon to be greatly reduced – and a tribute of sorts:

> our expected separation arose from an imperative duty I owed to obey the call of my family and my Country to marry, and <u>not</u> from the least diminution in an attachment which had stood the test of 28 years and which, but for <u>that</u> circumstance, would unquestionably have kept up the connexion, until it became the lot of one or other of us to be removed from this world.[7]

The Duke, encouraged by Prince Leopold, again pressed his suit on Victoire. On 25 January 1818, she accepted. 'I am,' she wrote, 'leaving an agreeable independent position in the hope that your affection will be my reward'.[8]

The couple were married twice, once in Germany and then in England, in the summer of 1818. The English marriage was a joint affair, shared with

ABOVE TOP *The Duke of Kent, Victoria's father, an engraving from the portrait by William Beechey. Prince Edward was fifty-one when he married. His bearing was 'soldier-like', but his sisters called him 'Joseph Surface', after the arch-hypocrite in Sheridan's play* School for Scandal.

ABOVE *The Duchess of Kent, Victoria's mother. The former Princess Victoire of Leiningen, was a thirty-year-old widow 'with not at all a <u>handsome</u> but a <u>very pretty</u> countenance', when she married the Duke of Kent, 'a man she had only seen once', in 1818.*

the Duke of Clarence and his bride, Princess Adelaide of Saxe-Meiningen. For the sake of the brides the ceremony was conducted in English and German. The Prince Regent gave both brides away and certainly the nuptials of the Duke of Kent were regarded as a good thing. Prince Leopold had been a popular husband for Princess Charlotte and her early death elicited public sympathy and Parliamentary bounty. His sister, it was presumed, would 'prove herself akin in virtue as in birth to her excellent and illustrious brother'.[9]

The Duke of Kent was fifty-one years old, stout and bewhiskered, but more intelligent than most of his family and with a degree of refined eloquence and worldly sophistication. He had a military background and his taste in music was for a band of wind instruments. A man of moderate personal habits but with a reputation for excessive harshness that amounted to sadism to his troops and a certain sentimentality towards animals, opinions about him were mixed. To his niece Princess Charlotte he had been a 'favourite and beloved uncle', whilst to the clerk to the Privy Council and acerbic political diarist Charles Greville he was 'the greatest rascal that went unhung'; when his daughter came to the throne nineteen years later people watched anxiously for 'the bad blood to come out'.

Following the marriage the Duke, his bride and her two children, Prince Charles who was then fourteen years old and eleven-year-old Princess Feodora returned to Victoire's tiny principality of Amorbach where it was cheaper to live. Far from erasing the debts that had been steadily mounting since the Duke was seventeen, the marriage had increased them. However, it is clear that, despite his calculation in marrying her, Edward had grown to love his new wife. He wrote to her on New Year's Eve following their marriage (though they were in the same place):

> This evening will put an end, dear well beloved Victoire, to the year 1818, which saw the birth of my happiness by giving me to you as my guardian angel. I hope that you will always recall this year with the same pleasure as I do, and that each time a new anniversary comes round, you will be as contented with your fate, as you make me hope you are today ... I would have wished to be at least able to say this to you in pretty verses but you know that I am an old soldier who has not this talent, and so you must take good will in accepting this little almanack. You will remember that it comes from your deeply attached husband, for whom you represent all happiness and all consolation. On that [note] let me tell you in the language of my country, <u>God bless you, love me as I love you</u> ...[10]

BELOW *A pencil sketch for the miniature of the very first portrait of Victoria, dated 2 November 1819, when she was nearly five months old. In the Duke's opinion, his daughter was 'a model of strength and beauty combined'.*

In the same letter the Duke also looked forward to 'the birth of a child who will resemble you', for Princess Victoire was pregnant. But then so too were the Duchess of Clarence, the Duchess of Cumberland and the Duchess of Cambridge.

As the Duke of Kent was George III's fourth oldest son, his heirs took precedence over the offspring of the Dukes of Cumberland and Cambridge but not, of course, over any of the Prince Regent or the Dukes of York and Clarence. It was therefore imperative that the Kents' child should be born on English soil. So, with the Duke acting as coachman to save money and financed by a collection of his friends who were backing this particular runner in the accession stakes, the seven-months-pregnant Duchess, accompanied by members of the household and a female obstetrician, Frau Siebold, who had qualified at the University of Göttingen, set off in a straggle of phaetons, landaus, barouches, post-chaises and a cabriolet for Calais in April 1819. The winds were against the motley party when they reached the French coast. They fretted for a whole week before it was possible for the royal yacht, grudgingly sent by the Prince Regent, to ferry them across the English Channel.

The Duke and Duchess and their retainers and possessions completed the 400-mile journey to Kensington Palace just a month before the birth of their daughter. She was a healthy baby – 'rather a pocket Hercules than a pocket Venus' wrote her proud father who also commented with approval on his observation of 'the process of maternal nutriement'. To many the notion of an aristocratic woman breastfeeding her baby rather than employing the customary wet nurse was 'astonishing'. Indeed the Duke's boast that his strong constitution and regular lifestyle gave him and his progeny the edge over his dissolute and weak kin seemed justified, particularly when the daughter born prematurely to the Duke and Duchess of Clarence lived for only seven hours.

Nevertheless Victoria's claim to the throne still seemed tenuous. Though Britain was not governed by Salic law – a woman could inherit the throne – a boy born to her parents or the offspring of her father's older brothers would take precedence. Her uncle Clarence was certainly still in the race and there was a possibility that her uncle York, or even the Prince Regent – though by now this seemed a very long shot – would outrank the infant.

The date of the new baby's christening was set for 24 June 1819 at three o'clock in the afternoon at Kensington Palace. The baby had four godparents: her grandmother, Augusta, the Dowager Duchess of Saxe-Coburg; her father's sister Charlotte, who was the widow of the King of Württemberg; Tsar Alexander I of Russia; and the Prince Regent. In the event only the Prince Regent attended in person and he showed his animosity towards his brother and his pretensions. He had already vetoed one of the names the Kents had chosen for their daughter – Georgiana, the feminisation of his own name. Now during the ceremony at the font erected in the Cupola room he indicated that two of their other choices – Charlotte and Augusta, again after the infant's godparents – were unacceptable. So the Archbishop of Canterbury was obliged to pause as the Prince gruffly allowed Alexandrina after the Tsar, rejected Elizabeth, but permitted Victoria, the anglicised version of her mother's name: 'give her her mother's name also then, but it cannot precede that of the Emperor'. The Archbishop pronounced her 'Alexandrina Victoria' as he made the sign of the cross on her forehead. It was regarded as unfortunate that the infant had two such unEnglish names, but the Duke of Clarence, a naval man, opined that the Navy would be pleased, believing that the child had been named in honour of Nelson's flagship HMS *Victory*.

When the Duke of Kent had been short of funds before he had taken his wife back to live in Germany. Clearly this was now no longer an option. If Victoria – or Drina as she was more usually known during infancy – was to be Queen of England one day, then she must be brought up in Great Britain and known to the British people. But it was obvious from his attitude that the Prince of Wales was not going to help the Duke and Duchess, and their debts were mounting. The Duke might consider that having provided the country with a likely contender for the throne – 'the nation is greatly my debtor' – that he would have been awarded an increased allowance, but no remuneration appeared to be forthcoming. So in October 1819 on the pretence that it was for his daughter's health, Kent removed his family to a rented house, Woolbrook Cottage, by the sea at Sidmouth in Devon.

The move may have been represented as being for the sake of the baby's health: it did nothing for the father's. The cold was 'intense, [with] a hard frost and everything covered in snow' and gales blew in from the sea. Proud of his robust constitution, the Duke took long, bracing walks in the rain even when he caught the same cold his infant daughter was suffering from. As was the medical convention of the day, the Duke, who was running a high fever, was bled and cupped (a heated cup would be placed over a cut and as the cup cooled blood would gush into it to fill the vacuum). As blood poured from his body he grew steadily weaker and by the time Prince Leopold arrived with Baron Stockmar in answer to his sister's pleas, on 22 January 1820, Leopold doubted if the Duke would survive the night. The Duke rallied sufficiently to sign his name shakily to a will that left all his property to his wife who was to be the sole guardian of their child. The next morning at ten o'clock he died of pneumonia. He was buried in the family vault at Windsor on 12 February 1820. His widow's request to be present was refused.

Less than a year after she had arrived in England the Duchess was a widow: she spoke little English, her baby was but eight months old; she had virtually no friends and from all the evidence the attitude of the family of her late husband was one of indifference, if not hostility. It took all the persuasion of her brother Leopold to stop her returning to Amorbach.

A week after the death of the Duke of Kent, on 29 January 1820, George III died. He had been king in name only for ten years and now the Prince Regent assumed the title as well as the role, and his estranged wife, Princess Caroline, became Queen of England. The new King immediately offered her a large sum to stay abroad, but, encouraged by the radical wing of the Whig party led by Lord Brougham, she resolved to return to England. The farce, which was always tragic, threatened to become dangerous with the 'public scorn' that Shelley identified attaching to the King and the people's sympathy drawn to the shunned Queen. The King petitioned Parliament to dissolve his

ABOVE *'The Queen's Matrimonial Ladder' by George Cruikshank, 1820. A comment on the relationship between George IV and Princess Caroline, with Britannia admonishing the foolish king for the disgrace that his marital saga brought on the monarchy.*

marriage and deprive Caroline of 'the title, prerogative, rights, privileges and exemptions of Queen Consort of this realm'. The case dragged on throughout the year: scurrilous pamphlets circulated in their thousands evidencing bribery and corruption in order to substantiate the case against the Queen. The Bill was abandoned. Caroline remained in England, a focus of opposition, a goad, and evidence of the low esteem into which the monarchy had fallen. The high – or low – point of the tragi-comedy came on 19 July 1821 when the legal Queen of England, who had been refused attendance at the Coronation, tried to force an entry to Westminster Abbey in the early hours of the morning. A month later she was dead.

The King neither wore the trappings of mourning nor mourned and within days, courtiers and the press were speculating about who he might choose for his new Queen. But the King had a new mistress, Lady Conyngham, who was much the same age as he, and in the opinion of the Princess Lieven had 'not a word to say for herself: nothing but a hand to accept pearls and diamonds with, and an enormous balcony to wear them on'.[11] George IV wanted domesticity and a quiet life: an aspiration in which his declining health played no small part. He had a serious attack of gout in 1822 and subsequently could only walk with difficulty. He was irritable, in pain and complained continually of his old age.

With the death of George III Princess Victoria moved up to third in line to the throne. It was a responsibility that her mother and those around her were to take very seriously.

Viscount Esher, who was to edit a selection of Victoria's early diaries 'under the direction' of her son Edward VII a decade after her death, framed the year of her birth:

> [The] year 1819 a year of deep despondency in England. Europe was quit of Napoleon, but had got Metternich and was ill pleased with the bargain. Great Britain, it is true, was free, but our people were overwrought by poverty and suffering. The storm-swell of the great Napoleonic wars still disturbed the surface of English life, and few realised that they were better off than they had been in the last decade ... On the very day that Princess Victoria was born, Byron was writing to John Murray from Venice ... clamouring for proofs of the first canto of *Don Juan*. In that year *Ivanhoe* was finished and in the hands of eager readers ... Keats had just finished *Endymion*. It was his last year in England before going south to die. And it was Shelley's *annus mirabilis*: the year in which he wrote *Prometheus* and *The Cenci* – an achievement, some have since said, unparalleled in English poetry since Shakespeare lived and wrote ... Wordsworth was at Rydal Mount completing *The White Doe of Rylston*. Southey was Poet Laureate. Three years before in the 'wild and desolate neighbourhood amid great tracts of bleak land enclosed by stone dykes sweeping up Clayton heights, Charlotte Brontë's eyes had opened on her sad world'. And halfway between Horncastle and Spilsby, on the lower slopes of a Lincolnshire wold, Alfred Tennyson was reading Pope's *Iliad* and himself 'writing an epic of 6,000 lines' ... At Shrewsbury School ... Charles Darwin, then a boy of

ten, had already begun to develop a taste for 'collecting' manifested in 'franks' and seals and coins. Under this galaxy of stars, some slowly sinking below the horizon, and others just rising above it, Princess Victoria was born.[12]

Victoria led a solitary childhood. Her mother was isolated by her poor command of English, by her relative poverty and by her concept of her role as mother of the future Queen of England. The Duke had made his wife his heir but he had left no land and a swarm of creditors. The Prince Regent fervently wished that his sister-in-law would return to Germany. He had snubbed and insulted his brother when he was alive and now he was dead George wanted no reminder that his unfavourite brother's daughter might succeed him to the throne.

Kensington Palace, where George allowed the Duchess and Victoria to remain, had become something of a Royal depository for the inconvenient. On the ground floor lived the Duke of Sussex between marriages – he sat all day in a velvet skull cap surrounded by a vast library of books and ticking clocks, for he was an avid collector of both. In another suite lived a fallen spinster, the unfortunate Princess Sophia, the King's now middle-aged sister who, in her youth, had an affair and bore a son to the King's elderly equerry, Colonel Garth. One of Victoria's earliest recollections of her childhood, recalled fifty years later, is of

crawling on a yellow carpet spread out for that purpose – and being told that if I cried and was naughty my 'Uncle Sussex' would hear me and punish me, for which reason I always screamed when I saw him![13]

LEFT *Kensington Palace, where Princess Victoria was born on 24 May 1819, and spent most of her childhood. The elegant palace was 'as quiet as possible, near the town and a view over the most magnificent Park', but the Duke of Kent's apartment was in a poor state of repair when he and his new wife took up residence in time for Victoria's birth.*

ABOVE *A drawing by Victoria of her governess, Lehzen. Victoria was an adept and prolific artist from childhood when she received regular instruction from the Royal Academician, Richard Westall, who also painted her portrait. Lehzen was her most readily available subject.*

On the death of Princess Charlotte, a sympathetic nation had granted Prince Leopold the very generous sum of £50,000 a year and he now settled a little more than five per cent of this largesse on his sister. However, this £3,000 a year enabled Lord Castlereagh to assure the House of Commons that there was no need to vote the Duchess and her daughter an allowance from the civil list since 'the Prince Leopold with great liberality, had taken upon himself the charge of the support and education of the infant Princess'.[14] This sum was supplemented by the £6,000 that the Duke of Kent had been granted on his marriage and which now reverted to the Duchess.

For companionship, the Duchess had her brother – in small measure for, though he paid weekly visits to Kensington Palace when he was in England, he often travelled abroad and as a widower in his late twenties had a string of amorous attachments, including a Prussian actress, Caroline Bauer, who he brought to England. However, Leopold, who had been in training himself for the role of Prince Consort, was correspondent to his sister and later to his niece, who found the wisdom and judgment of her 'dear uncle' of inestimable value as she was growing up.

The Duchess's conviction that she was the mother and guardian of the future Queen of England moulded the pattern of Victoria's life at Kensington Palace. She recognised the disrepute in which the monarchy was held and was determined to keep her daughter uncontaminated by lax morals and dissolute ways – and be seen to be doing so. Her determination that it was *her* daughter who would one day be queen also caused her to be distant with the Duchess of Clarence, a kind woman – and a fellow German speaker – who called regularly and could have proved a valuable friend. Adelaide's second child, whom the King had allowed to be named both Georgiana and Elizabeth, had died less than three months after her birth in 1820, but the Duchess was still young and the Duke had proved his abilities to procreate more than ten times already. As far as the Duchess of Kent was concerned the Clarences represented a constant threat to her own daughter's accession.

Despite her sister-in-law's manner and her own tragedies, Adelaide was always affectionate to her niece and the first letter ever received by Victoria was from her aunt in May 1821 on her second birthday:

> My dear little heart – I hope you are well and don't forget Aunt Adelaide, who loves you so fondly.
> Loulou and Wilhelm [two children of the Duchess of Clarence's sister] desire their love to you, and Uncle William also.
> God bless and preserve you is the constant prayer of your most affectionate Aunt, Adelaide[15]

Victoria recalled her early childhood:

> We lived in a very simple, plain manner; breakfast was at half-past eight, luncheon at half-past one, dinner at seven – to which I came generally

(when it was no regular large dinner party) – eating my bread and milk out of a small silver basin. Tea was only allowed as a great treat in later years.[16]

'Up to my 5th year I had been very much indulged by everyone, and set pretty well <u>all</u> at defiance', recalled Victoria,

> Old Baroness de Späeth, the devoted Lady of my Mother, my Nurse, Mrs Brock, dear old Mrs Louis <u>all</u> worshipped the poor little fatherless child whose future was then still very uncertain, my Uncle the Duke of Clarence's child still being alive, and the Duchess of Clarence had one or two others later. At 5 years old Miss Lehzen was placed about me, and though she was most kind, she was very firm and I had a proper respect for her. I was naturally very passionate, but always most contrite afterwards.[17]

The Princess who was 'not fond of learning as a little child – and baffled every attempt to teach me my letters ...' was instructed by Fräulein Lehzen, a strong-minded intelligent daughter of a Lutheran minister, who had been the governess of Victoria's half-sister Feodora, and was to play an important part in Victoria's life, even after she ascended the throne. A tutor was also engaged in 1823, a clergyman, the Reverend George Davys, who

> wrote some short words on cards for Princess Victoria and endeavoured to interest her by making her bring them to me from distant parts of the room as I named them ... The Duchess seems to be very anxious for the improvement of her little daughter and had promised her a reward if she said a good lesson. The Princess asked for the reward before she began the lesson.[18]

In 1830, the Duchess declared a wish to 'put to the test' – or more likely to demonstrate – the efficacy of the provision that Parliament had made in 1825

BELOW *A few of Victoria's collection of 132 miniature wooden dolls which she dressed, with the help of Lehzen, as figures from the court or characters from operas. A solitary child, surrounded by adults, these painted figures peopled the Princess's world at Kensington Palace.*

for her daughter's education. She wrote to the Bishops of London and Lincoln sending evidence. The Archbishop of Canterbury, among others, to whom the Duchess made appeal pronounced himself satisfied that

> Her Highness's education in regard to the cultivation of intellect, improvement of talent, and religious and moral principle is conducted with so much care and success as to render any alteration in the system undesirable.[19]

Others were warm in their praise. A visitor – a Whig – to Prince Leopold's home Claremont, near Esher noted:

> The little Princess is the most delightful, intelligent and lively child. She lives a good deal with grown up people as she sits thro' half the dinner, which is her supper. She is very observing, not at all shy, and seems to have amazing spirits ... I think her very pretty; her features are grown more delicate. She is still short for her age, tho' she has certainly grown lately, but from being stout, her hair turned up and her dress very womanly, the effect is shorter than she really is ... [she] is very amusing; her manner is very good and she is at the same time very natural.[20]

The Tory Lady Wharncliffe was also impressed:

> Her Mother's conduct is the most sensible thing I ever saw ... the way she brings the child gradually forward quite perfect ... She [the Princess] is really very accomplished by taste, being very fond both of music and

RIGHT *A sketch by Victoria of a sedate riding party in Tunbridge Wells, where the Princess had enjoyed several visits, 13 February 1834. Riding was one of her greatest pleasures. When she was thirteen, Victoria wrote of an occasion in Wales when 'we galloped over a green field which we had already done several times. Rosa [her pony] went an enormous rate; she literally flew ... It was a delightful ride.'*

drawing, but fondest of all of her Dolls … I look to her to save us from Democracy, for it is impossible she should not be popular when she is older and more seen.[21]

In fact her position – and the attitude of her mother – was more complex than these observations might suggest. Parliament may have recognised the likelihood that Victoria would succeed to the throne; that did not mean that this was a universally recognised – or accepted – fact. Her contact with her uncle, the King, was very limited.

ABOVE *A portrait of Princess Feodora, Victoria's half-sister, by W.C. Ross. In 1826, the sisters visited George IV at Windsor and, Victoria recalled, the sixty-four-year-old King paid so much attention to the eighteen-year-old Feodora that 'some people fancied he might marry her'.*

> I remember going to Carlton House, when George IV lived there as quite a little child before a dinner the King gave … In the year '26 (I think) George IV asked my Mother, my Sister and me down to Windsor for the first time; he had been on bad terms with my poor father when he died – and took hardly any notice of the poor widow and the fatherless girl, who were so poor at the time of his [the Duke of Kent's] death … We went to Cumberland Lodge, the King lived at the Royal Lodge … When we arrived … the King took me by the hand, saying 'Give me your paw'. He was large and gouty but with a wonderful dignity and charm of manner. He wore the wig which was much worn in those days.[22]

It was at least another year before Victoria visited Windsor Castle again. Perhaps the account of the acute aristocratic observer Princess Lieven, has the measure of things:

> We spent nearly the whole of last week at Windsor. It was a family reunion, the first to my knowledge. The little future Queen was there. In spite of the caresses the King lavished on her, I could see that he did not like dandling on his knee this little bit of the future, aged 7.[23]

On 26 June 1830 George IV died. He was succeeded by his brother, William, Duke of Clarence, as William IV. The new King and his wife, Adelaide, had no surviving children. Eleven-year-old Princess Victoria was now next in the line of succession.

The Duchess of Kent, however, insisted that as yet her daughter was 'not aware of the station that she is likely to fill'. The Princess had to be trained for her position so that when

> … Her innocent mind receives the impression of Her future fate, she receives it with a mind formed to be sensible of what is expected from Her, and it is to be hoped, she will be too well grounded in Her principles to be dazzled with the station she is to look to.

This meant constant surveillance:

> I … never had a room to myself until I was nearly grown up – always slept in my Mother's room till I came to the Throne. At Claremont, and in the small houses at the bathing places, I sat and took my lessons in my Governess's bedroom.[24]

ABOVE *Princess Victoria and her mother, the Duchess of Kent, drawn by Sir George Hayter. Victoria's journal for 14 February 1834, when she was fourteen, records that she and her mother sat for Hayter from 2.30 to 4.30 in the afternoon. Six further similar sittings were required for the portrait's completion.*

Victoria's isolation was intensified when Feodora, to whom she was very close, married Prince Ernest of Hohenlohe-Langberg and left for Germany when Victoria was ten. A letter from Feodora to Victoria, written in 1843, recalls their 'melancholy childhood':

> When I look back on those years, which ought to have been the happiest in my life ... I cannot help pitying myself. Not to have enjoyed the pleasures of youth is nothing, but to have been deprived of all intercourse, and not one cheerful thought in that dismal existence of ours, was very hard. My only happy time was going or driving with you and Lehzen; then I could speak and look as I liked. I escaped some years of imprisonment, which you, my poor darling sister, had to endure after I was married.[25]

The day after the accession of William IV, the Duchess of Kent wrote to the Prime Minister, the Duke of Wellington, urging that Victoria should be treated as heir apparent and that her increased allowance should be in her, the Duchess's, control. Her wish was granted on 15 November 1830 when the Lord Chancellor introduced a Regency Bill naming Victoria as heir to the throne – unless the King and Queen Adelaide produced a child. But Victoria was still a child of eleven so provision had to be made for a Regent. The Lord Chancellor pronounced:

> The manner in which Her Royal Highness, the Duchess of Kent, has hitherto discharged her duty in the education of her illustrious offspring ... gives us the best ground to hope most favourably of Her Royal Highness's future conduct. Looking at the past, it is evident we cannot find a better guardian for the time to come.[26]

It was, the Duchess proclaimed, her first happy day since the death of her husband. But her task now was to make her Regency effective by securing the greatest possible influence over her daughter. In this she was aided, if not manipulated, as Victoria and other members of the royal family were later to claim, by Sir John Conroy, a good-looking Irishman of considerable charm who had been her husband's equerry. Their strategy was to keep the young princess away from the court – and her benign uncle and aunt – yet in the public eye. Her royal status was to be evidenced; but no one was to think that her mentors were the present King and Queen. It was the Duchess of Kent who stood beside the heir presumptive.

To this end the Duchess refused to attend the Coronation of William IV or to allow her daughter to attend the ceremony. It was an extraordinary act and caused furious speculation in the press. Meanwhile Victoria and the 'Conroyals', as her mother and Sir John were known, embarked over the next three years on a series of royal 'progresses' such as the Tudor court had undertaken, staying at the great houses of the land: Blenheim, Badminton,

Chatsworth, Hatfield, Eaton Hall and Alton Towers, and seeing Britain's historical sites such as Stonehenge, York, Canterbury, Bath and Oxford where 'we were most WARMLY and ENTHUSIASTICALLY received. They hurrayed and applauded us immensely for there were all the students there; all in their gowns and caps'.[27] They were seen by the people in the industrial areas of Birmingham, Worcester, Leeds and Coventry where the 1832 Reform Act was to extend the franchise and admit to the electorate Britain's 'new wealth' as a small counterbalance to the landed interest. It was a far cry from her usual topography and social landscape. 'We have just changed horses at Birmingham', Victoria wrote in her journal, which her mother had given her when she was thirteen and she was to write daily for the rest of her life:

> ... and we visited the manufactories which are very curious. It rains very hard. We just passed through a town where all the coal mines are and you see the fire glimmer at a distance in the engines in many places. The men, women, children, country and houses are all black. But I cannot by any description give an idea of its strange and extraordinary appearance. The country is very desolate every where; there are coals about, and the grass is quite blasted and black. I just now see an extraordinary building flaming with fire. The country continues black, engines flaming, coals in abundance, every where smoking and burning coal heaps, intermingled with wretched huts and carts and little ragged children ...[28]

The King was displeased at these peregrinations. On 22 August 1835 he wrote to his sixteen-year-old niece:

> I hope the newspapers will not inform me of your travelling this year –
> I cannot and therefore do not approve of your flying about the Kingdom as you have done these last three years, and which if attempted I must and shall prevent in future. It is your real good and permanent happiness I have really at heart and I therefore write these my sentiments as being the best advice I can give.[29]

But the Duchess was still determined to continue with the 'progresses', despite the fact that the journeys proved 'not only disagreeable to [Victoria] ... but that it makes you even unhappy; that the fatigue of it will make you ill,

BELOW *The unseemly squabble for the crown. A 'hen-peck'd' William IV is sat upon by his wife, Princess Adelaide; Prince George, Duke of Cambridge, leans on the sceptre, whilst the Duchess of Kent is already tossing the orb to Princess Victoria.*

that you dislike it.'[30] The battles continued during the years of the under-age heir apparent. The tension between her mother and her uncle embarrassed and distressed the Princess and frequently made her ill. During a serious illness in the autumn of 1835, the Duchess and Sir John Conroy tried to make Victoria sign a document appointing him as her private secretary: 'I resisted in spite of my illness and their harshness, my beloved Lehzen supporting me alone'.[31]

By the time she was sixteen Victoria knew what was at stake. According to legend, five years earlier in 1830, her governess had slipped a genealogical table into the history book *Howlett's Tables of the Kings and Queens of England*, which her pupil was studying. Many years later, Lehzen recounted that the Princess, finding it, declared 'I see I am nearer the throne than I thought' and added, 'Many a child would boast, but they do not know the difficulty. There is much splendour, but more responsibility. I will be good', she vowed to her governess.[32]

As Victoria approached her majority the hostilities between the King and the Duchess and Conroy became more barbed – and more public, though William went out of his way to welcome his niece warmly on all occasions and express the wish that he saw more of her. On 20 August 1836, William, in London to prorogue Parliament, paid a surprise visit to Kensington Palace, where he found that, contrary to his express instructions, the Duchess had appropriated seventeen rooms for her own use: he upbraided her loudly in public. The next day at a dinner for one hundred people to celebrate his birthday, at which the Duchess and Victoria were both present, the King replied to the loyal toast:

> I trust in God that my life may be spared for nine months longer, after
> which period, in the event of my death, no Regency would take place. I
> should then have the satisfaction of leaving the royal authority to the
> personal exercise of that Young Lady [pointing to the Princess], the Heiress
> presumptive of the Crown, and not in the hands of a person now near me,
> who is surrounded by evil advisers and who is herself incompetent to act
> with propriety in the station in which She would be placed … Amongst
> many other things I have particularly to complain of the manner in which
> that Young Lady has been kept away from my Court; she has been
> repeatedly kept from my drawing-rooms, at which She ought always to have
> been present, but I am fully resolved that this shall not happen again. I
> would have her know that I am King, and I am determined to make my
> authority respected, and for the future I shall insist and command that the
> Princess do upon all occasions appear at my Court as it is her duty to do.[33]

The King did live to see his niece come of age on 24 May 1837 – for royalty were considered to reach their majority at eighteen. The journal entry for her birthday reads:

> Today is my 18th birthday! how old! and yet how far I am from being
> what I should be. I shall from this day take the <u>firm</u> resolution to study
> with renewed assiduity, to keep my attention always well fixed on whatever

I am about, and to strive to become every day less trifling and more fit for what, if Heaven wills it, I'm someday to be![34]

Less than a month later Victoria wrote to her uncle Leopold:

> You know, of course, dear Uncle, how <u>very ill</u> the King is; it may <u>all be over any moment</u>, and yet <u>may</u> last a few days. Consequently we have not been out anywhere in public since Tuesday 6th, and since Wednesday all my lessons are stopped, as the news may arrive very suddenly ...[35]

On 19 June 1837 Victoria wrote again:

> The King's state ... is <u>hopeless</u>; he may <u>perhaps</u> linger a few days, but he cannot recover <u>ultimately</u>. Yesterday the physicians declared he could not live to the morning, but to-day he is a little better; the great fear is his <u>excessive</u> weakness and no <u>pulse</u> at all. Poor old man! I feel sorry for him; he was always personally kind to me, and I should be ungrateful and devoid of feeling if I did not remember this.[36]

In the early hours of Tuesday 20 June 1837 King William IV died at Windsor Castle at the age of seventy. His short reign had lasted for just seven years.

At around five o'clock that same morning a sleepy porter on the gate of Kensington Palace was aroused by insistent knocking. The visitors were on 'business of State to the Queen' they said. Victoria's journal for that morning reads:

> I was awoke at 6 o'clock by Mamma, who told me that the Archbishop of Canterbury and Lord Conyngham were here, and wished to see me. I got out of bed and went into my sitting room (only in my dressing gown), and <u>alone</u> saw them. Lord Conyngham (the Lord Chamberlain) then acquainted me that my poor Uncle, the King, was no more and had expired at 12 minutes p. 2 this morning, and consequently I am <u>Queen</u> ... Since it has pleased Providence to place me in this station, I shall do my utmost to fulfil my duty towards my country; I am very young and perhaps in many, though not in all things, inexperienced, but I am sure, that very few have more real good will and more real desire to do what is right than I have.[37]

BELOW *Tuesday 20 June 1837: 'I ... went into my sitting room (only in my dressing gown), and alone saw them [the Lord Chamberlain, Lord Conyngham and the Archbishop of Canterbury] ... Lord Conyngham knelt down and kissed my hand, at the same time delivering to me the official announcement of the poor King's demise ... I am Queen.'*

CHAPTER TWO

VIVAT VICTORIA REGINA!

I SHALL TODAY ENTER on the subject of what is to be done when the King ceases to live', her uncle, Leopold, King of the Belgians, had written to Princess Victoria on 17 June 1837,

> The moment you get the official communication of it, you will entrust Lord Melbourne with the office of retaining the present Administration as your Ministers … The fact is that the present Ministers are those who will serve you <u>personally</u> with the greatest sincerity and, I trust, attachment. For them, as well as for the Liberals at large, you are the only Sovereign that offers them <u>des chances d'existence et de durée</u>. With the exception of the Duke of Sussex, there is no <u>one</u> in the family that offers them anything like what they can reasonably hope from you, and your immediate <u>successor</u> with the mustaches [the Duke of Cumberland] is enough to frighten them into the most violent attachment to you.[1]

The Princess did not have long to wait. On the morning of the King's death three days later, she

> received a letter from Lord Melbourne in which he said he would wait on me at a little before 9. At 9 came Lord Melbourne, whom I saw in my room, and of course, <u>quite</u> ALONE as I shall <u>always</u> do all my Ministers. He kissed my hand and I then acquainted him that it had long been my intention to retain him and the rest of the present Ministry at the head of affairs, and that it could not be in better hands than his. He then again kissed my hand. He then read to me the Declaration which I was to read to the [Privy] Council, which he wrote himself and which is a very fine one. I then talked with him a little longer after which he left me. He was in full dress. I like him very much and feel confidence in him. He is a very straightforward, honest, clever and good man.[2]

Lord Melbourne, the Prime Minister, was a Whig aristocrat, a habitué of the political salons at Holland House and a guest at the fine houses and the sprawling landed estates of England. At the accession he was fifty-five, still handsome, urbane, charming, erudite and tolerant. The second son of William Lamb, he was a long-serving parliamentarian: he had sat in the House of Commons in the Whig interest from 1806 until his father's death removed him to the Lords in 1829. He was appointed Home Secretary in 1830 and became Prime Minister in 1834 after Lord Grey was forced out of office. He was a consensual politician and though his usual advice was 'why not leave it alone?' he led a reforming ministry of toleration towards Dissenters and active reform of local government with the Municipal Corporations Act of 1835, which complemented at local level the work wrought nationally by the 1832 Reform Act. He was also a consummate politician, managing to hold together for six years a disparate party of Whigs, Radicals and Irish members, swaying on a slight parliamentary majority.

LEFT *'What is the finest sight in this world?' wrote the novelist Horace Walpole, at the end of the eighteenth century. 'A Coronation. What do people most talk about? A Coronation.' The coronation portrait of Queen Victoria, 28 June 1838, painted by Sir George Hayter.*

BELOW *A commemorative jug produced for the proclamation of Victoria Regina on 20 June 1837. In fact, the official Proclamation of the Sovereign took place the following day at St James's Palace, and subsequently at Trafalgar Square, Temple Bar, Wood Street and the Royal Exchange. At her request the Queen was named as Victoria: Alexandrina, her other baptismal name, was dropped.*

The poet Henry Bulwer-Lytton captured Melbourne:

> Sincere, yet deeming half the world a sham
> Mark the rude handsome manliness of Lamb!
> … few
> Guess right the man so many thought they knew:
> … A sage good-humour based on love of ease,
> A mind that most things undistrurbed'ly weighed
> Nor deemed the metal worth the clink it made.
> Such was the man, in part, to outward show;
> Another man lay coiled from sight below —[3]

The man 'coiled from sight below' gave Melbourne his aura of melancholy. His wife had been the unstable Lady Caroline Ponsonby, who had had a tempestuous – and very public – infatuation for the poet Byron. When Byron had rejected her advances she had become seriously mentally unbalanced and thereafter was confined to the Lamb's country home in Hertfordshire. Though the couple had separated, Melbourne continued to visit her regularly until her death in 1828. Two of the three children of the marriage had died in infancy and the first born, Augustus, who was retarded, died in 1836 at the age of twenty-nine.

To Charles Greville the bond that developed almost instantaneously between the tyro Queen and the experienced elder statesman was entirely explicable. For Victoria's part:

> No man is more formed to ingratiate himself with her than Melbourne.
> He treats her with unbounded consideration and respect, he consults her
> tastes and her wishes, and he puts her at her ease by his frank and natural
> manners, while he amuses her by the quaint, queer, epigrammatic turn of
> mind, and his varied knowledge on all subjects … Her reliance on
> Melbourne's advice extends at present to subjects quite besides his
> constitutional functions, for the other day someone asked her permission to

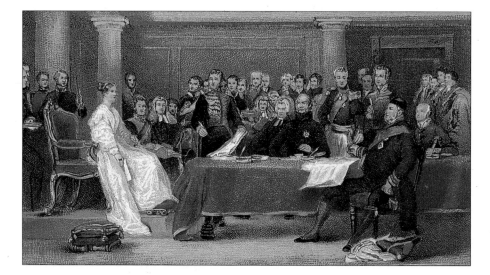

RIGHT *The Proclamation of 'little Victory', as Thomas Carlyle dubbed the new Queen. In Sir David Wilkies's painting of the Proclamation, reproduced here as a chromo-lithograph, Victoria, who was in mourning for the death of the King, is portrayed dressed in white, symbolising her innocence and youth – and thus distancing the new monarch from her dissolute and tarnished forebears.*

dedicate some novel to her, when she said she did not like to grant permission without knowing the contents of the work, and she desired Melbourne to read the book and let her know if it was fit she should accept the dedication.[4]

Whereas for Melbourne:

I have no doubt that he is passionately fond of her as he might be of his daughter if he had one, and the more because he is a man with a capacity for loving without having anything in the world to love. It is become his province to educate, instruct, and form the most interesting mind and character in the world. No occupation was ever more engrossing or involved greater responsibility.[5]

At eleven o'clock in the morning of 20 June, briefed by Melbourne, the Princess attended her first Privy Council, in the red saloon at Kensington Palace. First the Dukes of Cumberland and Sussex, the Chancellor, the Prime Minister and the Archbishops of Canterbury and York saw her alone in a side room to inform her officially of the news that she had heard at six o'clock that morning. Then the proclamation was read to the more than 200 Privy Councillors who had been summoned, and finally the new Queen, dressed in stiff black bombazine, entered. She bowed to those present and in a 'clear, distinct and audible voice' read out the declaration that Melbourne had written in which she pledged her allegiance to 'the wisdom of Parliament and upon the loyalty and affection of My people', to divine providence and to the established religion and religious toleration.[6]

Greville, who was present as the new Queen swore in her Privy Councillors, thought that she

ABOVE *Lord Melbourne, a sketch by Queen Victoria. 'I like him very much,' she wrote of her Prime Minister, on the morning of her accession, 'and feel confidence in him. He is a very straightforward, honest, clever and good man'.*

seemed rather bewildered at the multitude of men who were sworn, and who came one after another to kiss her hand, but she did not speak to anybody, nor did she make the slightest difference in her manner, or show any in her countenance, to any individual of any rank, station, or party.

[He] particularly watched her when Melbourne and the Ministers and the Duke of Wellington and Peel approached her. She went through the whole ceremony, occasionally looking at Melbourne for instruction when she had any doubt what to do, which hardly ever occurred.

He also observed how 'she blushed to the eyes' as her uncles the Dukes of Cumberland and Sussex kissed her hand and swore allegiance, 'as if she felt the contrast between their civil and their natural relations'.[7]

Greville concluded that on her first official engagement Victoria had behaved with 'perfect calmness and self possession, but at the same time with a graceful modesty and propriety particularly interesting and ingratiating', and others present were likewise impressed. Sir Robert Peel 'said how amazed he was at her manner and behaviour, at her apparent deep sense of her situation, her modesty, and at the same time her firmness. She appeared to be awed but not daunted.' The Duke of Wellington concurred and 'added that if she had been his own daughter he could not have desired her to perform her part better'.

Indeed the only dissenting voice in the room seems to have come from the Radical, Lord Brougham, who was in such a pet about the incorrect use of grammar in the proclamation, that he voiced his pedantry to Peel 'with whom he was not [usually] in the habit of communicating'.[8]

That first night as monarch, Victoria took her dinner upstairs 'alone' and for the first time in her life she slept on her own: 'went down and said goodnight to Mama, etc.' she wrote in her journal.

Despite her composure, the new Queen was little more than a month past her eighteenth birthday. She had spent an isolated childhood and little time at court. Victoria had every intention of fashioning the monarchy to her mould, but she was innocent of the complex and hazardous task that she had before her. As Baron Stockmar observed: 'Whenever the sceptre changed hands, it was to be apprehended that the compass might be wanting to so inexperienced a mariner.'[9]

But Victoria had more than one 'compass', and each had a different directional pull. She was aware of at least some of the difficulties. On that first evening she wrote, 'My dear Lehzen will always remain with me as my friend, but will take no situation about me, which is good'. Victoria's court could not be seen to be peopled with the old German influence; her reign was to represent a decisive break with the Hanoverian tradition and all that it had come to mean with her uncles. The same caution had to be exercised with her uncle Leopold: 'The irksome position in which you have lived, will have the merit to have given you the habit of discretion and prudence as in your position you can never have too much of either', wrote the King of the Belgians to his niece on the eve of her accession and gave her some advice which Victoria invariably tried to follow:

> 1. I should advise you to say as often as possible that you are born in England. George III gloried in this, and as none of your cousins is born in England, it is in your interest de faire reporter cela fortement …
> 2. You never can say too much in praise of your country and its inhabitants.
> 3. … The Established Church I also recommend; you cannot, without pledging yourself to anything particular, say too much on the subject.
> 4. Before you decide on anything important I should be glad if you would consult me; this would also have the advantage of giving you time. In politics most measures will come in time within a certain number of days; to retrace or back out of a measure is on the contrary extremely difficult, and almost always injurious to the highest authority.[10]

No doubt mindful of his niece's impetuousness – and quick temper, inherited she thought from her maternal grandmother – Leopold returned to this theme on many occasions. And though he might have been reticent about

ABOVE *Leopold, King of the Belgians, a pencil and wash sketch by S. Diez. Although Victoria had 'expressed a wish' that her uncle, who dispatched almost daily advice about her monarchical rights and duties, attend her crowning, 'mature reflection' made him 'think that a King and Queen at your dear coronation might perhaps be an hors d'oeuvre, and I think … it might be better to pay our respects at some other period'. Victoria acquiesced, and proposed an August visit instead.*

being seen to interfere, he had already 'carefully weighed the situation ... and arranged that in May 1837 from her eighteenth birthday, Stockmar [who had been Leopold's physician and then secretary, and had helped draw up the Belgian constitution] should reside in England, as the trusty helper and adviser of the Princess'.[11]

'I recommend to your kind attention what Stockmar will think it his duty to tell you', wrote Victoria's uncle,

> he will never press anything, never plague you with anything, without the thorough conviction that it is indispensable for your welfare ... You will recollect that I pressed upon you repeatedly how necessary it was for you to continue your studies on a more extended scale, more appropriate to the station you were destined once to fill. No one is better qualified to direct your studies for the next few years than Stockmar, few people possess more general information, and very, very few have been educated, as it were, by fate itself since 1816. There is no branch of information in which he may not prove useful ...[12]

What some branch of his political learning had suggested to the German polymath was that the Whig Prime Minister was not an altogether good influence on the young Queen:

> [Stockmar] found in [Melbourne] too great an inclination to yield to party interests. Instead of impressing upon his illustrious pupil, the great maxim, that she was Queen of the entire people, and that it was her duty to hold herself free from the bonds of any party, he contributed by sins, partly of omission, partly of commission, to her attitude assuming the appearance of her being only Queen of the Whigs, not to say that particular faction of the Whigs, who just then happened to be in power.[13]

Stockmar's analysis echoed the comments made by the *The Times*, a Tory-supporting paper, the morning after Victoria's first Privy Council when it thundered of the Declaration that Melbourne had written for her:

> We have seldom heard of any political expedient more unprincipled, more treacherous, or unfeeling than this. It is an actual trepanning of their innocent Sovereign into a course of policy subservient to their [the Whigs] own selfish interests.

The 'rage of party' was a site that Victoria was to occupy frequently during the early years of her reign. Woven into this politically difficult situation in an irksome and personal way, was her relationship with her mother who sought to maintain some influence over

BELOW *'The Saviour of her Country', Queen Victoria is represented as Joan of Arc in a cartoon at the time of her accession. It was not against a foreign army that hopes were pinned on Albion's answer to the Maid of Orleans, but rather to distance the monarchy from her unpopular Hanoverian forebears and unite the nation – in the Whig interest. Rural citizens rejoice, Melbourne looks approving, whilst the Tory Wellington and the Duke of Cambridge slink away.*

THE BRITISH JOAN OF ARC; (THE SAVIOUR OF HER COUNTRY.)

Victoria. The Duchess of Kent, like other commentators, stressed her daughter's youth, gender and inexperience:

> You are untried, you are liked for your youth and your sex and the hope that is entertained, but all confidence in you comes from your mother's reputation.

As Queen, the Duchess insisted, Victoria needed the continued protection of her mother and she also needed a politically disinterested man of experience and ability as her personal secretary: 'that person, I must repeat to you again your father considered to be Sir John Conroy'.[14]

But Victoria had no intention of complying with either injunction. On the day of her accession she rebuffed her mother, choosing to take up all her duties 'alone'. It was a pattern that was to be repeated with the Duchess enjoying neither intimacy with nor influence over her daughter as Queen.

> It is plain to see that [the Duchess of Kent] is overwhelmed with vexation and disappointment. Her daughter behaves to her with kindness and attention, but has rendered herself quite independent of the Duchess, who painfully feels her own significance.[15]

Greville reported in his journal. The Duchess of Kent continued to bombard her daughter with advice, notes and requests and Victoria's journals from the first years of her reign are peppered with despairing remarks about 'Ma's' letters and scenes.

On the morning of Victoria's accession Conroy appeared to throw in the towel. 'I am completely beaten', he declared to Stockmar and announced that his public life was at an end and that he intended to retire into private life, but that he required compensation for his services to the Duchess and his loss of earnings. 'My reward for the Past I conceive should be – a peerage, the red ribbon and a pension from the Privy Purse of £3,000 year.' It was an excessive demand, but it was granted – at least the pension was. Conroy was promised an Irish peerage, but eventually had to settle on a baronetcy. In fact, Conroy did not retire; he remained at Kensington Palace for a further two years, but the Queen remained adamant in her refusal to treat with him, or allow him any official function – or presence at official functions.

The office of the Queen's private secretary, instigated when George III became so myopic that he could no longer read State papers or write letters, was allowed to lapse. Whilst Lehzen took charge of the Queen's personal matters, Melbourne himself took control of her affairs of state. It was hardly a situation that pleased the Duchess of Kent who hissed 'Take care Victoria, you know your Prerogative! take care that Lord Melbourne is not King …'[16]

BELOW *Victoria and her mother. The Duchess of Kent had moved from Kensington to Buckingham Palace with her daughter, since it was not possible for Victoria to live as a* femme seule *without a woman of comparable rank. The alternative to this enforced mother-daughter intimacy which Victoria found irksome, was a 'schoking' one: marriage.*

The first year of her reign caused Victoria great pleasure: she was growing in confidence and whenever she attended a State occasion, such as her Proclamation on 21 June, the dissolution of Parliament on 17 July or the Lord Mayor's Banquet in November, the crowds acclaimed her. She wrote to Feodora on the occasion of the banquet:

> It is really most gratifying to have met with such a reception in the greatest capital in the world and from thousands and thousands of people. I really do not deserve all this kindness for what have I yet done. I may, may I not, my dearest sister, be proud of my country and my people.

On 13 July, Victoria had moved from Kensington Palace, which was now no longer large enough nor grand enough for the Queen's residence, cluttered as it was with other minor royals and remote from Parliament and her Ministers, to Buckingham Palace. It had been bought by George III whose children – all except the eldest – had been born there, and it had been extensively – and very expensively – modernised by George IV according to the design of his architect, John Nash. The work was finally completed by William IV just before he died. Though 'I rejoice to go into B.P. for many reasons', Victoria wrote

> it is not without feelings of regret that I shall bid adieu for ever … to this my birthplace where I have been born and bred, and to which I am really attached! … I have had pleasant balls and delicious concerts here … I have gone through painful and disagreeable scenes here, 'tis true, but I am still fond of the poor old Palace.[17]

As she predicted, Victoria enjoyed life at Buckingham Palace – at first – despite the doors that did not fit, bells that did not ring, chimneys that smoked and the 'noxious effluvia' of the drains. She found it an excellent place to hold concerts and indulge her love of opera and balls where she would energetically dance the quadrille until the early hours of the morning. That summer – 'the pleasantest summer I EVER passsed in my life … I shall never forget the first summer of my Reign' – was spent at Windsor Castle, where she was able to ride. Victoria had always been an excellent horsewoman and when she lived at Kensington Palace would frequently ride her horse to Hampstead Heath for a gallop.

But as Queen it was not all pleasure. On her accession Leopold had suggested a routine to her:

> The best plan is to devote certain hours to [business]; if you do that, you will get through it with great ease. I think you would do well to tell your Ministers that for the present you would be ready to receive those who should wish to see you, between the hours of eleven and half-past one.

Victoria, once again, heeded his advice and took her work very seriously. Creevey recorded that:

BELOW 'A Cabinet Lecture'. Queen Victoria and her Prime Minister, Melbourne. 'How I wish I had time to take minutes of the very interesting and highly important conversations I have with my Uncle [Leopold] and with Lord Melbourne; the sound observations they make, and the impartial advice they give me would make a most interesting book … Uncle and he perfectly agree in Politics, which are the best there are.'

A CABINET LECTURE.

> According to Lehzen who has been Vic's governess from the cradle, there
> never was so perfect a creature. She said that now Vic was at work from
> morning to night, and that, even when a maid was combing out her hair, she
> was surrounded by official boxes and reading official papers.[18]

When writing her journal, Victoria noted that communications from Lord
Melbourne 'occur every day and generally 2 or 3 times a day though the
[Minister] with whom I communicate oftenest after Lord Melbourne is Lord
Palmerston [the Foreign Secretary]'.[19] Palmerston schooled the young
sovereign in diplomatic niceties, the language of foreign despatches and the
history of international relations. He had 'atlasses' drawn to help and gave
her a copy of the *Almanach de Gotha*. Though her duties were time-consuming
they did not appear to oppress the new monarch.

> I have so many communications from the Ministers, and from me to them,
> and I get so many papers to sign every day, that I always have a very great
> deal to do … I delight in this work.[20]

wrote the new Queen who marvelled that when at an audience to receive
'various foreign Ambassadors [I] had my hand kissed nearly 3000 times!'

Victoria also took her family and financial responsibilities seriously. On her
accession one of her first thoughts had been for William IV's widow, her
Aunt Adelaide, and in her first note to her she addressed her still as 'Queen'.
'I will not be the first to call to give her that title' she had reproved the
Archbishop of Canterbury, who had pointed out that Adelaide should now
be addressed as 'Dowager Queen'. She insisted that the royal widow should
be allowed to remain at Windsor Castle as long as she wanted.

Following her accession Victoria's financial circumstances were
transformed. After considerable debate during which 'the Duke of Wellington
and Sir Robert Peel [even though they were Opposition Ministers] …
behaved very well; they have helped us [the Whigs] a great deal', Parliament
passed a new Civil List Bill which granted Victoria an allowance of £385,000
a year. The sum was to remain the same for the rest of her reign, though
additional amounts were granted on the birth of royal children. It was a
generous disposition, and the votes against were only nineteen in the House
of Commons and one (Lord Brougham) in the House of Lords, but the
Queen had hefty expenses in maintaining her residences and household of
over 445 staff, which included the Lord Chamberlain who grossed £2,000 a
year whilst the royal dentist took home £100; four Physicians to the Person
received £214 apiece whilst the Surgeon to the Household received £400 a
year and the Apothecary £414, for free medical treatment was one of the
perks of royal domestic service – and one which did not come cheap to the
Queen with one quarter's surgeon's bills submitted in September 1838
totalling £150 – treatment that would have been way beyond the pocket of
working people. In addition the annual salary bill covered a 'Rat Killer at
£80 a year, a Chimney Sweep who received £111 a year, a Stove and Fire
Lighter, £64, a Body Linen Launderess who earned £170 a year whilst the

Linen Women at Windsor Castle got £60 to the £66 her counterparts at Buckingham Palace were paid. Of what might be called out-of-house staff, the Poet Laureate [Southey at the time] received £72 a year and the principal painter £39'.[21]

Victoria was determined to settle the debts of her father who had died owing considerable sums. The debts of her mother were less straightforward and tended to multiply on closer scrutiny. *The Times* estimated in March 1838 that due, it claimed, to Conroy's mismanagement, the Duchess of Kent owed some £80,000, a sum that would have absorbed her daughter's Privy Purse of £60,000 for more than a year. The Duchess's allowance was increased by Parliamentary decree, and a new controller was appointed, who found that there was an absence of accounts for over ten years and capital sums appeared to have gone missing.

The expense to the nation of running a royal family, particularly in the lean years following the Napoleonic Wars and the extravagances of George IV, made the cost of the Coronation a sensitive issue. Indeed, William IV had been so alert to these sentiments that he had wanted to do without one altogether. This had not been considered appropriate, but his was a budget affair costing only £50,000. It had been so low key that wits had designated it a 'half crownation'. However, it was presumed that public enthusiasm for the young Queen would be so great that Parliament voted a grant of £200,000 to mount a spectacle with Westminster Abbey decorated magnificently in crimson and gold, a two-day fair in Hyde Park, fireworks and illuminations. The Coronation Banquet, which William IV had dispensed

LEFT *The People's Celebration. A woodcut of the fair in Hyde Park at the time of the Coronation. 'Crowds in the street and all so friendly ... the preparations for Fairs, Balloons, &c in the Parks quite changes all ...'*

with, was not to be revived, but the formal state procession, which the capital had not witnessed since the Coronation of George III in 1760, was to be reinstated at a cost of £26,000 so that as many of the nation as possible could see the pomp and majesty of the monarchy as their Queen rode through the streets in the State Coach, and, it was hoped, would recognise it as evidence of a new page turned in the annals of the British royal family.

The nation seemed to have come to London on Thursday 28 June 1838, the day of Victoria's Coronation when, she recorded:

> It was a fine day, and the crowds of people exceeded what I have ever seen; many there were the day I went to the City, [for the Lord Mayor's Banquet] it was nothing – nothing to the multitudes, the millions of my loyal subjects who were assembled in <u>every</u> spot to witness the Procession. Their good-humour and excessive loyalty was beyond everything and I really cannot say how proud I feel to be the Queen of <u>such a Nation</u>. I was alarmed at times for fear that the people would be crushed and squeezed on account of the tremendous rush and pressure.[22]

It was estimated that approaching half a million people flocked to see the Coronation, swelling the existing population of London to around two million souls. For Greville it seemed as if

BELOW The Coronation Procession: 'I found my eight train-bearers ... all dressed alike and beautifully, in white satin and silver tissue, with wreaths of silver corn-ears in front, and a small one of pink roses round the plait behind, and pink roses in the trimming of the dresses. After putting on my Mantle, and the young ladies having properly got hold of it, and Lord Conyngham holding the end of it, I left the robing room and the Procession began.'

> the population had been on a sudden quintupled; the uproar, the confusion, the crowd, the noise are indescribable. Horsemen, footmen, carriages, squeezed, jammed, intermingled, the pavements blocked up with timbers, hammering and knocking, and falling fragments stunning the ears and threatening the head; not a mob here and there, but the town all mob, thronging, bustling, gaping and gazing at everything, at anything, at nothing.[23]

Though the Coronation coincided with the start of 'railway mania', in mid-1838 only 200 miles of track traversed the country. Accounts of the occasion tell how 'the roads are covered, the railways loaded with arriving multitudes,' and report of 'stoppages in every street, and hundreds of people waiting on the line of road from Birmingham, to get lifts on the railway in vain ... not a fly or a cab to be had for love or money. Hackney coaches £8 or £12 each, double to foreigners!'[24]

Almost all the houses along the route from Hyde Park Corner to Westminster Abbey had scaffolding stands erected to command a view of the procession as it passed – at a cost. Victoria

> reached the Abbey amid deafening cheers a little after 1/2 p.11; I first went into the robing room quite close to the entrance, where I found my eight Train-bearers …

The Duchess of Richmond had designed the young ladies' dresses and had been 'determined … that I would have no discussion with their Mammas about it'.

The boys of Westminster School, as was their traditional privilege, shouted out 'Vivat Victoria Regina!', the Archbishop of Canterbury presented Victoria as 'the undoubted Queen of this realm' and was answered by the whole congregation, including for the first time members of the House of Commons, acclaiming nine times 'God Save Queen Victoria' as she turned herself first to the north, then to the south and the west before taking an oath to uphold the Protestant religion as established by law.

> The sight was splendid; the banks of Peeresses quite beautiful, all in their robes, and the Peers on the other side. At the beginning of the Anthem … I retired to St Edward's Chapel, and put on the Supertunica of Cloth of Gold, which was put over a singular sort of little gown of linen trimmed with lace. I also took off my circlet of diamonds and then proceeded bare-headed into the Abbey; I was then seated upon St Edward's chair where the Dalmatic robe was clasped round me by the Lord Great Chamberlain. Then followed all the various things; and last (of those things) the Crown being placed on my head; – which was, I must own, a most beautiful impressive moment; <u>all</u> the Peers and Peeresses put on their Coronets at the same instant. My excellent Lord Melbourne, who stood very close to me throughout the whole ceremony, was <u>completely</u> overcome at this moment, and very much affected; he gave me such a kind, and I may say <u>fatherly</u> look. The shouts, which were very great, the drums, the trumpets, the firing of the guns, all at the same instant, [in the parks and at the Tower of London to let the crowds know that the crowning was taking place] rendered the spectacle most impressive. The Enthronization and the

ABOVE *The Imperial Crown. The crown made for George IV was too heavy for the nineteen-year-old Queen, so a new, lighter one of less than half the original 7lb was refashioned with diamond and pearl-encrusted gold circlets over a blue velvet cap, incorporating all the precious stones, including the heart-shaped ruby worn by Henry V at Agincourt, and topped by a Maltese cross set with a large sapphire.*

Homage of, 1st all the Bishops, then my Uncles, and lastly of all the Peers, in their respective order was very fine … poor old Lord Rolle, who is 82 and dreadfully infirm, in attempting to ascend the steps, fell and rolled quite down, [which provided an opportunity for a play on words from commentators] but was not in the least hurt; when he attempted to reascend them I got up and advanced to the end of the steps, in order to prevent another fall. After the Homage was concluded I left the Throne, took off my Crown and received the Sacrament; I then put on my Crown again and reascended the Throne, leaning on Lord Melbourne's arm … There was another present at this ceremony, in the box immediately above the Royal Box, and who witnessed it all; it was Lehzen, whose eyes I caught when on the Throne, and we exchanged smiles …

Finally, after a ceremony lasting nearly five hours, at about 1/4 p. 4 I re-entered my carriage, the Crown on my head and Sceptre and Orb in my hand, and we processed the same way as we came – the crowds if possible having increased. The enthusiasm, affection and loyalty was really touching, and I shall remember this day as the proudest of my life.[25]

ABOVE *An admission ticket to Westminster Abbey for the Coronation of Queen Victoria on 28 June 1838.*

It had not been a flawless ceremony: the crown was 'excessively heavy', despite the fact that the 7lb-crown worn by William IV at his Coronation had been broken up and refashioned into a smaller ornament which weighed less than 3lb; it included the heart-shaped ruby that had been worn by Henry V at Agincourt. The ruby ring, which the Archbishop of Canterbury had to place on the Queen's index finger, had been made to fit her little finger. The Archbishop forced it on and 'the consequence was that I had the greatest difficulty to take it off again' and the royal hand had to bathed in iced water. Greville recorded, 'nobody knew what was to be done except the Archbishop and [the sub dean of Westminster, Lord John Thynne] (who had rehearsed), Lord Willoughby (who is experienced in these matters), and the Duke of Wellington, and consequently there was continual difficulty and embarrassment, and the Queen never knew what she was to do next'.[26] Victoria herself records that the officiating clergy were 'remarkably maladroit' and at one point when the orb was placed in her hand she asked the Bishop of Durham who had put it there 'What am I to do with it?' It was very heavy, but the only answer Victoria got was 'Your Majesty is to carry it, if you please in your hand'. In fact the Bishop had given it to her too early. 'The Archbishop … ought to have delivered the Orb to me, but I had already got it and he (as usual) was so confused and puzzled and knew nothing – and went away.'[27]

Greville thought that 'the Queen looked very diminuted and the effect of the procession itself was spoilt by being too crowded; there was not interval enough between Queen and Lords going before her'. But he also realised that this was not really the heart of the matter 'so much has been done for the people; to amuse and interest <u>them</u> seems to have been the principal object'.[28] The day had been a royal pageant, evoking and confirming tradition, precedent and a hierarchical status based on the landed interest. It had also been a confirmation that Britain had a constitutional monarchy based on the will and consent of the people, and the oath Victoria swore that day bound her, as Queen, to respect the rule of law, the freedom of her subjects and the privileges of the Established churches.

When he dined with her later that same evening, before she saw the day out 'on Mamma's balcony looking at the fireworks in Green Park, which were quite beautiful', Lord Melbourne told his Queen 'You did it beautifully, – every part of it, with so much taste; it's a thing that you can't give a person advice upon; it must be left to a person'.[29]

But as Thomas Carlyle watched the Queen drive away from the Abbey in her golden coach, he had reflected:

> Poor little Queen, she is at an age when a girl can hardly be trusted to choose a bonnet for herself; yet a task is laid upon her from which an Archangel might shrink.[30]

LEFT *A pencil sketch by Sir George Hayter of the Archbishop of Canterbury in the act of crowning the Queen. The artist, who was commissioned for 2,000 guineas to depict the Coronation, sat in the Lord Chamberlain's box in Westminster Abbey, sketching throughout the ceremony. This particular sketch however, was rejected, as Victoria did not consider it proper to be depicted with her head bowed.*

CHAPTER THREE

THE ROYAL CONNECTION

She saw no purple shine,
For tears had dimmed her eyes;
She only knew her childhood's flowers
Were happier pageantries!
And while the heralds played their part,
Those million shouts to drown –
'God save the Queen' from hill to mart, –
She heard through all her beating heart,
And turned and wept –
She wept to wear a crown!

LEFT *Victoria riding with her Prime Minister in Windsor Great Park, detail from a painting by Sir Francis Grant. 'I have had delicious rides which have done me a world of good,' the Queen recorded in her journal for 3 October 1837. 'Lord Melbourne rode near me the whole time. The more I see of him and the more I know of him, the more I like and appreciate his honest character. I have seen him in my Closet for Political affairs, I have ridden out with him, ... I have sat near him constantly at and after dinner, and talked about all sorts of things ... I am very fond of him ...'*

IN HER POEM 'Victoria's Tears', Elizabeth Barrett Browning had misconstrued the signs at Victoria's Proclamation. Her childhood had not been a happy pageant and the tears she shed on this occasion were of emotion – and happiness – at being declared Queen. She had taken up the reins of state with enthusiasm and application, and the first year of her reign seemed one of unalloyed satisfaction to her. She was eighteen; she was a woman; she was Queen of England in a country where women enjoyed no political, and only very circumscribed legal, rights. She could command when her sisters could not vote. The fact of her gender – *Her* Majesty for the first time in over 120 years – had already had the parliamentary clerks scrabbling for the feminisation of the dictat '*Le roy le veult*'. It meant that the connection between Hanover and England had been broken – which seemed to cause relief in most quarters – since as Hanover had Salic law, there could no longer be a joint monarchy; hence her uncle, the Duke of Cumberland, became King of Hanover.

Victoria's youth was an attribute. It was moving to see so slight a figure assume the responsibility of the highest office in the land, and the contrast between her fresh innocence and her world-weary, elderly, dissolute predecessors was striking. But though the Coronation may have suggested that being Queen was also a job, there is little evidence that she fully understood or had had explained to her the full significance of the various ceremonies. Victoria's journal at this time is a jumble of impressions and emotions. Yet again, her uncle Leopold had given her pertinent advice:

BELOW *The singularity of a female monarch. The new Queen coyly asks the Duke of Norfolk, Earl Marshall of England, the authority on ceremony and protocol, how (or rather where) she should wear the Order of the Garter, an insignia traditionally worn around the thigh. 'Honi Soit Qui Mal Y Pense' (Shamed Be He Who Thinks Evil Of It) is the motto of the Order.*

> Monarchy to be carried on requires certain elements, and the occupation of the Sovereign must be constantly to <u>preserve these elements</u>, or should they have been too much weakened by untoward circumstances, to contrive by every means to <u>strengthen them again</u>. You are too clever not to know, that it is not the being <u>called</u> Queen or King, which can be of the <u>least consequence</u>, when to the title there is not also annexed the power indispensable for the exercise of those functions.

HONI SOIT QUI MAL Y PENSE!

ABOVE *Sir John Conroy. The 'Flora Hastings affair' gained its vindictive edge largely because Victoria regarded Lady Flora, lady-in-waiting to her mother and a friend of Sir John, as an enemy, even a dangerous spy, in the 'Conroyal' camp.*

ABOVE *Lady Flora Hastings, a silhouette cut by Victoria. Lady Flora was the eldest child of the Tory Marquis of Hastings.*

> All trades must be learned, and nowadays the trade of a constitutional Sovereign, to do it well, is a very difficult one.[1]

The second year of her reign was to bring home to Victoria the truth of Leopold's sober analysis.

The Duchess of Kent's lady-in-waiting, Lady Flora Hastings, came from a distinguished Tory family and in Victoria's eyes was part of the Conroy faction, and thus not entirely to be trusted. Early in 1839 it was observed that the 31-year-old spinster's figure was ballooning. Court gossip suggested that she was pregnant and Victoria had 'no doubt that she is – to use the plain words – with child!!' And as far the Queen was concerned the 'horrid cause of all this is the Monster and demon incarnate,'[2] whose name she could not bring herself to write, Sir John Conroy, with whom Lady Flora had shared a post-chaise all the way from Scotland on her return journey from a Christmas visit to her family.

Lord Melbourne became involved and sent for the Queen's physician, Sir James Clark, who, in a statement printed in *The Times* on 6 October 1839, was 'bound to admit … that the appearance of Lady Flora in some degree countenanced [the rumours]'. But as he had only 'examined the state of the abdomen over the dress', he was unable to 'satisfy myself as to the nature of the enlargement'. Sir James requested that he 'might be permitted to lay my hand upon her abdomen with her stays removed. Lady Flora refused.'

The gossip at court 'swelled into a report, and finally into a charge'. It was only when she was faced with an ultimatum from the 'ladies of the Palace' that a medical opinion had to clear her, or she would have to leave the court, since 'it is quite impossible that the Queen should admit the Lady into her presence until her character is cleared', that Lady Flora submitted to a full medical examination by two royal physicians.[3] When their work was complete they issued a statement that in their opinion 'although there is an enlargement of the stomach … there are no grounds for suspicion that pregnancy does exist, or ever did exist'.[4] She was a virgin and had 'the satisfaction of possessing a certificate' to prove it.

Lady Portman, the Queen's lady-in-waiting who had been the spokesperson in the affair went to see Lady Flora to apologise for the aspersions that had been cast upon her virtue. She admitted that the Queen had been fully aware of the pressure put on Lady Flora, who replied that she was surprised that 'knowing my family as she does, she could have entertained those suspicions'.[5]

Victoria sent a note regretting the whole incident and offered to visit the wronged courtier. When Lady Flora felt in a fit state to see her a week later, Victoria found she was 'dreadfully agitated … and looked very ill', but Lady Flora had agreed that 'for Mamma's sake she would suppress every wounded feeling and would forget it etc'.[6]

But that was not quite how the Hastings family saw it. With his sister's honour besmirched, Flora's brother wanted an explanation of why the affair had been so grievously mismanaged. He challenged Lord Melbourne – whose characteristic action had been to hope that the whole matter would somehow blow over – to a duel, insisted on an audience with the Queen herself, and throughout the spring laid charges at the feet of all those at the 'polluted Court' who he thought might have fermented the gossip. By early March

> the whole town has been engrossed for some days with a scandalous story at Court ... the Court is plunged in shame and mortification at the exposure, that the palace is full of bickerings and heart-burnings, while the whole proceeding is looked upon by society at large as to the last degree disgusting and disgraceful.[7]

It was all too drearily familiar and by then the papers had got hold of it. The Queen was incensed by the behaviour of the Hastings family and the rift between Victoria and her mother deepened as the Duchess complained of a plot against a lady of her household. The Queen was also insensitive to the situation of Lady Flora herself; she refused to accept how ill she was, despite Melbourne's insistence, and complained that it was 'disagreeable and painful to me to think there was a dying person in the house'. When it was clear that the end was imminent Victoria postponed a planned ball at the Palace and went to see her:

> I went in alone; I found poor Lady Flora stretched on a couch looking as thin as anyone can be who is still alive; literally a skeleton, but the body very much swollen like a person who is with child ... she ... said how very grateful she was for all I had done for her ...[8]

A week later, on 5 July 1839, Lady Flora died of cancer of the liver. The Queen obstinately told Melbourne that she 'felt no remorse, I felt I had done nothing to kill her'. The scandal continued to smoulder. The Hastings family returned the £50 Victoria had sent to Lady Flora's maid. Statements from the parties involved, and the correspondence between Lord Hastings and Lord Melbourne, appeared in the press, which declared that Victoria had been badly advised, whilst a rash of anonymous pamphlets and booklets talked of 'foreign conspiracies' (referring to Lehzen who, it was alleged, had largely orchestrated the campaign of vilification), a Queen 'betrayed' by her advisors, her mind too full of balls and parties to govern effectively. She was hissed at when she appeared in public and the epithet 'Mrs Melbourne' was hurled at her. Greville concluded:

> The whole affair has done incredible harm, and has played the devil with the Queen's popularity and cast dreadful odium and discredit at Court, especially in the country where a thousand exaggerated reports are rife. It is next to impossible to repair the mischief because so much mystery is still thrown over the transaction at its origin. The public take it up (as it took Q. Caroline) on the principle of favouring an injured person, and one who appears to have obtained no reparation for the injuries inflicted on her.[9]

Meanwhile another scandal which would further suggest the Queen's inexperience and lack of understanding of the 'trade of the Sovereign' was

ABOVE *Queen Victoria, a silhouette self-portrait. 'We [Victoria and Lord Melbourne] spoke of many things; I asked if he liked my headdress which was done in plaits round my ears, for I know in general he only likes the hair in front crepe in 2 puffs. He said, looking at me and making one of his funny faces, 'It's pretty; but isn't it rather curious – something new?'*

brewing. 'I really thought my heart would break', she wrote in her journal for 7 May 1839:

> he [Lord Melbourne] was standing near the window; I took that kind, dear hand of his, and sobbed and grasped his hand in both of mine and looked at him and sobbed out, 'You will not forsake me'.

What had occasioned this 'state of agony, grief and despair [that] may be easier imagined that described! All, all my happiness gone' was the intelligence that she had learned that morning from Melbourne who had

> to acquaint your Majesty that the division upon the Jamaica Bill, which took place about two this morning, was two hundred and ninety-nine against the measure and three hundred and four in favour of it [in fact the division was 294 to 289] ... a cabinet will be summoned early this morning, and Lord Melbourne cannot conceal from your Majesty that in his opinion [this leaves] your Majesty's confidential servants no alternative but to resign their offices into your Majesty's hands.[10]

The matter that had finally sundered the fragile Whig majority was an important one. In 1833 slavery had been abolished throughout the British Empire. The sugar planters of Jamaica had refused to comply. Faced with the revolt, Melbourne proposed to suspend the Jamaican constitution for a period of five years during which time the island would be under direct rule from Britain exercised through a Governor General and Council. Opposition

RIGHT *Victoria fails to balance a see-saw resting on the back of John Bull by pushing down the left-hand end on which sits the Tory Wellington, whilst on the other end, Melbourne, the Whig leader, rises aloft. A comment on the Queen's partiality for the Whigs in an 1838 cartoon.*

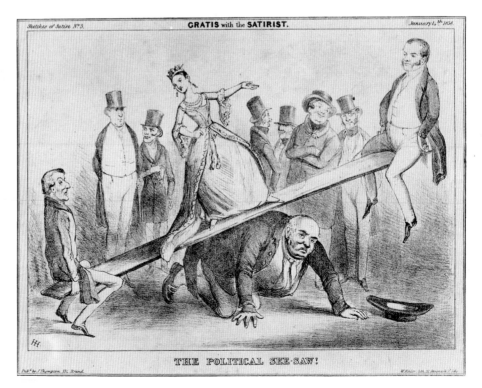

to this proposal had united the Radicals who were opposed in principle to direct rule, and the Tories who supported the plantation owners. Melbourne considered that a majority of five was too narrow to legislate on such a fundamental issue and, since the Government could not 'give up the Bill either with honour or satisfaction to their own consciences' nor achieve greater support for the measure, they should resign. Melbourne realised how 'painful and embarrassing' this would be for the Queen, but expressed the hope that she would 'meet the crisis with that firmness that belongs to your character, and with that rectitude and sincerity which will carry your Majesty through all difficulties'. He advised his Sovereign:

> at once to send for the Duke of Wellington. Your Majesty appears to
> Lord Melbourne to have no other alternative. The Radicals have neither
> ability, honesty, nor numbers ... There is no party in the State to
> which your Majesty can now resort, except that great party that
> calls itself Conservative.[11]

The Queen, who always wrote of the Whig government as if they were her home team 'we won ...', 'we may lose ...', was distraught. On waking the next morning

> all – all that had happened in one short eventful day came most forcibly to
> [the Queen's] mind and brought back her grief ... she couldn't touch a
> morsel of food last night, nor can she this morning.[12]

That morning the Queen saw the Duke of Wellington and told him that as

> his party had been instrumental in removing [the present Ministry] ... she
> must look to him to form a new Government. The Duke answered that he
> had no power whatever in the House of Commons, 'that if he was to say
> black was white [presumably black was black], they would say it was not,'
> and then he advised me to send for Sir Robert Peel, in whom I could place
> confidence, and who was a man of honour and integrity.

When the Queen expressed the hope that 'he would at all events have a place in the new Cabinet' at first the Duke pleaded that he was 'so deaf, and so old and unfit for discussion' that he would rather not do it, but finally agreed that he would. The Queen then

> wrote to Peel, who came after two, embarrassed and put out. The Queen
> ... asked Sir Robert to form a new Ministry. He does not seem very
> sanguine; says entering the Government in a minority is very difficult; he
> felt unequal to the task, and far from exulting in what had happened, as he
> knew what pain it must give me ... [Peel] is such a cold, odd man she can't
> make out what he means. He comes to me to-morrow at one to report
> progress in the formation of the new Government. The Queen doesn't like
> his manner – oh! how different, how dreadfully different, to that frank,
> open, natural and most kind, warm manner of Lord Melbourne ... The
> Queen was very much collected, and betrayed no agitation during these two
> trying Audiences. But afterwards again all gave way.[13]

ABOVE *Her Majesty's Unwelcome Opposition. The Duke of Wellington and Sir Robert Peel, after the painting by Franz Xaver Winterhalter. Peel was a reserved man with a formal, stiff, awkward manner and 'a deficiency in worldly dexterity and tact, and in knowledge of character'.*

Melbourne congratulated his protégé on her 'proper and judicious conduct' and made a fist at reassuring her about Peel:

Sir Robert is the most cautious and reserved of mankind. Nobody seems … to know him, but he is not therefore deceitful or dishonest. Many a very false man has a very open sincere manner, and vice versa.[14]

Even if he had felt he could have been more fulsome, Melbourne would have had an uphill task. Victoria saw the Tories as 'enemies' and Peel as their representative, and, given that he was likely to be her closest Minister, as a particular antagonist – she confessed that she liked the patrician Duke of Wellington 'far better'. The son of a Lancashire cotton magnate rather than the landed classes, Peel spoke with a northern accent and was not a man at ease in drawing-room society. As Melbourne had reminded the Queen 'he (Peel) is not a man who is accustomed to talk to Kings; a man of quite a different calibre; it's not like me; I've been brought up with Kings and Princes. I know the whole family and I know exactly what to say to them; now he has not that ease …'[15] As the historian Monica Charlot has pointed out Peel was not a courtier; he was of the new breed of professional, managerial politicians,[16] a new sort of Tory, soon to be known universally as Conservatives. And above all he was not Melbourne. In these negotiations Lord Melbourne generally behaved scrupulously:

I would strongly advise your Majesty to do everything to facilitate the formation of the Government. Everything is to be done and endured rather than run the risk of getting into the situation in which they are in France, of no party being able to form Government and conduct the affairs of the country.[17]

The 'everything' included negotiations over the Ladies of the Bedchamber. It was an issue the Queen had raised at her first audience with Wellington. He did 'not give any decisive answer about it'. She raised it again with Peel who again 'would give no answer, and said nothing should be done without my knowledge or approbation'.[18]

The issue involved members of the Queen's staff whose husbands were Peel's political opponents in Parliament. Peel felt that if he became Prime

Minister he had no desire to

> give to the World the spectacle of a Court entirely hostile to him, consisting
> of ladies whose husbands were his political opponents, thereby creating an
> impression that the confidence of the Crown was bestowed on his enemies
> rather than on himself.[19]

To an incoming Tory government the Ladies of the Bechamber could be a
focus of opposition and intrigue. In addition the posts offered a new
administration opportunities for placement and patronage. But to Victoria,
who maintained that this was all irrelevant since she 'never talked politics
with them, and that they were related, many of them, to Tories', it was an
encroachment on her royal prerogative by political enemies she didn't want
in power anyway. It should not be forgotten that Lady Flora was a Tory; the
two issues became entangled. Melbourne reinforced her feelings:

> [he] begs to suggest that if Sir Robert Peel presses for the dismissal of
> those of your Household who are not in Parliament, you may observe that
> in so doing he is pressing your Majesty more hardly than any Minister
> pressed a Sovereign before … When Sir Robert Peel himself became
> Minister in 1834, no part of the Household were removed except those
> who were in Parliament.[20]

But Peel did press his case: 'Sir Robert Peel has behaved very ill', the Queen
wrote to Melbourne,

> and has insisted on my giving up my Ladies, to which I replied I never
> would consent, and I never saw a man so frightened … he was quite
> perturbed – but this is <u>infamous</u> … I was calm but very decided, and I
> think that you would have been pleased to see my composure and great
> firmness; the Queen of England will not submit to such trickery. Keep
> yourself in readiness, you may be needed soon.

Her next missive to Melbourne that same day assured him that she
had not been rash in her opinions

> … the Queen felt this was an attempt to see whether she could be led
> and managed like a child; if it should lead to Sir Robert Peel refusing to
> undertake the formation of the Government, which would be absurd,
> the Queen will feel satisfied that she has only been defending her own
> rights, on a point which so nearly concerned her person, and which,
> if they had succeeded in, would have led to every sort of unfair attempt
> at power.

At one o'clock the next morning Melbourne wrote that following
'much discussion' in Cabinet, he advised the Queen to reply to Peel
that 'she could not adopt a course which she conceives to be contrary
to usage, and which is repugnant to her feelings'. Since Peel had made
the matter one of confidence in the Queen's support of him, he wrote
a convoluted reply setting out 'his impression with respect to the
circumstances which have led to the termination of his attempt to

BELOW *'The British Beehive'. The
Queen and the royal family sit atop
a hierarchy which is underpinned
by the constitution, the church, the
press, agriculture, industry, trade
and manual workers with the
foundations of capital and the
armed forces. George Cruikshank
originally drew the cartoon in
1840, the year of Victoria and
Albert's marriage, but amended it
in 1867 to take account of the
controversy over the extension of the
franchise contained in the second
Reform Bill of that year.*

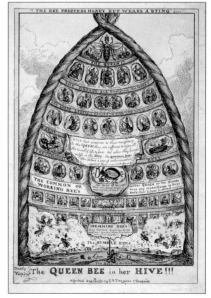

49

form an Administration for the conduct of your Majesty's service'.[21] In effect he returned the commission. Since this was the course the Whigs had advocated they were 'bound in honour to do all consistently with our public duty to support her'. Victoria recounted the story to Leopold, concluding:

> You will easily imagine that I firmly resisted this attack on my power, from these people who pride themselves upon upholding the prerogative! I acted quite alone, but I have been, and shall be, supported by my country, who are very enthusiastic about it, and loudly cheered me on going to church on Sunday. My Government have nobly stood by me, and have resumed their posts, strengthened by the feelings of the country …[22]

Not everyone saw it quite like that. Indeed, sixty years later the Queen herself admitted: 'Yes, I was very hot about it and so were my ladies as I had been so brought up under Lord Melbourne; but I was <u>very</u> young, only 20, and never should have acted so again – Yes! it was a mistake.'[23]

But at the time Victoria had seen the matter as a personal affront and its resolution as a personal triumph, but there were important constitutional issues at stake. The Government might be 'hers'; but it was also the people's and rumblings of discontent in the country would soon indicate that what was foremost in the popular mind was not the situation of a bevy of royal dressers and maids of honour but the 'condition of England' question.

A matter of days after the Ladies-of-the-Bedchamber crisis, Victoria wrote in her journal: 'This day I <u>go out of my</u> TEENS and become 20! It sounds so strange to me!' She voiced the pieties usual on such occasions about being thankful and resolving to be good and equal to her station, but the truth was that the 'station' was becoming more of a burden than it had seemed less than two years ago and Her Majesty was out of sorts. 'It was a most beautiful, bright day', she recorded on the morning after her 20th birthday, 'yet the 1st impression, I know not why – beautiful as it looked and green and bright – is always a triste one.'[24] She lamented having to remain in London into the summer 'which when the Opera was over, I should dislike, as I hated <u>not</u> going out, and staying at home every day'. ('Lord M' pointed out that in the *country* she must stay at home, so that put an end to that discussion.) She complained of feeling tired and didn't know why, she complained about being 'quite muzzed with reading so many despatches' ('though Lord M explained that <u>I</u> need not read them all through')[25] and she complained of 'my disliking this meeting of Ministers; my disliking to hear nothing else but Politics and always Politics' (again the patient Melbourne agreed this was 'disagreeable' and he himself preferred to talk of poetry and literature, but added sagely that people seldom liked what they did best).

In addition to her other discontents Victoria found to her 'horror' that she was putting on weight. She now weighed 8 stone 13lb, 'an incredible weight for my size' which was less than 5 feet. Already at twenty the barrel-like figure with a girth that almost equalled its height, which is our image of the Queen today, was foreshadowed. Larger dresses had to be sent from Paris. The

LEFT *Victoria's first visit to Covent Garden as Queen, accompanied by her mother, Lady Sutherland, Lord Conyngham and Lord Albermarle to see Byron's* Werner *in November 1837. 'I met with the same brilliant reception, the house being <u>so</u> full that there was a great piece of work for want of room and many people had to be <u>pulled</u> out of the Pit by their wrists and arms into the Dress Circle ... it was the oddest thing I ever saw.'*

young Queen, who was clearly depressed, was rising later, bathing less and finding difficulty in summoning up the energy to brush her teeth. Melbourne advised her to walk more. But she said she got stones in her shoes. 'Have them made tighter', was Lord Melbourne's practical suggestion.

The problem was her isolation. 'I said a young person like me must <u>sometimes</u> have young people to laugh with.' Melbourne was well aware of that: 'Nothing so natural', he replied 'with tears in his eyes', as she pointed out that 'I had <u>that</u> so seldom'. 'You must take care of your health', he urged, 'you complain of that languor increasing and dislike of exertion; now, it would be a dreadful thing for you if you were to take a dislike for business', which, Victoria assured him, 'she never should'. 'You lead rather an unnatural life for a young person', he empathised, 'it's the life of a man'. 'I did feel it sometimes', Victoria admitted.[26]

A way of ameliorating this isolation and 'unnatural' existence, would be for Victoria to marry – it would have the added bonus that she would no longer have to live in the same establishment as her mother, the Duchess of Kent.

However, in the summer of 1839 the Queen had told Melbourne 'I wished, if possible, never to marry'. For the question of marriage was yet another pressure. It was, naturally, a matter of speculation at court and in the country. But who could a Queen regnant marry? The field was hardly wide open. 'I don't think a foreign prince would be popular', opined Melbourne. 'But I ... couldn't and wouldn't like to marry a subject', countered Victoria. Melbourne agreed: 'What ever family he belonged to ... they would be the object of jealousy. No I don't think that would do'.[27] The Duke of Cambridge had been pressing the charms of his son, Prince George, but this acned young man held no attraction for the Queen. Her uncle, William IV, had wanted Victoria to marry one of the sons of the Prince of Orange but she found Prince William and Prince Alexander 'very plain ... they look heavy, dull and frightened and are not at all prepossessing' when they had paid a visit to England in May 1836.[28] Someone who did appeal to her was the Grand Duke Alexander of Russia, the eldest son of Tsar Nicholas I, who had visited at the end of May 1839. 'I really am quite in love with the Grand Duke', she had observed, 'he is a dear delightful young man'.[29] But as heir to the throne of All the Russias, Alexander was not in the market for playing Prince Consort in Britain.

However, Victoria's 'beloved uncle', Leopold, had other plans. He had already taken up a scheme from his mother, the Dowager Duchess of Saxe-Coburg, that her two grandchildren – the 'little May flower', Princess Victoria, and Prince Albert, son of Leopold's older brother, Ernest, Duke of Saxe-Coburg and Gotha, should marry. Leopold agreed that this proposed union made a great deal of sense. He had

> formed the highest opinion of his young, handsome, very amiable, and highly gifted nephew, Prince Albert, and ... had come to the happy conclusion that no Prince was so well qualified to make his niece happy, and fitly to sustain the arduous and difficult position of Consort to the Queen of England.[30]

BELOW The Rosenau, a modest hunting lodge on the edge of the Thuringen forest, a few miles from Coburg, the former captial of the Duchy of Saxe-Coburg and Gotha. The Duke and his family spent their summers at the Rosenau and it was there on 26 August 1819 that Prince Albert was born. Frau Siebold, the midwife and obstetrician who delivered him, had delivered his cousin, Victoria, in London three months previously.

Albert was born at the summer lodge of his parents on the edge of the forest of Thuringen in the Duchy of Saxe-Coburg and Gotha. His father, Ernest had married the seventeen-year-old Princess Louise of Saxe-Gotha-Altenburg in 1817. They had two sons, Ernest born in 1818 and Albert the following year. It was not a happy marriage. The Duke, who was sixteen years older than his wife, was a notorious womaniser, and when Albert was five years old his mother abandoned her children and ran off with an army lieutenant whom she married after her divorce from the Duke in 1826. The little Princes never saw their mother, who died in 1831, again. Albert, who had been her favourite, grew up a sensitive, shy, scholarly and somewhat frail child.

In 1836 when the matter was of some portent, Leopold had sent Stockmar to look Albert over and give his views as to his suitability for the girl who, would before long, be Queen of England. Stockmar was impressed too:

> Albert is a handsome youth, who, for his age, is tolerably developed, with pleasant and striking features; and who, if nothing interferes with his progress, will probably in a few years be a fine and powerful man, with a pleasant, simple and yet distinguished bearing. Externally, therefore, he has everything attractive to women, and what must please at all times, and in all countries. It may also be considered as a fortunate circumstance that he has already a certain English look about him.

> The only question, therefore, is in reference to his mind ... He is said to be prudent, cautious and already very well informed. He must not only have great capacity but true ambition, and a great strength of will. To pursue so difficult a political career a whole life through requires more than strength and the wish to do it; for such a task is required that sustained earnestness which, as a matter of course, sacrifices mere pleasure to that that is truly useful. If the mere consciousness of filling one of the most influential positions in Europe does not satisfy him, how often will he feel tempted to repent his adventure. If he does not, from the very first, undertake his new functions as a serious and difficult task, upon the thorough fulfilment of which his honour and happiness depend, he is not likely to succeed.

BELOW *Prince Albert of Saxe-Coburg when a child. As an infant Albert was reputed to be 'as pretty as an angel'. His mother, betrayed by her husband's frequent and public infidelities, left his father for an army officer when Albert was only five – and in bed with whooping cough. He never saw her again.*

In Stockmar's opinion, two objectives had to be accomplished:

> The first is, a well-planned system of education for his future career, with special reference to the peculiar land and people where he would be called upon to dwell; and the second is, that he should win the affection of the Princess before he asks her in marriage, and that his suit should be founded only on this sentiment of affection.[31]

The first goal was to be achieved by sending Albert (and Ernest) abroad for their education. Coburg was clearly too small and incestuous a place; Berlin was considered but rejected since 'a certain dissoluteness is as endemic in Berlin as influenza', whilst 'Vienna is ... not at all a suitable school for a German prince'. Stockmar recommended Brussels where the boys could 'pursue their studies ... under the superintendence of their uncle'.

The princes studied in Brussels for nearly a year: Albert studied history and modern languages and mathematics. In April 1837, the princes then continued their studies at Bonn University for eighteen months, where Albert applied himself to history, political economy, philosophy, Roman law and the natural sciences in an institution that was considered one of the most enlightened in Europe.

Phase two of the grand design was put into action in 1836. Stockmar wrote: 'Now is the right moment for the first appearance in England', and asserted that: 'If the first favourable impression is made, the foundation stone is laid for the future edifice'.[32]

On 18 May 1836 Princess Victoria noted in her journal: 'At a 1/4 to 2 we went down to receive my Uncle Ernest, Duke of Saxe-Coburg-Gotha, and my Cousins, Ernest and Albert, his sons...' Always susceptible to male good looks, she continued:

Ernest ... has dark hair, and fine dark eyes and eyebrows, but the nose and mouth are not good ... Albert, who is just as tall as Ernest, but stouter, is extremely handsome; his hair is about the same colour as mine; his eyes are large and blue, and he has a beautiful nose and a very sweet mouth with fine teeth; but the charm of his countenance is his expression, which is most delightful ... full of goodness and sweetness, and very clever and intelligent.[33]

Victoria professed herself 'delighted' with her cousins:

They are so natural, so kind, so <u>very</u> good and so well instructed and informed; they are so well bred, so truly merry and quite like children in their manners and conversation.

And on the last day of the visit, which had lasted for over three weeks, she wrote of Ernest and Albert

I do love [those <u>dearest</u>, beloved Cousins] so VERY VERY dearly; <u>much more dearly</u> than any other cousins in the <u>world</u> ... they have both learned a great deal, and are very clever naturally clever, particularly Albert, who is the most reflecting of the two, and they like very much talking about serious and instructive things and yet are so <u>very very</u> merry and gay and happy, like young people ought to be ...[34]

Unsurprisingly, Victoria 'cried bitterly, very bitterly ...' when they left. But the visit had not been an unqualified success: Albert had found the constant partying and late nights exhausting. He had written to his stepmother: 'The climate of this country, the different way of living, and the late hours do not agree with me'.[35]

Despite Stockmar's advice that 'it must be a "*condition sine qua non*" that the real intention of the visit should be kept secret from the Princess as well as the Prince, that they may be perfectly at ease with each other',[36] Victoria was aware of Leopold's intention. She wrote to the King of the Belgians of the visit in a letter Albert's father was commissioned to deliver:

I must thank you, my beloved Uncle, for the prospect of <u>great</u> happiness you have contributed to give me, in the person of dear Albert. Allow me, then, my dearest Uncle, to tell you how delighted I am with him, and how much I like him in every way. He possesses every quality that could be desired to render me perfectly happy ... He has, besides, the most pleasing and delightful exterior and appearance you can possibly see.[37]

That Victoria and Albert were to marry was an understanding, rather than a formal commitment, though they wrote letters to each other between their first meeting in June 1836 and 1838, and Leopold certainly kept the prospect firmly in view. But in January 1838 Victoria dashed his hopes of an early union: she announced that she was 'not yet quite grown up …' nor was Albert and 'it would not do, were I to marry a boy, for so I rate a man of 18 or 19' and she could not marry Albert until he was 'perfect in the English language; [he] ought to write and speak it without fault, which is far from being the case now …'[38]

When Melbourne quizzed her on the situation in April 1839 Victoria

mustered up courage and said that my Uncle's great wish – was – that I should marry my Cousin Albert … he said 'Cousins are not very good things,' and then 'Those Coburgs are not popular abroad; the Russians hate them.' I then said, who was there else? We enumerated the various Princes, of whom not one, I said, would do. For myself, I said at present my feelings were against ever marrying. 'It's a great change in the situation', he said. 'It's a very serious thing, both as it concerns the Political effect and your own happiness.' I praised Albert very much; said he was younger than me. I said Uncle Ernest pressed me much about it; Lord M said if one was to make a man for it, one would hardly know what to make; he mustn't be stupid – nor cunning. I said, by all that I had heard, Albert would be just the person … I said he would come with his older brother in the autumn … I said, why need I marry at all for 3 or 4 years? did he see the necessity? I said I dreaded the thought of marrying; that I was so accustomed to have my own way, that I thought it was 10 to 1 that I shouldn't agree with any body. Lord M said, 'Oh! but you would have it still' (my own way) …[39]

BELOW *Prince Albert, a portrait by W.C. Ross, 1839. 'Albert really is quite charming, and so excessively handsome, such beautiful blue eyes, an exquisite nose, and such a pretty mouth with delicate moustachios and slight but very slight whiskers',* enthused Victoria on the day after the arrival of her Saxe-Coburg cousins at Windsor.

With the next visit of the Saxe-Coburg cousins approaching, Victoria was anxious to clarify the situation. On 15 July 1839, she wrote to her uncle Leopold:

First of all, I wish to know if <u>Albert</u> is aware of the wish of his <u>Father</u> and <u>you</u> relative to <u>me</u>? Secondly, if he knows that there is <u>no engagement</u> between us? I am anxious that you should acquaint Uncle Ernest, that if I should like Albert, that I can make <u>no final promise this year</u> for, at the <u>very earliest</u>, any such event could not take place till <u>two or three years hence</u>. For, independent of my youth, and my <u>great</u> repugnance to change my present position, there is <u>no anxiety</u> evinced in <u>this country</u> for such an event, and it would be more prudent, in my opinion, to wait till some such demonstration is shown, – else if it were hurried it might produce discontent.

Though all reports are most favourable, and although I have little doubt I shall like him, still one can never answer

BELL'

RUMOURED MARRIAGE of the QUEEN.

The *Morning Post* of Thursday published the following statement respecting the marriage of her Majesty :—

It is our duty this day to make to the British people an announcement which they will receive with intense interest, and we hope and believe with unanimous satisfaction. We have received from a correspondent resident at the court of Brussels, and enjoying the entire confidence of that court, a communication which enables us to state, in the most distinct and positive terms that a matrimonial alliance is about to take place between her Britannic Majesty and his Serene Highness the Prince Albert Francis, second son of Ernest, the reigning Duke of Saxe Coburg Saalfield.

The august prince whom so high and so auspicious a destiny awaits will shortly arrive in this country, accompanied by their Majesties the King and Queen of the Belgians. He will arrive, we believe we may venture to say, to depart no more. He will arrive, we ardently hope, to impart new lustre and security to the British crown, and to constitute the domestic happiness and sustain the social virtues of the illustrious lady by whom, in the ordination of a gracious Providence, the British crown is long, we trust, to be worn.

The Prince Albert Francis of Saxe Coburg was born on the 26th of August, 1819. He is, therefore, three months two days younger than her Majesty.

The father of th[e] Saalfield, was h[is] father, Fran[...] on the fi[...]

ABOVE *Speculation in* Bell's *Weekly Messenger of 24 August 1839, reporting a rumour emanating in Brussels, that 'a matrimonial alliance' was about to take place between 'Her Britannic Majesty and his Serene Highness the Prince Albert Francis second son of Ernest, the reigning Duke of Saxe-Coburg-Saalfield'. It was premature: Victoria was loath to pledge herself to the cousin she had not seen for three years, whilst Albert was made anxious by reports that Victoria was 'incredibly stubborn'.*

beforehand for <u>feelings</u>, and I may not have the <u>feeling</u> for him which is requisite to ensure happiness. I <u>may</u> like him as a friend, and as a <u>cousin</u>, and as a <u>brother</u>, but not <u>more</u>; and should this be the case (which is not likely) I am <u>very</u> anxious that it should be understood that I am <u>not</u> guilty of any breach of promise, for <u>I never gave any</u>. I am sure you will understand my anxiety, for I should otherwise, were this not completely understood, be in a very painful position. As it is, I am rather nervous about the visit, for the subject I allude to is not an agreeable one to me.[40]

The situation was not particularly 'agreeable' to Prince Albert either, for he, too, was in a 'painful position'. 'I am ready to submit to this delay', he had told Leopold,

only if I have some certain assurance to go upon. But if after waiting, perhaps, for three years I should find the Queen no longer desired the marriage, it would place me in a very ridiculous position, and would to a certain extent ruin all prospects of my future life …[41]

The visit finally took place on Thursday 10 October 1839:

At 1/2 p. 7 I went to the top of the staircase and received my 2 dear cousins Ernest and Albert – whom I found grown and changed and embellished. It was with some emotion that I beheld Albert – who is <u>beautiful</u>.[42]

Unfortunately 'having no clothes' (their trunk had not arrived) the cousins could not appear at dinner, nor at the reception planned to welcome them. But later – 'despite their *négligé* – they came to be presented to Lord Melbourne, who tactfully agreed with the Queen that Albert was 'like me', and that the thought had 'struck [him] at once'.

The next day, Victoria eulogised in her journal: 'Albert really is quite charming, and so excessively handsome'. They took to the floor that evening and Victoria danced two quadrilles with 'dearest Albert, who dances so beautifully' and she had an opportunity to watch him waltz and gallop, noting that he 'holds himself so well with that beautiful figure of his'[43] (the couple could not dance these together for Albert was not of Victoria's royal status and therefore his arm could not encircle the royal waist – which was why Victoria had had to develop a fondness for the uncoupled quadrille).

The next day the Queen went horse-riding in Windsor Great Park, trotting between Lord Melbourne and Prince Albert and she 'talked a good deal' to Albert. The following day, being a Sunday, the Queen went to church – again Albert was in the party and he 'enjoyed the music excessively and thought it quite beautiful'. Later that afternoon Victoria confessed to Melbourne that:

seeing my cousins … had a good deal changed my opinion (as to marrying), and that I would decide soon, which was a difficult thing. 'You would take another week' said Lord M; 'Certainly a very fine young man, very good-looking', in which I most readily agreed.[44]

After dinner the Queen enjoyed a domestic interlude with her cousins and Lord Melbourne, looking at pictures, talking, playing games and sitting 'on the sofa with dearest Albert' as his pet greyhound, Eôs, 'came in again and yawned'. 'A delightful evening', the Queen concluded.

On Monday while Ernest and Albert went shooting Victoria recorded that:

At 1 came Lord Melbourne … After a little pause I said to Lord M that I had made up my mind (about marrying dearest Albert). – 'You have?' he said; 'well, then, about the time?' Not for a year, I thought; which he said was too long; that Parliament must be assembled in order to make a provision for him, and that if it were settled 'it shouldn't be talked about', said Lord M; 'it prevents any objection, though I don't think there'll be much; on the contrary', he continued with [customary] tears in his eyes, 'I think it'll be very well received; for I hear there is an anxiety now that it should be; and I'm very glad of it; I think it is a very good thing, and you'll be much more comfortable; for a woman cannot stand alone for long, in whatever situation she is in' … Then I asked, if I hadn't better tell Albert of my decision soon, in which Lord M agreed. How? I asked, for that in general such things were done the other way.[45]

But in the event, it seemed possible:

At about 1/2 p. 12 I sent for Albert [the Queen wrote in her journal for Tuesday 15 October 1839]; he came to the Closet where I was alone, and after a few minutes I said to him, that I thought he must be aware <u>why</u> I wished them to come here, – and that it would make me <u>too happy</u> if he would consent to what I wished (to marry me). We embraced each other, and he was <u>so</u> kind, <u>so</u> affectionate … I really felt it was the happiest brightest moment in my life. I told him it was a great sacrifice, – which he wouldn't allow; I then told him of the necessity of keeping it a secret, except to his father and Uncle Leopold and Stockmar … and also that it was to be as early as the beginning of February. I then told him to fetch Ernest, which he did and he congratulated us both and seemed very happy. I feel the happiest of human beings.[46]

BELOW *Victoria proposes marriage to Albert, 15 October 1839. 'I said to him, that I thought he must be aware <u>why</u> I wished him to come [to the Closet] – and that it would make me <u>too happy</u> if he would consent to what I wished (to marry me).'*

5 7

CHAPTER FOUR

'MY BELOVED ALBERT ...'

ALBERT HAD SUGGESTED A HONEYMOON during which time the couple could 'retire from the public eye for at least a fortnight – or a week'. But Victoria, who was having to contemplate what would be the concern of her future life 'namely of reconciling the authority of a Sovereign with the duty of a wife', was firm; a three-day trip to Windsor after the wedding was the only romantic interlude that could be allowed. 'You forget, my dearest Love', Queen Victoria chided her betrothed,

> that I am the sovereign and that business can stop and wait for nothing. Parliament is sitting, and something occurs almost every day, for which I may be required, and it is quite impossible for me to be absent from London; therefore two or three days is already a long time to be absent.[1]

The question of the honeymoon was but one of the many delicate issues that had to be broached after the Queen had proposed to her Prince and before they were to be married four months later. At first they had an idyllic few days of enchantment with each other. 'I love him more than I can say', Victoria wrote to her uncle Leopold on the evening of her proposal,

> and I shall do everything in my power to render the sacrifice he has made (for a sacrifice in my opinion it is) as small as I can ... these last few days have passed like a dream to me, and I am so much bewildered by it all that I hardly know how to write; but I do feel very, very happy.

They walked and rode together, danced and talked. Victoria played the piano for Albert and one evening the couple

> played at that game of letters out of which you are to make words, and we had great fun about them. Albert gave 'Pleasure', and when I said to the people who were puzzling it out, it was a very common word, Albert said, But not a very common thing ...[2]

Even her duties were made more pleasurable for the Queen. Later that week she was signing her official papers and writing her journal:

> my dearest Albert came to me ... such a pleasant happy time. He looked over my shoulder and watched me writing to the Duchess of Northumberland and the Duchess of Sutherland; and he scraped out some mistakes I had made. I told him I felt so grateful to him and would do everything to make him happy. I gave him a ring with the date of the ever dear date to me 15th engraved in [the date of their engagement]. I also gave him the little seal I used to wear. I asked if he would let me have a little of his dear hair.[3]

All too soon Albert had to return to Saxe-Coburg to put his affairs in order. On 14 November Victoria kissed his 'dear soft cheek', which was 'fresh and pink like a rose', wept at the parting and turned to contend with the

LEFT *A detail from the painting by Sir George Hayter of the marriage of Queen Victoria and Prince Albert in the Chapel Royal at St James's Palace on 10 February 1840. 'I do not think it possible for anyone in the world to be happier, or as happy as I am', wrote Victoria of her wedding day.*

innumerable constitutional and political matters and issues of etiquette connected with her impending marriage. But, within a couple of days a letter arrived from Calais to sustain her:

> I need not tell you that since we left all my thoughts have been with you at Windsor and your image fills my whole soul. Even in my dreams I never imagined that I should find so much love on earth. How that moment shines for me when I was close to you with your hand in mine. Those days flew so quickly, but our separation will fly equally so.[4]

On 23 November, more than a month after the lovers had agreed to marry, Victoria made an official announcement. The Privy Council was summoned and the Queen, wearing a bracelet containing a portrait of Albert, entered and in a 'clear' voice, but with trembling hands, read the Declaration of Marriage, in which she informed the Council of a decision 'which deeply concerns the welfare of My people and the happiness of my future life'.

> It was rather an awful moment, [she confessed to her fiancé] to be obliged to announce this to so many people, many of whom were quite strangers, but they told me I did it very well, and I felt so happy to do it.[5]

That perfect happiness was to be marred somewhat over the next few weeks by the wranglings over Albert's future status, role and responsibilities as husband of the Queen.

As soon as the news was public rumours began to circulate that the Queen's husband-to-be was a Roman Catholic. The usual form of words for a Declaration was that the sovereign was 'marrying into a Protestant country', but this could not be said of Coburg since, in Melbourne's words, at least one branch had 'collapsed in Catholicism'. So, in composing the Declaration, Melbourne, not wishing to meet trouble halfway, had elected simply not to mention Albert's religious persuasion. Victoria reported angrily to Albert:

> The Tories make a great disturbance (saying) that you are a Papist, because the words 'a Protestant Prince' have not been put into the Declaration – a thing that would be quite unnecessary, seeing that I cannot marry a Papist.[6]

The Act of Settlement deprived the British sovereign of the crown if he or she married a Catholic. At Melbourne's request Albert obliging supplied 'a short History of the House of Saxe-Coburg, who our direct ancestors are, and what part they took in the Protestant, or rather Lutheran religion' showing that the main line of the Coburgs had never looked to Rome since Luther's edict, but it was a sensitive issue that cut across a number of British susceptibilities. The Oxford Movement was in many eyes dangerously 'Romish' and Papist. What had begun as a defence of the spiritual independence of the Church of England against secular interference from the government in 1833 had, by 1839, developed into an attack on the Established Church with its call for a return to spiritual values and

ABOVE *A Royal Romance. This engraving shows Victoria and Albert at about the time of their wedding in February 1840, on sheet music of the 'Cellarius Waltz'. 'It is quite a pleasure to look at Albert when he ... waltzes, he does it so beautifully, holds himself so well with that beautiful figure of his', wrote the Queen.*

Episcopalian hierarchy. And, of course, there were the interests of the Irish Catholics, on whose support in the House of Commons the Whigs relied, to placate. There was an element of xenophobia, manifest perhaps particularly in the case of Leopold who was seen to be 'behind' the proposed marriage. He was still drawing a hefty British pension of £50,000 a year on account of his brief marriage to Charlotte, even though he now ruled another country and was married to a French Catholic Princess. Had Victoria settled on one of the Prince of Orange's sons for a husband, as the old King had wanted, she would have made a connection with the Netherlands, England's traditional ally, who over a century before had provided a Protestant monarch for the throne at a time of religious and civil disturbance.

Despite the outcry, Melbourne did not insert a reference to Albert's religion into the speech Victoria made announcing her betrothal when she opened Parliament on 16 January 1840. Though she had been nervous, as she wrote to Albert the following day, in the event 'everything went off extremely well ... perhaps never, certainly not for a long time, have I been received so well; and what is remarkable, I was not nervous, and read the speech really well.' Greville agreed: he thought her reception was 'much better than usual'. But nevertheless 'the Tories began immediately afterwards to conduct themselves very badly and to plague us'.[7] In the House of Lords the Duke of Wellington carried an amendment to the address censuring Ministers for having failed to declare publicly that the Prince was a Protestant and was able to take Holy Communion in the form prescribed by the Church of England. Greville was distressed to see the Duke 'descend to such miserable humbug, and was in hope that he was superior to it, and would have put down the nonsense that lead to his sanction'.[8] But there were real issues at stake. The Bedchamber Crisis was fresh in Tory minds and many believed that: 'the real obstacle to the Tories coming into office was the Queen ... her violent and undisguised antipathy to Peel rendered him extremely reluctant to take office'.[9]

Would her husband wean her away from what many Tories regarded as an excessive dependence on Melbourne and Whig partisanship? Was Albert the right man for the job? After all, as Wellington had said, the public had a right to know something about him other than his name, and they didn't know much – except, perhaps, the politicians' well-aired prejudices. The Tories were concerned whether at twenty-one Albert could be expected to be mature enough to provide the ballast that, in their opinion, their young – and rather foolish – Queen needed. *The Times* commented on their wedding day:

> If the thing were not finally settled indeed, one might without being unreasonable, express a wish that the consort selected for a Princess so educated and hitherto so unfairly guided, as Queen Victoria – should have been a person of riper years, and likely to form more sound and circumspect opinions.

BELOW *England quakes. An anxious cartoon about Albert's status published in* Cleave's *shortly before the royal wedding. 'Am I not to be your lord and* master' *he demands, and acting out the patriarchal role insists – or threatens – 'I will interfere in the affairs of the state, and have considerable influence in the army also – and all in defiance of you or old Jack [John] Bull.'*

To the ultra Tories, who regretted that England did not have Salic law so that *their* man, the Duke of Cumberland, could have succeeded, the fact that Albert was a possible Catholic and a mere boy, was nothing as compared to the fact that he was a foreigner and a penniless one at that. In this they found an echo on the streets. A popular ballad ran:

> He comes the bridegroom of Victoria's choice
> The nominee of Lehzen's vulgar voice;
> He comes to take 'for better or for worse'
> England's fat queen and England's fatter purse.

The questions of a title and an income for Albert were contentions that rumbled on throughout the months of the betrothal. Leopold pressed for his nephew to be given a peerage on the grounds that it 'would make Albert's foreigness disappear as much as possible'. But Victoria replied:

> The whole Cabinet agree with me in being strongly of opinion that Albert
> should not be a Peer; indeed I see everything against it and nothing for it;
> the English are very jealous at the idea of Albert's having any political
> power, or meddling with affairs here

which, she added, 'I know from himself he will not do'.[10] While Melbourne may have been opposed to a peerage for Albert on grounds of political expediency, Victoria had a grander title in mind – that of 'King Consort'.

There was also the question of royal precedence, which came up during the debate over the Bill for Albert's naturalisation in January 1840. English constitutional law seemed to have made no provision for the position of the husband of a Queen regnant and therefore a clause was inserted into the Bill to give the Prince precedence after the Queen – in other words above that of their future children – and her present uncles. But Melbourne's attempt to slip this clause into what might have otherwise been regarded as a routine measure was unsuccessful.

Brougham supported Wellington's objection that the wording of the Bill would give Albert 'unconditional precedence over every eldest son and heir-apparent of a sovereign, and therefore, in the event of the Queen dying without issue, over the eldest Prince of the King who would be called to the succession, i.e., Ernest Augustus of Hanover'.[11] The ultra Tories led by the Duke of Cumberland, who refused to give precedence to what he designated 'a paper Royal Highness', also objected fervently to the clause. Finally, the Government had to drop the issue to get the Bill through the Parliament. Constitutional experts were consulted on Royal precedence and the Queen was finally able to declare that the matter was one of royal prerogative – a prerogative that she exercised nearly twenty years later.

If Albert had been philosophical about the reluctance to grant him a title the most telling rebuff that he was to suffer before he arrived in his adopted land, was over the question of his annuity. A proposal was put forward in the House of Commons on 24 January 1840 by Lord John Russell that Her Majesty be enabled to grant an annual income of £50,000 out of the Consolidated Fund for a provision to Prince Albert to commence on the day of his marriage with Her Majesty and to continue during his life.[12]

On a Tory motion, supported by Peel, the Radicals and 'a great proportion' of Whigs, the vote was a majority of 104 in favour of a reduction to £30,000. Greville was not surprised:

Everybody (except those who have an interest in defending it) thinks the allowance proposed for Prince Albert very exorbitant: £50,000 a year given for pocket money is quite monstrous and it would have been prudent to propose a more moderate grant for the sake of his popularity.[13]

Victoria was distressed: fearing that 'they made [Albert] believe abroad that we wanted to degrade him here'. Leopold's annuity was very much in the mind of Colonel Sibthorp, who had moved that the allowance should be ·slashed. In Committee he proposed that if Albert were to survive Victoria and then marry a Catholic, or fail to reside in Britain for a minimum of six months a year, then he should forfeit the annuity. Leopold was incensed:

I must confess that I never saw anything so disgraceful than the discussion and vote in the Commons. The whole mode and way in which those who opposed the grant treated the question was so extremely vulgar and disrespectful, that I cannot comprehend the Tories. The men who uphold the dignity of the Crown to treat their Sovereign in such a manner and on such an occasion! ... Clearly, as you are Queen Regnant, Albert's position is to all intents and purposes that of a male queen Consort, and the same privileges and charges ought to be attached to it which were attached to Queen Adelaide's position ... I can only conclude by crying shame, shame![14]

It was left to Melbourne to point out that there was a wider context to the debate than royal precedence and status: the condition of England question.

The years between 1839 and 1842 were ones of particular political turbulence since the advocacy of political reform was given an urgency by harsh social and economic conditions. A bank crisis in 1837 had slowed down the railway boom; the harvests of 1837 and 1838 had been poor leading to increases in the already high price of bread, and the hardships had been exacerbated by a bitter winter. The Poor Law Amendment Act of 1834, passed in an effort to save on poor relief, discouraged outdoor relief whilst making the workhouse an option only the destitute would contemplate. Thus employers were able to keep wages low, making life even harsher and more humiliating for the poor. Various Radical members of Parliament joined with members of the London Working Men's Association to press for reform. A Charter was drawn up to formulate demands made on behalf of the working classes for democracy. The Chartists' six demands – universal male suffrage, annual Parliaments, the abolition of property qualifications for Parliamentary candidates, the payment of MPs, vote by secret ballot and equal electoral districts – did nothing directly to alleviate the living conditions of the poor.

However, their realisation would have given the working classes a voice in the governance of their country: 'required, as we are universally, to support and obey the laws, nature and reason entitle us to demand that in the making of laws, the universal voice shall be implicitly listened to'.

In November 1839 a Chartist uprising in South Wales marched on Newport to protest against the arrest of a Chartist leader. They attacked a military detachment quartered there and in the ensuing fracas, several soldiers were injured and protesters killed when the military opened fire. The trial of the Chartist leaders opened in early 1840 amidst rumours of more disturbances to come – possibly a march on London. A week before the debate on Albert's allowance, three of the leaders were found guilty of high treason and sentenced to death by hanging and quartering. The sentence was due to be carried out in the weeks before the royal wedding and the political atmosphere was tense. Melbourne, who lost his kindly, avuncular approach when confronted by Chartist demands, had to be persuaded by the Lord Chief Justice to commute the sentences to one of transportation.

Nevertheless, though Melbourne was unsympathetic towards the Chartists he was aware of the correlation between what was happening at court and what was afoot in the nation. He wrote to Leopold:

> This match does not come off at quite a good moment. The times are somewhat unpropitious. Party spirit runs high, commerce suffers, the working classes are much distressed. Your Majesty well knows how the feelings of nations, which have the power of manifesting public opinion, are affected by these circumstances.[15]

While Parliament was debating Albert's religion, status and income there were further disagreements over his personal staff. At the end of November Victoria wrote briskly to Albert that Melbourne

> has told me that young Mr Anson (his Private Secretary), who is with him, greatly wishes to be with you. I am very much in favour of it, because he is an excellent young man and very modest, very steady, very well-informed, and will be of much use to you.

But Albert was not in favour of this arrangement. It was essential he wrote that he surround himself with superior men 'either of high rank, or very rich, or very clever, or who have performed important services for England' not party placemen.[16] The Prince, 'saw in the proposal an intention',

> on the part of the Whigs to establish their influence over him. Not wishing, at first starting, to have himself thus ostentatiously decorated with the Whig colours, and determined to adhere to his principle of not identifying himself with a party, he energetically opposed the appointment.[17]

Victoria shot back:

> My dear Albert, I must tell you quite honestly that it will not do. You may entirely rely upon me that the people who will be about you will be absolutely pleasant people of high standard and good character ... You may

rely upon my care that you shall have proper people and not idle and not too young, and Lord Melbourne has already mentioned several to me who would be very suitable.[18]

Albert thought it might be more appropriate to have some fellow Germans, who would stand aside from British politics, in his entourage. He tried to make Victoria understand his predicament:

I am leaving my home with all its old associations, all my bosom friends … Except yourself I have no one to confide in. And is it not even to be conceded to me that the two or three persons who are to have charge of my private affairs should be persons who already command my confidence.[19]

But his objection was to no avail. Though Victoria might have been 'distressed to tell you what I fear you do not like, but it is necessary, my dearest, most excellent Albert', she wrote to him later in December that it 'will … not do to wait till you come to appoint all your people'. The Queen had decided who they would be. In the event Albert was to get on very well with Anson and found him 'a faithful, devoted and honest servant, wholly above party intrigues'.[20]

Finally, the waiting was over. Prince Albert arrived at Buckingham Palace in the afternoon of 8 February 1840. He had had 'a terrible crossing' but when the storm-tossed boat arrived at Dover the Queen, who had been ill herself in the last few days – it had been feared that she might have caught measles – on seeing 'his dear dear face again put me at rest about everything'.[21] On the night of her accession, Victoria had rejoiced in the fact that she had slept alone for the first time in her life, but on the morning of her wedding to Albert she was happy to surrender that particular privilege: 'Monday, February 10', she recorded in her journal, 'the last time I slept alone.'

The day of the wedding did not dawn fair. 'A dreadful day', recorded Greville, 'torrents of rain and violent gusts of wind'. Albert and Victoria were to be married in the Chapel Royal in St James's Palace. Westminster Abbey had been ruled out as a possible venue 'as that would be like a 2nd Coronation'. Victoria wrote an account of the wedding in her journal

BELOW *The condition of England question: 'A Trial Between Right and Might'. A broadsheet showing Queen Victoria holding the scales of justice which are unbalanced by the poor man's moral claim to cheap bread, weighed against the vested interests of land, law and church. The dragon of monopoly lies slain at Victoria's feet, a plea for the repeal of the Corn Laws, protecting British agriculture against foreign competition to the detriment of the poor.*

At 1/2 p. 12 I set off [from Buckingham Palace], dearest Albert having gone before. I wore a white satin gown with a very deep flounce of Honiton lace, imitation of old. I wore my Turkish diamond necklace and earrings, and Albert's beautiful sapphire brooch ... I never saw such crowds of people as there were in the Park, and they cheered most enthusiastically. [This was the first Royal wedding for more than a century not to be held in private and late at night. The government had considered it prudent for the people to have an opportunity to see the Queen's new husband as well as to pay for him.] When we arrived at St James's I went into the dressing-room where my 12 young Train-bearers were, dressed all in white with white roses, which had a beautiful effect. Here I waited a little till dearest Albert's Procession had moved into the Chapel. I then went with my Train-bearers and ladies into the Throne-room, where the Procession formed ... The Ceremony was very imposing, and fine and simple, and I think OUGHT to make an everlasting impression on every one who promises at the Altar to <u>keep</u> what he or she promises. Dearest Albert repeated everything very distinctly. I felt so happy when the ring was put on, and by Albert. As soon as the Service was over, the Procession returned as it came, with the exception that my beloved Albert led me out ...[22]

Among the throng in the Chapel – 300 were present – there were 'but 3 Tories there', wrote Florence Nightingale, who was in London on a visit and joined the crowds to see, and in her case be scornful about, the occasion:

Ld Melbourne pressed the Queen to ask more, told her how obnoxious it was. Queen said 'It is MY marriage and I will only have those who can sympathise with me'. She asked D. of Wellington as a public character; Ld Liverpool and the Jenkinsons as her private friends and Ld Ashley because

RIGHT *The arrival of the Coburg princes, Albert and Ernest, at Dover on 7 February 1840, after a painting by Knell. The crossing was 'terrible' and the anxious bridegroom was, in his own words, 'the colour of a wax candle', as he stepped ashore in his new homeland to a welcome from several thousands cheering on the quayside.*

he married a Cowper [a niece of Melbourne] – but not even the Duchess of Northumberland.[23]

The couple signed the register in the Throne-room and Victoria gave each of her Train-bearers

ABOVE *Victoria's sketch of herself on her wedding day, wearing a wreath of orange blossom encircling a veil of Honiton lace. Work on the bridal attire provided short-term employment for 200 people, and the designs were destroyed so that no one could emulate the royal bride.*

as a brooch a small <u>eagle</u> of turquoise. I then returned to Buckingham Palace alone with Albert; they cheered us really most warmly and heartily; the crowd was immense; and the Hall at Buckingham Palace was full of people; they cheered us again and again. The great Drawing-room and Throne-room were full of people of rank, and numbers of children were there ... I went and sat on the sofa in my dressing-room with Albert; and we talked together ... then we went down where all the Company was assembled ... My health and dearest Albert's were drunk ... I went upstairs and undressed and put on a white silk gown trimmed with swansdown, and a bonnet with orange flowers ... Lord Melbourne came to me ... 'Nothing could have gone off better,' he said, and of people being in such good humour ... I pressed his hand once more, and he said 'God bless you, Ma'am', most kindly, and with such a kind look.[24]

At that moment 'Albert came up and fetched me downstairs', and Melbourne, who 'had been much affected' throughout the day in effect relinquished his role of closest advisor and confidante of the Queen, to her husband. The couple 'took leave of Mamma and drove off at near 4; I and Albert alone which was SO delightful'.

The couple were to honeymoon at Windsor Castle. The crowds on the road were so great that they did not reach the Castle till eight o'clock.[40] As the coach drew into Windsor crowds lined the streets, and the houses 'glowed with crowns, stars and all the brilliant devices which gas and oil could supply'.[25] The Queen was exhausted and

had such a sick headache that I could eat nothing and was obliged to lie down ... for the remainder of the evening, on the sofa, but ill or not, I <u>never, never</u> spent such an evening!! My <u>dearest dearest dear</u> Albert sat on a footstool at my side, and his excessive love and affection gave me feelings of heavenly love and happiness I could never hoped to have felt before! He clasped me in his arms, and we kissed each other again and again. His beauty, his sweetness and gentleness – really how can I ever be thankful enough to have such a <u>Husband</u>! ... to be called names of tenderness, I have never yet heard used to me before – was bliss beyond belief! Oh! this was the happiest day of my life! – May God help me to do my duty as I ought and be worthy of such blessings.[26]

The next morning, Victoria wrote a note to her Prime Minister about her 'most gratifying and bewildering' wedding night. Greville, had his intelligence too: he had heard that the newly-weds

were up very early on Tuesday morning walking about, which is very contrary to her former habits. Strange that a bridal night should be so short; and I told Lady Palmerston [who was herself newly married – a fact that made Victoria 'smile' since the couple were 'both of them above fifty'[27]] that this was not the way to provide us with a Prince of Wales.[28]

A street ballad circulating at the time of the wedding raised an intriguing issue:

Since the Queen did herself for a husband 'propose',
The ladies will all do the same, I suppose;
The days of subserviency will be past,
For all will 'speak first' as they always did last!
Since the Queen has no equal, 'obey' none she need,
So of course at the altar from such vow she's freed;
And the women will all follow suit, so they say –
'Love, honour', they'll promise, but never – 'obey'.[29]

In fact, Victoria *had* promised 'to obey' during the wedding ceremony. In 1856, she wrote about the difficulties, in the early years of her marriage, in reconciling the anomalies of being Albert's wife and his sovereign:

It is a strange omission in our <u>Constitution</u> that while the <u>wife</u> of a <u>King</u> has the highest rank and dignity in the realm after her husband assigned to her by law, the <u>husband</u> of a <u>Queen regnant</u> is entirely ignored by law. This is the more extraordinary, as a husband has in this country such particular rights and such great power over his wife, and as the Queen is married just as every other woman is, and swears to obey her lord and master, as such, while by law he has no defined position ... when I first married, we had much difficulty on this subject ...[30]

The rank, position and, above all, the role of the 'King Queen' had come sharply into focus within days of their return to Buckingham Palace, after the couple's brief honeymoon, and the resumption by Victoria of her monarchical duties. Three months later Prince Albert explained to a friend: 'In my home life I am very happy and contented; but the difficulty of filling this place with proper dignity is that I am only the husband, and not the master of the house.'[31] Albert had been educated for a role of responsibility at the insistence of Leopold who was confident of what the job entailed:

The Prince ought in business as in everything to be necessary to the Queen, he should be to her a walking dictionary on reference on any point which her own knowledge or education have not enabled her to answer.

But to be able to do this,

there must be no concealment from him on any subject [and the serious-minded young Prince must] studiously imbibe that information on every subject, which may enable him to be ready and fit to render advice under any circumstances.[32]

But this 'dual monarchy' was not developing. The Prince's Private Secretary, Anson, persuaded Lord Melbourne to discuss the matter with Victoria:

ABOVE *The wedding of Queen Victoria to Prince Albert on 10 February 1840. The bride, dressed in white satin trimmed with lace, was radiant, and the groom, who wore the uniform of a British Field Marshal, entered the Chapel Royal at St James's Palace to the strains of 'See the Conquering Hero Comes'.*

I [Melbourne] have spoken with the Queen, who says that the Prince complains of a want of confidence on trivial matters and on all matters connected with the politics of this country. She said it proceeded entirely from indolence; she knew it was wrong, but when she was with the Prince she preferred talking on other subjects. I told Her Majesty that she should try to alter this, and that there was no objection to her conversing with the Prince on any subject she pleased. My impression is that the chief obstacle in Her Majesty's mind is the fear of difference of opinion, and she thinks that domestic harmony is more likely to follow from avoiding subjects likely to create difference.[33]

But Albert was still refused the key to the despatch boxes and Victoria continued to converse long with her Ministers – alone. The Queen's reluctance to divide her prerogative grew markedly less, however, in the next few months when she found that she was pregnant. She was not pleased:

I am really upset about it ... I have always hated the idea and I prayed God night and day to be left free for at least six months ... I cannot understand how anyone can wish for such a thing, especially at the beginning of a marriage.[34]

But by September that year Albert, in the schoolmasterly way he increasingly came to use when referring to – and addressing – his Queen-wife, was able to report that he had 'come to be extremely pleased with Victoria during the past few months. She has only twice had the sulks ... altogether she puts more confidence in me daily'.[35]

LEFT *'Almost all the way [to Windsor where Victoria and Albert were to honeymoon briefly] the road was lined and thronged with spectators, twenty-two miles of it, every soul turning out from the towns and villages' to cheer the royal newly-weds.*

As her pregnancy progressed, Anson claimed Albert had become 'in fact tho' not in name, Her Majesty's Private Secretary' and messages from Melbourne increasingly included reference to Albert's views, as did Victoria's replies. Albert's aim was, as he told the Duke of Wellington:

> to be the natural head of the family, superintendent of her household, manager of her private affairs, her sole confidential advisor in politics, and only assistance in her communication with the officers of the Government, her private secretary and permanent Minister.[36]

It was an awesome competence.

In June that year Albert had been named Regent should Victoria die leaving an infant heir. 'I am to be Regent – <u>alone</u> – Regent without a Council', he wrote to his brother. 'You will understand the significance of this matter and that it gives my position here in the country a fresh importance'.[37] In August he sat in an armchair next to the Throne at the prorogation of Parliament and was awarded the freedom of the City of London that same month: on 11 September 1840 he was admitted to the Privy Council. Earlier, on 1 June, he had made his first public speech in English. He had addressed a gathering of what he estimated to be 'five or six thousand people' on the subject of slavery – 'the blackest stain on civilised Europe'. Since slavery had been abolished throughout the Empire, the Anti-Slavery Society was considered to be above party, and Albert accepted the invitation to be its president.[38] It gave him a cause and went some way to alleviating the *ennui* he frequently felt with his new life. Melbourne reported

BELOW *A cartoon ridiculing Albert as Victoria's poodle, as she walks with Melbourne. His private secretary, Anson, was concerned that no outlet was being provided at Court for Albert's abilities and energies. 'If you required a cypher in the difficult position of Consort of the Queen', he wrote, 'you ought not to have selected the Prince; having got him you must make the most of him.'*

> The Prince is bored with the sameness of his chess every evening. He would like to bring literary and scientific people about the Court, vary the society, and infuse a more useful tendency into it. The Queen, however has no fancy to encourage such people. This arises from a feeling on her part that her education has not fitted her to take part in such conversation; she would not like conversation to be going on in which she could not take her fair share, and she is far too open and candid in her nature to pretend to one atom more knowledge than she really possesses on such subjects; and yet, as the world goes, she would, as any girl, have been considered accomplished, for she speaks German well and writes it; understands Italian, speaks French fluently, and writes it with great elegance. In addition to this old Davys instilled some Latin into her during his tutorship. The rest of her education she owes to her own natural shrewdness and quickness, and this perhaps has not been the proper education for one who was to wear the Crown of England.[39]

Despite her distaste at being pregnant, the Queen bloomed as she 'grew to a great size' and nine months and eleven days after their wedding, Victoria and Albert's first child was born. Albert and the Duchess of Kent were present and in an adjoining room waited Melbourne and some of her Privy Councillors ready to inspect the newborn and confirm that it had not been smuggled

Outrage on her Majesty.

QUEEN AND PRINCE ALBERT,
Driving in their Phaeton.

LEFT *On 10 June 1840, Queen Victoria was fired at as she rode with Prince Albert in an open carriage along Constitution Hill. The would-be assassin, Edward Oxford, was apprehended by the father of the pre-Raphaelite painter, Millais, who had just doffed his cap to the Queen. Victoria was unhurt and Oxford, the first of a number of insane assailants she was to encounter, was committed to an asylum.*

into the royal bed in a warming pan. The birth was earlier than expected and the wet nurse had to be rushed to the Palace from the Isle of Wight, for the Queen did not intend to feed her infants as she herself had been nourished. Both Victoria and Albert had very much hoped for a son, but again, briefly, a girl was next in line of succession to the throne of England and 'what the country cares about is to have a life more, whether male or female, interposed between the succession and the King of Hanover', wrote Lord Clarendon. And Albert's status was now that of father of the heir to the throne.

Leopold wrote with warm congratulations. Victoria thanked her uncle for his good wishes and spoke of 'his little grand-niece [who] is flourishing; she gains daily in health, strength and, I may add, beauty; I think she will be very like her dearest father ...'[40] but was dismissive of his wish to see her become

> 'Mamma d'une <u>nombreuse</u> famille' for I think you will see with me the great inconvenience a <u>large</u> family would be to us all, ... independent of the hardship and inconvenience to myself; men never think, at least seldom think what a hard task it is for us women to go through this <u>very often</u>.[41]

However, Victoria did 'go through this very often'. With a passionate marriage and a stoical acceptance that 'God's will be done, and if He decrees that we are to have a great number of children, why we must try to bring them up as useful and exemplary members of society',[42] she was pregnant again within three months of the birth of the Princess Royal. She had four children in the first five years of marriage and in all bore nine healthy children in an age when childbirth was frequently hazardous, even for the well to do, and infant mortality was high.

BELOW *A report of the birth of Victoria and Albert's first child from the* Worcestershire Gazette *of 28 November 1840. 'Precisely at 10 minutes to 2 o'clock Mrs Lilly entered the room where the Privy Councillors were assembled, with the "Young Stranger", a beautiful, plump and healthful Princess wrapped in flannel.'*

The Princess Royal was christened Victoria Adelaide Mary Louisa, on the first anniversary of her parent's marriage, though she was known by the family as Pussy as a child, and as she grew up as Vicky.

Victoria's next pregnancy was more tiresome, but on 9 November 1841 she was delivered of a son, a male heir to the throne who was called Albert (Edward) after his father but always known as Bertie. A second daughter, Alice, was born in 1843; a son Alfred (known as Affie) in 1844; two more daughters followed, Helena in 1846 and Louise in 1848; then two more sons, Arthur born in 1850 and Leopold three years later. The last child, Beatrice, who was always known as 'Baby' was born in 1857 when Victoria was thirty-eight and Vicky was shortly to be married.

The growing royal nursery meant a number of changes both public and domestic to the Queen's life. First there was the care and education of the royal children – a matter to which Albert in particular devoted a great deal of serious thought and strict administration. He hardly needed Stockmar's strictures that 'the education of the royal children from the very earliest beginning should be thoroughly <u>moral</u> and thoroughly <u>English</u>'.[43] Initially, Lehzen played an important role in caring for Princess Victoria, as indeed she still did for the infant's mother. She had been devoted to and protective of Victoria since she was a child, never taking a day's holiday, and after seventeen years must have found the changed circumstances contingent on Victoria's marriage hard to adjust to.

For his part, Albert was suspicious of and increasingly hostile towards the influence he imagined Lehzen (who he referred to as 'the old hag' in letters to his brother) had on his wife. He had suggested to Melbourne that she was the reason why Victoria was so reluctant to share the confidences of State with him, though Melbourne dismissed the idea that 'the Baroness is the cause of the want of openness … her name to me is never mentioned by the Queen'.[44]

This did nothing to assuage Albert's conviction that his wife's former governess had a bad effect on her character and was a schemer who sought to influence his children as she had been allowed to influence his wife. Albert accused Victoria of being 'infatuated' with her 'oracle' and pressed her to discharge Lehzen from her service. Finally, Victoria, who found the tension most distressing, agreed and, on 23 September 1842, Lehzen left the Palace and retired on a royal pension to live with her sister in Hanover.

Lady Lyttleton, who had been appointed as one of the Queen's ladies-in-waiting on her accession, and was herself the mother of five, was given authority over the royal nurseries in 1842 and a period of tranquillity ensued. She

ACCOUCHEMENT OF HER MAJESTY.
BIRTH OF A PRINCESS.

(London Gazette Extraordinary.)

Buckingham Palace, Nov. 21.

This afternoon, at ten minutes before two o'clock, the Queen was happily delivered of a Princess; his Royal Highness Prince Albert, her Royal Highness the Duchess of Kent, several Lords of Her Majesty's Most Hon. Privy Council, and the Ladies of Her Majesty's Bedchamber, being present.

This great and important news was immediately made known to the town by the firing of the Tower guns; and the Privy Council being assembled as soon as possible thereupon at the Council-chamber, Whitehall, it was ordered that a form of thanksgiving for the Queen's safe delivery of a Princess be prepared by his Grace the Archbishop of Canterbury, to be used in all churches and chapels throughout England and Wales, and the town of Berwick-upon-Tweed, on Sunday, the 29th of November, or the Sunday after the respective ministers shall receive the same.

Her Majesty and the young Princess are, God be praised, both doing well.

(From the Court Circular.)

Her Majesty was taken unwell at an early hour on Saturday morning, and the medical gentlemen were in consequence summoned to Buckingham Palace.

The Duchess of Kent was sent for at half-past eight o'clock by his Royal Highness Prince Albert. Her Royal Highness immediately went to the Palace, and remained with Her Majesty throughout the day until six o'clock in the evening.

Sir James Clark left the Palace to give the requisite information to Viscount Melbourne. The noble Viscount and the Lord Chancellor arrived at the Palace before ten o'clock.

Summonses were sent to the principal Cabinet Ministers and the great officers of state in town, and expresses were forwarded to the Marquis of Lansdowne, Lord President of the Council, at his seat, Bowood Park, Wilts, and to the Earl of Clarendon, Lord Privy Seal, at Watford.

Some of the Cabinet Ministers and great officers of state arrived before twelve o'clock, and between twelve and one o'clock the Archbishop of Canterbury and the Bishop of London arrived at the Palace.

Her Majesty was safely delivered of a princess at ten minutes before two o'clock p.m. Their Royal Highnesses Prince Albert and the Duchess of Kent were in the room at the time, together with Sir James Clark, Dr. Locock, Dr. Ferguson, and Mr. Blagden, the medical attendants on Her Majesty.

In an adjoining room, the door being open, were the following Councillors—his Grace the Archbishop of Canterbury, the Lord Bishop of London, the Lord High Chancellor, Viscount Melbourne, First Lord of the Treasury, the Earl of Erroll, Lord Steward of the Household, Viscount Palmerston, Secretary of State for Foreign Affairs, Lord John Russell, Secretary of State for the Colonies, and the Earl of Albemarle, Master of the Horse.

The infant Princess having been brought into the room where the Ministers and Great Officers of State were assembled, their Lordships took their departure from the Palace shortly afterwards.

Information of the auspicious event was despatched by a messenger to Her Majesty the Queen Dowager at Sudbury Hall, and one of the Equerries in Waiting conveyed the joyful intelligence to the Royal family in town.

Shortly before four o'clock Prince Albert, attended by Lord Robert Grosvenor and the Hon. Colonel Cavendish, left the Palace to attend a Privy Council.

At the Council it was ordered that a form of thanksgiving for the Queen's safe delivery of a Princess should be prepared by his Grace the Archbishop of Canterbury for England and Wales.

The Council broke up at half-past four o'clock, and Prince Albert returned to the Palace, attended by Lord Robert Grosvenor and the Hon. Colonel Cavendish.

The Duchess of Kent left the Palace in the early part of the evening, but returned about nine o'clock.

On Sunday forenoon the following bulletin was issued:—

" Buckingham Palace, Nov. 22, 10 o'clock a.m.

" The Queen has passed an excellent night. Her Majesty and the infant Princess are going on favourably in every respect.

"JAMES CLARK, M.D.
"CHARLES LOCOCK, M.D.
"ROBERT FERGUSON, M.D.
"RICHARD BLAGDEN."

The following details respecting the auspicious event are ..... a paper possessing to be published under ..... sanction of the Royal Family, and ..... sources of information in all ..... collected, confirmed that the Queen was 'very fond' of her children, but 'severe in her manner and a strict disciplinarian in her family'.

Vicky was a 'remarkably intelligent' and precocious child. She was reading Gibbon's *Decline and Fall of the Roman Empire* and learning Latin before she was five. She was also high-spirited and wilful and Lady Lyttleton thought rather too much was expected of her: 'Poor little body! She is always expected to be good, civil and sensible', and was somewhat 'over-watched and over-doctored' by her anxious parents.[45] She was the special favourite of Albert who spent much time playing with and teaching the child, whose intelligence he came to regard as superior to that of her mother.

The Prince of Wales was not his sister's equal in quickness and learning and sorely tried those who tried to get him to apply himself to his letters. Lady Lyttleton described him as being 'extremely shy and timid, with very good principles, and particularly an exact observer of the truth'.[46] She appreciated his qualities of kindness and sociability, but his parents, particularly his father, were always disappointed by their eldest son. They failed to recognise his charm and intuitive intelligence and engaged a series of unsuitable tutors to mould Bertie into the monarch Albert thought he should become.

Next came 'good, amiable Alice' as her mother labelled the exceptionally pretty, rather shy, unsure third child, followed by 'Affie' who, it always had to be remembered, would be king should anything befall his older brother.

The older children often accompanied their parents on their trips at home and abroad and were gradually initiated into their royal roles. As a toddler Vicky was held up to 'look at the people' as she rode in the royal carriage and before he was three Bertie attended a review in Windsor Great Park to welcome Tsar Nicholas I of Russia. When the Queen contracted chicken-pox in 1849, Vicky and Bertie accompanied their father to the ceremonial opening of the Coal Exchange in the City of London.

ABOVE *Prince Albert holding the infant Princess Royal, 'a perfect little child ... but alas a girl and not the boy, as we had so hoped and wished for. We were, I am afraid, sadly disappointed'. Yet as she grew older it was the intellectual Princess Vicky who was to particularly delight her Papa, and her brothers who would frequently disappoint him.*

But it was not all state occasions and good behaviour. The royal children had young parents who enjoyed playing parlour games with them and taking them to the zoo, or the theatre, or letting them stay up to hear the fine musicians who played at Windsor or Buckingham Palace. Both Victoria and Albert were music lovers and Mendelssohn, who paid several visits and sang with the royal couple, was only one of the composers and singers who gave concerts for the royal family. For Victoria, who had had such an isolated and austere childhood her growing 'tribe' were 'though often a source of anxiety and difficulty, ... a great blessing and cheer & brighten up life'.

As their family grew Victoria and Albert decided that they wanted a private country residence of their own to use as a retreat away from official business and politics, and where they could spend holidays as a family. Buckingham Palace and Windsor Castle were both state residences with restricted space and limited privacy. Osborne House, on the Isle of Wight, standing in an estate of 800 acres and with a commanding view over the Solent, seemed ideal. The royal couple rented the property for a year in 1843 to see how they liked it, and when they found they did, negotiated to buy it out of the Queen's own money. Victoria was enchanted, as she wrote to Melbourne:

> It is impossible to see a prettier place with woods, valleys and points de vue, which would be beautiful anywhere; but all this near the sea (the woods grow into the sea) is quite perfection; We have a charming beach all to ourselves. The sea was so calm and blue that the Prince said it was like Naples. And then we can walk about anywhere by ourselves without fear of being followed and mobbed, which Lord Melbourne will understand is delightful.[47]

The Royal Children in the Nursery

ABOVE *'Dear Papa always directed our nursery and I believe that none was better', wrote the Queen of the creation of the royal 'family' with its exaltation of domestic and bourgeois values. It was a middle-class domesticity far removed from the aristocratic insouciance of Victoria's regency uncles.*

Though the situation was delightful, the house was too small, Prince Albert considered, for a royal residence. He was very interested in architecture and, working with the Norfolk builder of Belgravia, Thomas Cubitt, drew up designs for a grand Italianate villa complete with loggias, towers and campaniles. The building materials used were very modern: cast-iron girders replaced wooden beams, a rather elementary central heating system was installed to supplement the fires, with insulation using crushed sea shells. The interior owed more to Germanic hunting lodges than the palazzos of Florence, though there was a great deal of statuary, including several of Victoria and Albert in various guises and neoclassical figures such as a fig-leaf bedecked version of William Theed's *Narcissus*. Royal group paintings and portraits by Sir Edwin Landseer, Franz Xaver Winterhalter and others adorned the walls of the ornately furnished rooms. The monograms 'V & A' were entwined above the door of every room in the house, except Albert's smoking room where the 'V' is absent. For Victoria, Osborne was a place of tranquillity and relaxation where she could enjoy her family and rejoice to see Albert busy yet relaxed away from the strains of court life.

> How happy we are here! And never do I enjoy myself more, or more peacefully than when I can be so much with my beloved Albert and follow him everywhere![48]

For Albert, Osborne was a place of learning, teaching and organising, where he could be 'partly forester, partly builder, partly farmer and partly gardener [and] a good deal upon my legs in the open air'.[49]

As he had reorganised the chaotic household at Buckingham Palace and Windsor, dispelling lax habits of household management and pilfering, rationalising accounting systems and portion control and doing something about the drains, so at Osborne. Albert planted and planned and soon made the home farm turn in a tidy profit. He also taught the princes to swim, sail, farm and build. They worked with builders and carpenters at the house who showed them their trade and filled in time sheets so that the royal children could be paid at the going rate, as they were for any produce yielded from the vegetable gardens they individually planted and reared. Bertie, Affie, Arthur and Leopold also boned up on military tactics in a model fort equipped with real firing cannons.

Meanwhile, the princesses scrubbed, washed and cooked in the Swiss Chalet built in the grounds and the Queen, who believed such an education in the domestic arts to be appropriate for 'girls of any rank', always aimed to have served at table a dish made by her daughters to tempt guests.

Since her 'progresses' in the mid-1830s with her mother and Sir John Conroy, Victoria had travelled little in Britain. In 1839 she had explained to Melbourne that she had 'a very strong dislike of travel'. 'You must do it one day'; he responded '... You should go to Scotland and Ireland'. In June 1842 she paid her first visit, with Albert, to her northern kingdom. They had been advised that Chartist disturbances made the North unsafe to journey through so they went by sea on the royal yacht. It took three days and three nights before the party 'came in sight of the Scotch coast, which is very beautiful, so dark, rocky, bold and wild, totally unlike our own coast'.[50] Despite the exhausting journey and schedule of parties, balls, dinners and presentations when they arrived, they were completely enamoured of Scotland. The home they were to acquire there was to become a much yearned for and often visited retreat by the couple, and later for Victoria a defining part of her life.

LEFT *The Swiss Chalet in the grounds of Osborne where the royal children, at the direction of their father, learned the household arts of cooking, gardening and thrift that they would rarely, if ever, need to pursue. The royal children laid the foundation stone of the house, which was reminiscent of the Swiss dairy farm of their father's childhood home, in 1853. The eight-year-old Prince Alfred proved a particularly enthusiastic labourer. The furnished chalet was officially handed over to the children on the Queen's birthday the following year.*

Victoria and Albert paid two more visits to the west coast of Scotland in 1844 and 1847 and invariably found themselves marvelling at the magnificent highland scenery through sheeting rain. They had already decided that they wanted to have a home of their own in Scotland, but as Victoria was experiencing twinges of rheumatism the idea of such a damp climate was not very appealing. She consulted her chief physician, Sir James Clark, who was a native of Banffshire and who recounted an encouraging tale. At the very moment that the royal party had been drenched in Ardeverike, Sir James's nephew had been basking in hot sun at the estate of Balmoral on the river Dee on the east coast. A survey was commissioned on the climatic conditions of Deeside by the meticulous Albert. When this was found to bear out the anecdotal evidence of the royal physician's relative, and Victoria had admired the sketches made for her by an Aberdeen artist, James Giles, the royal couple decided to secure a lease on Balmoral – the name of which is thought to derive from the Celtic and mean 'majestic dwelling place'. They eventually purchased the castle in June 1852 at a cost of 30,000 guineas.

The royal family spent their first holiday at Balmoral in the summer of 1848. They received a magnificent welcome with impromptu arches erected all along the road from Aberdeen. The Queen, wearing a tartan shawl, arrived at Balmoral in the early afternoon and found it 'a pretty little castle in the old Scottish style [with] a picturesque tower and a garden in front and a high wooded hill; at the back there is a wood down to the Dee; and the hills rise all around'. After lunch they climbed the wooded hill opposite and looked down on their new home:

> The view … is charming. To the left you look towards the beautiful hills surrounding Loch-na-Gar, and to the right, towards Ballater, to the glen (or valley) along which the Dee winds, with beautiful wooded hills, which reminded us very much of Thürginerwald [Albert's childhood home]. It was so calm, and so solitary, it did one good as one gazed around; and the pure mountain air was most refreshing. All seemed to breathe freedom and peace, and to make one forget the world and its sad turmoils.[51]

BELOW Scottish sport – a stag shot by Prince Albert sketched by Queen Victoria during her annual summer visit to Balmoral. 'What a delightful day!' the Queen recorded in her journal, 'but sad that it should be our last day! Home by half-past six. We found our beautiful stag had arrived, and admired him much.'

But again, as far as Albert was concerned, the existing building did not provide a sufficiently 'majestic dwelling place'. Plans were afoot for a new, much larger castle to be built, which would also provide more suitable accommodation for guests and for the Minister-in-Attendance who was obliged to drag himself the 600 miles north when the Queen and her family sought their Highland solitude.

When the fastidious and often carping Greville was summoned to Balmoral in September 1849 even he was impressed:

> much as I dislike Courts and all that appertains to them, I am glad to have taken this expedition, [which entailed him leaving London at 5 p.m. on Monday, travelling by

various trains to Perth and then road to Balmoral arriving exactly at 2.30 p.m. on Wednesday as he had been bidden] and to have seen the Queen and Prince in their Highland retreat, where they certainly appear to great advantage. The place is very pretty, the rooms very small. They live there without any state whatever; they live not merely like private gentlefolks, but like very small gentlefolks, small house, small rooms, small establishment. There are no soldiers, and the whole guard of the Sovereign and the whole Royal family is a single policeman who walks about the grounds to keep off impertinent intruders or improper characters ... They live with the greatest simplicity and ease. The Prince shoots every morning, returns for luncheon, and then they walk and drive. The Queen is running in and out of the house all day long and often goes about alone, walks into cottages, and sits down and chats with the old women ... In the evening we withdrew to the only room there is besides the dining-room, which serves for billiards, library (hardly any books in it) and drawing-room. The Queen and Prince and her ladies ... soon went back to the dining-room, where they had a Highland dancing-master, who gave them lessons in reels.[52]

For Victoria and Albert these Scottish holidays were a respite from the cares of state, and in Albert's case from a project that was taking shape that called on all his talents for diplomacy, organisation, design and sheer hard work.

BELOW *'The Ascent of Loch-na-Gar' after the watercolour by Carl Haag. On 6 September 1850, Victoria wrote of a 'delightful expedition' to Ben-na-Bhourd in the Scottish highlands. 'The view from the top was magnificent and most extensive ... on the other side rose Loch-na-Gar, still the jewel of all the mountains here' as it towered above Balmoral Castle.*

CHAPTER FIVE

ROYAL CONSTRUCTIONS

'**M**Y DEAREST UNCLE,' wrote Victoria to Leopold on 3 May 1851, 'I wish you <u>could</u> have witnessed the 1st May 1851, the <u>greatest</u> day in our history, the <u>most beautiful</u> and <u>imposing</u> and <u>touching</u> spectacle ever seen, and the triumph of my beloved Albert. Truly it was astonishing, a fairy scene. It was the <u>happiest, proudest day</u> in my life, and I can think of nothing else.'[1]

The 'spectacle' was the Great Exhibition. In the summer of 1849 the Prince Consort had first proposed an international exhibition that would be a showcase for all that was finest in art and industry. He described the concept of a 'Great Exhibition of the Works of Industry of all Nations' at a banquet given by the Lord Mayor of London to launch the project on 21 March 1850. The purpose of the exhibition was to celebrate 'the realisation of the unity of mankind' which was being brought about by scientific discovery and invention – the new civilisation. There was an enthusiastic response from the guests present who included a number of foreign ambassadors of those countries that, it was hoped, would be exhibitors. Queen Victoria was predictably impressed too:

> Albert made a really beautiful speech ... and it has given the greatest
> satisfaction and done great good. He is indeed looked up to and beloved,
> as I could wish he should be ... People are much struck at his powers
> and energy.[2]

Unfortunately not everyone saw Albert's vision quite like that. *The Times* was not at all in favour of the proposed 'vast pile of masonry', a huge edifice using 19 million bricks, that was suggested in the *Illustrated London News* in June 1850, forecasting that it would turn the exhibition into something 'between Wolverhampton and Greenwich Fair', and introduce vulgar commerce into Hyde Park (the proposed site), not to mention the hordes of trippers who would despoil its verdant landscape. *The Times* predicted that it would become 'a bivouac of all the vagabonds of London so long as the Exhibition shall continue ...', whilst the protectionists in Parliament accused 'the object of [the Exhibition's] promoters is to introduce among us foreign stuff of every description – live and dead stock – without regard to quantity or quality. It is meant to bring down prices in this Country, and to pave the way for the establishment of the cheap and nasty trash and trumpery system.'[3]

It looked for a time as if the exhibition might be stymied by lack of cash, for subscriptions were slow to come in at first. However, by the summer of 1850 the subscriptions – including a contribution of £1,000 from the Queen, and £500 from Albert, were on target. So, once Parliament agreed the site all that was needed was a plan for the building, and time was running out if the exhibition was to open as planned in May 1851. Architects from all over the world sent in proposals for the design, but the one finally chosen

LEFT Joseph Paxton's ingenious scheme for the Great Exhibition allowed the trees to be enclosed within the great glass edifice, which provided a pleasant setting for refreshments – even if the sandwiches 'were the worst and smallest ever tasted', as a visitor complained.

BELOW 'The Industrious Boy', a Punch cartoon of June 1850 depicting Prince Albert, cap in hand, appealing for funds for the Great Exhibition. The slow response of industry and commerce was at odds with the Prince's grandiose vision 'to give ... a true test and a living picture of the point of development at which the whole of mankind has arrived ... and a new starting-point from which all nations will be able to direct their future exertions'.

ABOVE *'All the World is Going to See the Great Exhibition'*, cartoon by George Cruikshank. On the opening day, 1 May 1851, 25,000 visitors thronged through the turnstiles: within a week the numbers had risen to 60,000 a day and by the time the exhibition closed on 15 October, it was estimated that 6 million people had visited the Hyde Park site.

was for a 'palace of glass' (held in place by iron girders), sketched by Joseph Paxton on a sheet of blotting paper during a railway board meeting in Derby. Paxton was the superintendent of the gardens of the Duke of Devonshire and had no professional architectural training. His imaginative design was based on the conservatory designed by him at Chatsworth which the Queen and Prince Albert had admired on a visit in 1843. The prefabricated materials meant that the edifice was very quick to erect and dismantle. Construction started on 26 September 1850 and the shell was finished by New Year's Eve. The construct soon came to be known as the 'Crystal Palace' after *Punch* used the designation, though the art critic John Ruskin saw it more as 'a cucumber frame between two chimneys'.[4] Composed of 293,655 panes of glass and an iron framework it covered an area more than three times larger than that of St Paul's Cathedral: it was more than a third of a mile long and so high that the fear that trees in Hyde Park would need to be felled was unrealised since the tall elms, and many of the birds who roosted in them, were enclosed in the structure. 'Try sparrow hawks', was the Duke of Wellington's solution. It worked.

There were 13,937 exhibitors: 7,381 came from Britain and the colonies and the remaining 6,556 from forty other countries. There were four categories: raw materials, machinery and mechanical inventions, manufacture and fine arts. Visitors could wander round the west 'nave' where the space was given over entirely to exhibits from Britain and the colonies, whilst housed in the east 'nave' were the exhibits from foreign countries and their colonies arranged according to latitude.

The Queen paid several visits to the Crystal Palace whilst it was in the process of construction and found it 'one of the wonders of the world ... fairy-like in appearance'. She was anxious that it should be the tremendous success she felt Albert deserved and was concerned about the criticisms of his project and the obstacles put in the way of its fulfilment.

> The triumph is <u>immense</u>, for up to the <u>last hour</u> the difficulties, the opposition, and the ill-natured attempts to annoy and frighten, of a certain set of fashionables and Protectionists, [who disliked the celebration of free trade implicit in the exhibition] were immense; but Albert's temper, patience, firmness and energy surmounted all, and the feeling is universal.[5]

The exhibition was to be truly international – though this did not please the King of Prussia any more than the Parliamentary protectionists. At first he refused his family's attendance on the grounds that 'international' meant

'Socialists and men of the Red colour'. Since revolutionary uprisings had swept Europe in 1848 both deposed – or temporarily deposed – monarchs and exiled political activists had sought shelter in Britain from the social and political discontent and nationalist fervour in their own countries.

Albert wearily recounted some of the objections to the exhibition:

> Mathematicians have calculated that the Crystal Palace will blow down in the first strong gale. Engineers that the galleries would crash in and destroy the visitors; Political Economists have prophesied a scarcity of food in London owing to the vast concourse of people; Doctors that owing to so many races coming into contact with each other the Black Death of the Middle Ages would make its appearance as it did after the Crusades; Moralists that England would be infected by all the scourges of the civilised and uncivilised world; Theologians that this second Tower of Babel would draw upon it the vengeance of an offended God. I can give no guarantee against these perils ...[6]

However, none of the warnings of the Cassandras came to pass. The Great Exhibition was a triumph. Nearly three-quarters of a million people lined the route to Hyde Park as the Queen drove to open the Great Exhibition on 1 May 1851, accompanied by Prince Albert, who was 'terribly fagged' by all the work the exhibition had required of him, and Vicky and Bertie in Highland dress. It was a success from the moment the first visitors flooded in to marvel at the soaring, light-filled building, containing waving palms, tinkling fountains, banks of flowers and miles of exhibits. The seventeen-year-old William Morris may have refused to go in and sat sulking outside in the carriage as his family gawped at the curlicued excesses of Victorian fine arts, but most people were as enchanted as their sovereign was – she dropped in most days. Whilst she pronounced herself to be impressed by the beauty and utility of overseas products, she was overwhelmed by the demonstration that in her view the British section proved 'that we are capable of doing almost anything'. The exhibition was entirely contemporary; it displayed only the

LEFT *Albert's intention for the 'Great Exhibition of the Works of Industry of all Nations' was not only to promote Britain as the workshop of the world, but also to improve technical education with the application of science to the arts and vice versa. The manufacturers of machinery showed themselves to be less concerned about competition than the landowners had in 1846 over competition from foreign corn.*

work of living artists, or very recently living artists, and state-of-the-art machinery and technology.

Six million visitors, the equivalent of nearly a third of the population of Britain at the time, paid an entrance fee that varied on different days from a pound down to sixpence, plus there were two free days between the May Day opening and the exhibition's close on 15 October. Thousands came by train, for by 1851 there were some 6,000 miles of railway line criss-crossing the country, whilst others came from Europe, the United States and the colonies by steam ship and yet more arrived by carriage or on foot.

When the doors closed for the last time on 'a very wet day' that the Queen considered 'appropriate to the really mournful ceremony of the closing of the Exhibition', it was estimated that it made a profit approaching £200,000.

Prince Albert suggested that land in Kensington Gore should be purchased and 'place on it four Institutions corresponding to the 4 great sections of the exhibition'.[7] The Government approved a loan to be added to the exhibition profits and the land, which was purchased in December 1852 and was sometimes labelled 'Albertropolis', now houses a complex of educational institutions including the Imperial College of Science, the Royal Colleges of Music and of Art, and the four museums of science, natural history, geology, and art and design.

The 'Crystal Palace' structure was sold for £70,000 to the London Brighton and South Coast Railway, which had it re-erected in slightly foreshortened form at the end of a specially constructed branch line in Sydenham, which was then in the Kent countryside. The transparent edifice continued to attract visitors for almost a century until it was destroyed by fire in 1936. In 1857 the South Kensington Museum opened on the Kensington Gore site, to house a selection of the finest exhibits from the Great Exhibition, selected 'entirely for the excellence of their workmanship', and this is the site on which the present-day Victoria and Albert Museum, opened in 1909 by Bertie (by then Edward VII), stands.

The Great Exhibition was regarded by many at the time, and the impression has persisted, as a microcosm of British achievement and world hegemony. It was a monument to British industrial confidence and prosperity. The new machinery for making textiles, Wedgwood pottery, pressing steel, James Nasmyth's steam hammer, the hydraulic press used for the construction of the bridge over the Menai Straits, the Ross telescope, Applegarth's printing press with its astonishing capacity for producing 10,000 sheets an hour, were all testimony to the age of mass production. But it was a fragile pinnacle of success and the criticisms of its conception and realisation indicate many of the tensions within mid-Victorian Britain. Increasing industrialisation raised the standard of living of many in Britain, but at the cost of urban overcrowding, long hours worked in inhuman conditions by many employees and in the future cycles of economic boom and depression.

Whereas the decade prior to the Great Exhibition had been politically volatile and socially troubled both at home and abroad, the ten years that followed were ones of continuing prosperity, but they were marred by political stagnation at home – and war abroad.

After the Bedchamber Crisis in 1839 it had become increasingly clear that the natural course of politics had been artificially diverted by the issue. The Whigs had run their course – they lost four by-elections in the early months of 1841 – and found it increasingly hard to govern what was becoming a nation beset with difficulties. The population of Britain had been increasing in what seemed Malthusian proportions – 14.3 per cent between 1831 and 1841 – and the shortages of food predicted by the 'dismal scientist' were apparent. The price of bread was beyond the pockets of the poorest and the tax on imported corn exacerbated the problem in the years of bad harvest that prevailed throughout the late 1830s and the 'hungry forties'.

In May 1841 Melbourne's budget introduced a fixed duty on corn and reduced the duty on imported sugar and timber. At a stroke he alienated both agricultural and commercial interests in Parliament and in a vote on sugar duties on 18 May, which divided the Whig supporters of Free Trade from the Tory protectionists, the Government was defeated. However, Melbourne did not resign. Sir Robert Peel then introduced a vote of confidence and after a debate that lasted five days the Government was defeated by one vote on 29 June 1841. Parliament was dissolved and a general election was called.

Anxious questions were raised: would it be the Bedchamber Crisis all over again? Had the Queen changed her views of the royal prerogative? Or Sir Robert Peel his of political necessities? Lord Melbourne urged compromise:

> ... it is of great importance that Sir Robert Peel should return to London
> with full powers to form an Administration. Such must be the final result,
> and the more readily and better it is acquiesced in the better.

> It must be recollected [he added] that at the time of the negotiation in
> 1839 Lord Melbourne and Sir John Russell were at the head of a majority
> in the House of Commons. That is not the case now.[8]

But, however much the Queen might accept the inevitable, it was not how she saw life. In politics she exercised her constitutional function by conflating her like or dislike of a member of her Government or Opposition with her view of whether or not their policies coincided with her predilictions and paid scant respects to wider issues of policy. It was the same with social questions. Whilst the Queen was often deeply sympathetic and generous to the sufferings and hardships of individuals she heard about – particularly if she knew them – and was generous in her philanthropy to good causes, she had little understanding of the social conditions or radical demands of the working classes. Thus she was opposed, for example, to legislation that aimed to improve the working conditions of factory workers, regarding it as a threat to Britain's competitive edge in the world of trade and industry. She was profoundly unreceptive to Chartist demands, which gathered momentum during the 1840s, and totally uncomprehending of the ideologies that informed political protest and extra parliamentary associations, seeing such manifestations merely as mob rule, the work of agitators that must be repressed with the utmost severity lest they threaten the peace of the kingdom, even though that peace might be exclusive and bought at the price of repression. As a female sovereign she imperiously defended her prerogatives and privileges, yet she did not identify with the 'woman question' and was out of sympathy with demands for increased legal and civil rights for women. Likewise foreign policy was to her a matter of individuals – increasingly frequently her relatives – behaving well or badly and she had little understanding of the wider canvas of burgeoning nationalist aspirations or struggles over resources or human rights.

The royal prerogative could be a dangerous card to play, and Leopold, who had frequently evoked it in 1839, reminded Victoria that her country had deposed a monarch before and that 'the Sovereign should be forcibly reminded by this fact that the Sovereign of a free people cannot be the Sovereign of a party.' Albert too subscribed to the tenet that the Crown must remain above party and refused to join in the cut and thrust of the forthcoming election which, in his view

> empties purses, sets families by the ears, demoralises the lower classes, and perverts many of the upper ... all the world is rushing out of town to agitate the country for or against.[9]

For Victoria, however, the Whigs were the natural ruling party and she embarked on a tour of their great houses, but to no avail. The general election gave an overwhelming victory to the Tories – or Conservatives as they were increasingly called. The section of the middle classes which the Whigs – or Liberals as the *Annual Register* now listed them – admitted to the franchise in 1832, had largely voted for the Opposition. The Queen was 'very sad, and God knows very wretched at times, for myself and my country ... I feel that my constant headaches are caused by annoyance and vexation.'[10]

When the Commons reassembled a vote of no confidence in the Whigs succeeded by a majority of ninety-one. Melbourne resigned as Prime Minister. 'After seeing him for four years with very few exceptions daily', the loss of Melbourne was a great blow to the Queen. Her first Prime Minister felt the loss of their personal and political intimacy too. 'I have seen you daily and I like it better every day', he said simply, 'but it is so different now from what it would have been in 1839'. Victoria now had a husband, whose 'judgment, temper and discretion' Melbourne held in high esteem: 'The Queen, no longer having Lord Melbourne to resort to in case of need, must from this moment consult and advise with the Prince'.[11]

The outgoing Prime Minister gave some advice to his successor, Sir Robert Peel, on how to treat the Queen:

> ... he should write fully to Her Majesty, and elementarily, as Her Majesty always liked to have full knowledge upon everything which was going on ... the Queen is not conceited; she is aware that there are many things she cannot understand, and she likes to have them explained

to her … she does not like long audiences, and I never stayed with her a long time …[12]

But the Queen confessed that she

was afraid that she could never be at ease with Peel, because his manner was so embarrassed, and that conveyed embarrassment also to her, which it would be very difficult to get over.

Melbourne hoped that this would wear off in time and Greville suggested that 'cultivating the Prince, with whom he [Peel] could discuss art, literature and the tastes they had in common' might help.[13] Greville observed the Queen with her new Prime Minister at Windsor following his first Privy Council.

She talked for some time to Peel, who could not help putting himself in his accustomed attitude of a dancing master giving a lesson. She would like him better if he would keep his legs still.[14]

Gradually the Queen did come to like Peel and respect his qualities of steely integrity and fair mindedness – for example, he had no objection and saw no disloyalty in Victoria and Melbourne keeping up a steady flow of letters after his demise, though the Prince and Baron Stockmar had been insistent that this was unwise and bordering on the unconstitutional.

Following the birth of Bertie, which was followed by a period of post-natal depression, Victoria withdrew a little from politics. Anson recorded:

I should say that her Majesty interests herself less and less about politics and that her dislike is less than it was to her present Ministers, though she would not be prepared to acknowledge it.[15]

Over ten years later, in 1852 on the day she was to open Parliament she confided to Leopold:

LEFT *The Great Chartist meeting held on Kennington Common in South London, 19 April 1848. The Chartists' six points for political reform were backed by what the* Morning Chronicle *called 'the cry of millions suffering under a diseased condition of society'. Parliament proved unresponsive to Chartist demands, but hunger kept the movement alive, and the European revolutions of 1848 gave it a fresh impetous. However, the Kennington meeting was a fiasco from which Chartism never recovered.*

I love peace and quiet – in fact, I <u>hate</u> politics and turmoil …Albert grows daily fonder of politics and business, and is so wonderfully <u>fit</u> for both – such perspicacity and such <u>courage</u> – and I daily grow to dislike them both more and more. We women are not <u>made</u> for governing – and if we are good women, we must <u>dislike</u> these masculine occupations; but there are times which force one to take an <u>interest</u> in them *mal gré bon gré* and I do, of course, intensely.[16]

ABOVE Punch*'s comment on the debate on Prime Minister Robert Peel's decision to repeal the Corn Laws which protected British agriculture against the import of cheaper foreign corn. The Irish famine of 1845 had been one of the factors that had converted Peel to free trade. His decision split his Conservative Party, but won the admiration of the Queen for 'his unbounded* loyalty, courage, patriotism and high-mindedness*'.*

Bad harvests throughout the early years of Victoria's reign, coupled with population growth and increasing industrial concentration, meant that domestic corn production was not sufficient to feed the population at a reasonable cost. Yet the Corn Law Act, passed in 1815 at the end of the Napoleonic Wars, kept cheaper foreign corn out by a series of tariffs designed to protect British agriculture. In 1838 a highly effective, middle-class pressure group, the Anti-Corn Law League, had formed in Manchester with the intention of getting the Corn Laws repealed. A new urgency informed the League's demands after the disastrous harvest of 1845 and the terrible Irish famine, which started in 1844 when a potato blight from the United States devastated crops of Ireland's staple food and left its people starving. By the autumn of 1845 Peel was convinced that the Corn Laws must be repealed. But many of his Cabinet, men of the landed interest and protectionists, were in violent disagreement. The Prime Minister informed the Queen of his intention to introduce a Bill to modify the Corn Laws – and also of the divisions within his Cabinet over the matter. On 28 November 1845 she wrote to him:

The Queen thinks the time is come when a removal of the restrictions upon the importation of food cannot be successfully resisted. Should this be Sir Robert's own opinion, the Queen very much hopes that none of his colleagues will prevent him from doing what it is <u>right</u> to do.

But the Cabinet was still divided and Peel journeyed to the Isle of Wight to tender his resignation to the Queen. She accepted with reluctance for she had come to greatly admire Peel, whom she praised as 'belonging to no party' – which was just as well, as far as she was concerned, since the party he led was not the Whigs but the Conservatives – 'fashionables', the 'claret-drinkers' and 'fox hunters'. Albert, too, saw in Peel's independence and intransigence a statesman above politics and was in the same degree of daily correspondence with the Tory leader as he had advised his wife that it was unwise for her to be with Melbourne. Albert's interest in agriculture and husbandry also allied him with the anti-protectionists who saw the modernisation of farming rather than the maintenance of protective tariffs as the way to alleviate the food crises.

The Queen invited Lord John Russell to form a government but after protracted negotiations and prevarication, Russell declared that he was unable to comply. On 20 December 1845 the Queen wrote:

> Sir Robert Peel has just been here [Windsor Castle]. He ... did not hesitate for a moment in withdrawing his offer of resignation. He said he felt it his duty at once to resume office, though he is deeply sensible of the difficulties with which he has to contend.

Victoria garnered a great deal of praise for her handling of this constitutional crisis. It was the exact reverse of the Bedchamber incident. The *Examiner* reported on 27 December 1845, that she had played a 'scrupulous constitutional role ... [and proved herself] warmly devoted to the interests of a people, and with so enlightened a sense of their interests'.

On 27 January 1846, with Prince Albert listening attentively in the gallery, which led to remarks about unconstitutional behaviour, party favouritism and royal support for Free Trade, Peel delivered, what the Queen later praised as a 'beautiful and indeed unanswerable speech' putting the case for the total repeal of the Corn Laws.[17]

The Bill split the Tory party, but after months of debate it passed its third reading in the House of Lords on 28 June 1846. That same night, however, Peel was defeated in the House of Commons on an Irish Coercion Bill, one of a series of occasional measures that sought to confer extraordinary powers on the executive in Ireland. It was the Commons hitting back over the Corn Laws. Peel could have sought the dissolution of Parliament and gone to the country for a larger majority, but such an election would have been fought on the issue of repression in Ireland where Peel had sought toleration, and the repeal of the Corn Laws was bound up figuratively if not economically with the Irish famine, for the situation in Ireland was worsening. Between 1846 and 1851 the population had fallen by two million from death and emigration, and, predictably, the politics grew gradually more bitter. 'Here the potatoes have turned out very bad and will lead to the greatest political complications. It is impossible to argue with famished people' wrote Prince Albert to his brother.[18]

Three days later Peel resigned. The Queen wrote to him from Osborne to

> seize the opportunity ... of expressing her <u>deep concern</u> at losing his services, which she regrets as much for the Country as for herself and the Prince. In whatever position Sir Robert may be, we shall ever look on him as a kind and true friend, and ever have the greatest esteem and regard for him as a Minister and as a private individual.[19]

BELOW *'Sir Robert Peel reading to Queen Victoria', a pen and wash sketch by Sir David Wilkie. Victoria's initial distaste for Peel, mainly because he wasn't a Whig, but compounded by his lack of social graces, soon changed to admiration for her Prime Minister's integrity. In 1844 she wrote 'Peel's resignation would not only be for us (for <u>we cannot</u> have a better and a <u>safer</u> Minister), but for the whole country, and for the peace of Europe – a great <u>calamity</u>.'*

Peel retired to the back benches. But four years later he was dead, thrown from his horse in July 1850 as he rode up Constitution Hill. He lingered for a few days and died in agony. The Queen and Prince Albert were devastated:

> That is one of the hardest blows that could have fallen on us and on the country … his value is now becoming clear even to his opponents; all Parties are united in mourning.[20] … My poor dear Albert … has felt, and feels, Sir Robert's loss <u>dreadfully</u>. He feels he has lost a second father.[21]

During the late 1840s and early 1850s, Victoria lost three of the politicians who had featured prominently in her life. First Melbourne died in November 1848. After leaving office he had remained leader of the Opposition in the House of Lords, but in October 1842 he had suffered from a stroke from which he had never fully recovered. Then in 1850 Peel died and two years later there was another loss. 'One cannot think of this country without the "Duke" our immortal hero', wrote Victoria in her journal on the death of the Duke of Wellington of a stroke – 'he seems to have gone out like a lamp' – at his home at Walmer Castle on 14 September 1852, aged eighty-three.

BELOW *The lying-in-state of the Duke of Wellington. The Duke, who had 'gone out like a lamp' on 14 September 1852, lay in Chelsea Hospital for three days, with his cocked hat and sword placed on the coffin. Pairs of soldiers from his regiments stood guard like statues and eighty-three candelabras – one for each year of his life – illuminated the magnificent scene. On the final day the public were admitted and in the chaos, as thousands crammed in to pay their last respects, three people were crushed to death.*

The hero of Waterloo, the 'Iron Duke' who, when he laid down his arms, became Tory Prime Minister, was given a state funeral. The Duke's body lay in state, with his cocked hat and sword placed on the coffin, and his array of medals and orders at the foot, for three days. For the funeral on 18 November – the five-foot tall cadaver had had to be refrigerated for the intervening two months – the bronze hearse was pulled by twelve black horses in full mourning dress, and was accompanied by representatives of the entire British army. The Duke's horse was in line – riderless. As the procession moved slowly to the roll of muffled drums from Chelsea Hospital to St Paul's Cathedral, a million and a half people, many of whom had waited through the night to be there, bowed their heads in the wind and rain as it passed. The Queen stood on the balcony of Buckingham Palace as the seemingly endless, solemn, sombre parade moved slowly past, honouring the man who was not only the nation's hero, but who had been present at her birth, by proxy at her christening, and on every important formal occasion throughout her life and after whom her third son, the Duke's godson, Arthur, was named.

> For this country, and for us, his loss ... is irreparable! ... He was the
> GREATEST man this country ever produced, and the most devoted and
> loyal subject, and the sternest supporter the crown ever had.[22]

The politician who was still very much alive and directed Britain's contentious foreign policy from the 1840s into the 1860s was Palmerston. Lord Palmerston was a Whig (though he had started out as a Tory). He, like Melbourne, was urbane, sceptical, epicurean – and an active and adept lover. In his youth he had been dubbed 'Lord Cupid' – though his love for the married Lady Cowper had been steadfast and when they finally married in 1839, after her husband's death, the twenty-six years they had left to them before Palmerston died, aged eighty in 1865, were ones of great happiness and companionship. However, Palmerston substituted Melbourne's tolerant languor for the prodigious hard work and the encyclopedic knowledge of a supremely professional diplomat with a strong, confident, sometimes bombastic, temperament, and a clear view of matters and of Britain's role in them.

In the early years of Victoria's reign Palmerston, as Foreign Secretary, had been patient and fastidious, though more patrician and less paternalistic than Melbourne in educating the young Queen into her role and the complexities of foreign affairs. But he was firm from the start that he informed and followed his own imperatives even if they conflicted with the views of the Queen. After her marriage Victoria began to assume a competency in foreign affairs that had little to do with the tutelage of her Foreign Secretary and a great deal to do with Albert's view of his own role and abilities. In 1841 the Queen complained that she had not received any despatch boxes for several days and wished them sent *every* day – and not to be sent drafts to approve after the originals had already been sent. 'This should never be done!' she decreed.[23] Victoria's view of 'the right of supervision and control belonging to the Crown in foreign politics' was reinforced by the visits the royal couple had begun to make to other 'Crowns' – their combined sets of relatives scattered throughout the royal houses of Europe.

Victoria journeyed abroad for the first time in August 1843 when she and Albert visited France at the invitation of Louis Philippe (whose sister's marriage to Leopold was only one filament in the dynastic web that enmeshed the House of Orléans and the Queen and the Prince).

The Queen's visit to France came at a fortuitous moment in soothing Anglo-French relations, following the rift over the so-called Eastern Question when Britain had sided with Russia, Prussia and Austria to prevent the French-backed Egyptian ruler from conquering the Ottoman Empire. It was a historic occasion. The last British monarch to pay a visit to a French monarch had been Henry VIII when he had appeared at the Field of the Cloth of Gold in 1520. Since George III British monarchs had stayed at home. When Victoria paid her first visit abroad she found 'Everything very different to England, particularly the population.'[24] The trip with its grand dinners, concerts, shopping expeditions and picnics, enchanted the Queen, whilst her host made as much as possible of its diplomatic possibilities by

RIGHT *At the invitation of Louis-Philippe, King of the French, Victoria paid her first visit abroad in August 1843. She and Albert stayed at the magnificent Château d'Eu in the Somme and the King arranged a series of grand picnics in the forest where as many as 70 people lunched in a clearing on a 'collation, composed of meats, pâtés, confectionary of the most recherché description, in fact everything that the most exquisite taste could suggest and wealth provide.'*

commissioning a number of paintings to commemorate the visit and assuring the Queen that he ardently sought close links with Britain to guarantee peace in Europe. Victoria was to repay this hospitality in an unexpected way when, in 1848, revolution in France forced the notably pear-shaped French King to flee to England. Wary of British political opinion as being seen to shelter foreign émigrés who had lost the trust of their own subjects, she nevertheless allowed the French exiles to settle at Claremont (which after all belonged to his brother-in-law, Leopold). Palmerston, who did not uphold the privileges of absolutist monarchs, but was rather a supporter of the liberal movements for constitutional reform and nationalist recognition that swept Europe that year, generously provided living expenses from 'secret service money … on condition that the royal family should not know where the money came from'.

Also, in the name of diplomacy, the Tsar of Russia paid a visit to Britain. Nicholas I was convinced of French ambitions in the East and therefore concerned to confirm the Russo-British pledge to support the Ottoman Empire against any such encroachments, and to judge if there was any prospect of detaching Britain from her alliance with France. Aware of Turkey's parlous state, he also intended to take action in the not far distant future. The Tsar arrived in London, with two days notice on 1 June 1844, Victoria found him

> … a <u>very striking</u> man; still very handsome; his profile is <u>beautiful</u>, and his manners <u>most</u> dignified and graceful; extremely civil – quite alarmingly so, as he is so full of attentions and <u>politesses</u>. But the expression of the <u>eyes</u> is <u>formidable</u>, and unlike anything I ever saw before. He gives me and Albert the impression of a man who is <u>not</u> happy, and on whom the weight of his immense power and position weighs heavily and painfully …

Reflecting after the Tsar had departed, Victoria ventured:

I was extremely against the visit [but Albert] and with great truth says [what] is the great advantage of these visits is that I not only <u>see</u> these great people but <u>know</u> them. I got to know the Emperor and he to know me ... He is stern and severe – with fixed principles of <u>duty</u> which nothing on earth will make him change; very clever I do <u>not</u> think him, and his mind is an uncivilised one; his education has been neglected; politics and military concerns are the only things he takes great interest in; the arts and all softer occupations he is insensible too, but he is <u>sincere</u>, I am certain sincere even in his most despotic acts, from a sense that that <u>is the only</u> way to govern.[25]

In fact Nicholas I was a most reactionary ruler, suppressing any liberal tendencies at home and quelling rebellion in Poland with great harshness.

The chasm between the Sovereign (and Prince Albert) and her Foreign Secretary increased. In 1845 Palmerston informed the House of Commons:

I do not depreciate the visit of sovereigns but however gratifying they may be, they do not impress me with such entire confidence with regard to the maintenance of our mutual peaceful relations as to justify any reduction in British armaments.[26]

They continued to have differences of opinion over foreign affairs such as in the dispute over the duchies of Schleswig and Holstein when Palmerston supported Denmark and they Schleswig; when Victoria and Albert supported the dominance of Prussia in Germany, Palmerston was more cautious and while they favoured Austrian hegemony in Italy, Palmerston was a fervent champion of Italian independence. Palmerston thought it legitimate for Foreign Ministers to communicate unofficially with parties that were aiming to overthrow the existing government: Victoria emphatically did not – and even the Prime Minister Lord John Russell saw that as 'impolitic and perilous' conduct.

In 1850 matters came to a head: first there was the Don Pacifico incident, when in January that year Palmerston ordered the British fleet to seize Greek shipping in the port of Piraeus in Greece in restitution for the losses suffered by a Portuguese Jew, born in Gibraltar and thus able to claim British citizenship when an anti-Semitic Greek mob had attacked his house. It had been an excessive claim; Palmerston's action was out of all proportion to the grievance and caused anger abroad and acute embarrassment at home. The Queen and Prince Albert shared these sentiments.

The Queen decided that the time had come when she should make clear what she expected from her Foreign Secretary:

She requires: (1) That he will distinctly state what he proposes in a given case, in order that the Queen may know as distinctly to <u>what</u> she has given her Royal sanction; (2) Having <u>once given</u> her sanction to a measure, that it

ABOVE 'Victoria the Guardian Angel'. A German caricature of Victoria affording asylum to the monarchs who had been displaced from their thrones by the liberal and nationalist revolutions that swept Europe in 1848. In fact, whilst Victoria was alarmed about the 'state of politics in Europe', she was critical of the French King who arrived at Newhaven: 'One does not like to attack those who have fallen, but the poor King L.P, has brought much of this on by that ill-fated return to a <u>Bourbon policy</u>. I always think he <u>ought not</u> to have abdicated.'

ABOVE *Henry Temple, 3rd Viscount Palmerston. Victoria and Albert's relationship with their flamboyant Foreign Secretary reached a nadir in the early 1850s. 'Foreign governments distrust and foreign nations hate Lord P.', wrote Albert in 1851, 'and he is not likely to change his nature in his sixty-seventh year'. But for a Sovereign to engineer the dismissal of a Minister, particularly one who was so popular with the people as 'our immoral one for foreign affairs', proved difficult.*

be not arbitrarily altered or modified by the Minister; such an act she must consider as failing in sincerity towards the Crown, and justly to be visited by the exercise of her Constitutional right of dismissing the Minister. She expects to … receive the Foreign Despatches in good time, and to have the drafts for her approval sent to her in sufficient time to make herself acquainted with their contents before they must be sent off.[27]

But by this time Palmerston, during a debate on the affair, had delivered a five-hour speech, which climaxed with the rousing sentiment that the principles on which the foreign policy of Her Majesty's Government must be conducted bound it 'to afford protection to our fellow subjects abroad' so, as a Roman could claim *Civis Romanus sum,*

so also a British citizen in whatever land he may be, shall feel confident that the watchful eye and the strong arm of England will protect him against injustice and wrong.[28]

The peroration 'drew loud and prolonged cheers' and the enthusiasm for 'Pam' throughout the country made it clear that foreign policy was not just the business of monarchs – and politicians – but that it stirred the people too.

In September there was another cause for conflict in the visit of the Austrian General Haynau whose reputation for atrocities in Italy made him an unwelcome visitor to many in Britain. On 5 September, whilst visiting a London brewery, draymen recognised Haynau as 'the Austrian butcher' and attacked him. The Queen thought that Palmerston should have written a more apologetic note to the Austrian Ambassador about the incident than he had; Palmerston disagreed explaining that revulsion at the General was not confined to the brewery workers of London but that he was known as 'General Hyæna' in Vienna too. As was to be expected, the Queen's protest was too late: when she received a draft, the original had already been sent. This time she insisted on the recall and repudiation of the despatch to the Ambassador.

In October 1851, Louis Kossuth, a Hungarian patriot arrived in England and made speeches denouncing the Emperors of Austria and Russia as the oppressors of Hungry. The Queen, alarmed that this might disrupt the friendly relations she was anxious to cultivate with both Emperors, advised Palmerston that Kossuth should not be received by him. In fact Kossuth had already been invited by Palmerston to his own home. Palmerston was incensed: 'There are limits to all things. I do not chose to be dictated to as to who I may or may not receive in my own house'.[29]

Again the Queen pressed for Palmerston's dismissal, but it was clear that his standing – and that of Kossuth – was high in the country. Lord John Russell was aware of this, and also of his own political difficulties. Who would replace Palmerston as Foreign Secretary? And if he lost Palmerston, might he well not lose the support of the Radicals on whom he depended too?

Palmerston's – temporary – nemesis came in December 1851 when, without consultation, he congratulated the French Ambassador on Napoleon III's *coup d'état*. The Queen was outraged – or seized her opportunity. In purporting to express the views of the Cabinet he had violated the 'policy of strict neutrality which had been laid down'. This time it was not a popular issue in the country and though Palmerston was able to demonstrate rational political reasons for his statement, Russell was able to point out that it was not his opinion that was at issue; it was his action in again acting unilaterally without prior Cabinet consultation and royal sanction. Palmerston refused to accept these conditions and Russell advised the Queen that in the circumstances she should inform Palmerston that she 'was ready to accept the Seals of Office and place them in other hands'. Which she did – with pleasure.

The 'Eastern Question' flared up again in February 1853 when the Tsar sent his troops to Constantinople to enforce his demands that Turkey give Russia political as well as religious rights over all Greek Christians in Turkey; the Turks refused. In July Russia occupied two Turkish dependencies, Wallachia and Moldavia, and in response Britain and France sent their fleets into the Dardanelles. Negotiations to reach a peaceful solution failed when Turkey refused the proposed compromise and, on 4 October, 1853, declared war on Russia. Whilst the Prime Minister, Lord Aberdeen, was prepared to continue to negotiate, the Queen decided that the current situation could be laid at the feet of 'the selfishness and ambition of one man': Tsar Nicholas I, the bellicose autocrat who had felt 'skinned' on his visit to Britain when he was forced to change out of his military uniform at a State banquet.

In December news reached London of what became known as the 'Massacre of Sinope' when the Russian fleet virtually destroyed the Turkish fleet in the port of Sinope on the Black Sea on 3 November. Only 400 Turkish seamen survived: 4,000 men perished. There was outcry in Britain – much of it directed against Prince Albert who was thought to be acting in the interests of Russia and also to have orchestrated Palmerston's resignation as Home Secretary, since Palmerston, it was believed, was the only one who would 'stand up to the Russian bear'. (In fact Palmerston had resigned on 15 December in protest at Aberdeen's proposal to extend the franchise, and was, to Palmerston's surprise accepted. A week later Palmerston effectively withdrew his resignation and Aberdeen reinstated him.) Xenophobic rumours spread of Albert's sinister influence on the Queen, the 'whisper in the ear' against an alliance with France, on behalf of the Coburg interest, not the British. Such was the disquiet that at the reassembly of Parliament at the end of January 1854 Lord John Russell and Lord Aberdeen in the House of Commons and Lord Derby in the House of Lords defended the Prince

Consort's constitutional correctness and loyalty to the Crown. The day before, in her Address from the Throne, the Queen had continued to speak of efforts to avert war and seek conciliation between Russia and Turkey. But by the middle of February she was writing 'War is, I fear, quite inevitable … Our beautiful Guards sail to-morrow. Albert inspected them yesterday'.

On 28 March 1854 Britain followed France in declaring war on Russia. Prussia, however, another of the guarantors decided to remain neutral. In September the Russians were routed by the Allies in the Battle of Alma. 'We are', the Queen wrote,

> and indeed the whole country is entirely engrossed in the Crimea. We have received all the most interesting and gratifying details of the splendid and decisive victory of the Alma; alas! it was a bloody one. Our loss was a heavy one – many have fallen and many are wounded, but my noble Troops behaved with a courage and desperation which was beautiful to behold.[30]

Lord Raglan, the Commander of the British troops in Crimea, then pressed for a march on Sebastopol, but he was overruled by the combined opinion of Sir John Burgoyne and the French Commander-in-Chief General Canrobert. In the meantime the Russians fortified Sebastopol and went on the offensive and a war that the British thought was almost won at Alma was to rage until March 1856.

The Crimean War is chiefly remembered for mismanagement and deficiencies in military command and support of the armed forces. On 25 October 1854 at Balaclava, the Turks fled in the face of the advancing Russians. The Russians – who in fact had been routed at the battle – prepared to commandeer the Turks' abandoned weapons. Ordered to stop the Russians, a British cavalry charge was led by Lord Cardigan. And so 'into the valley of death rode the six hundred' straight into the Russian guns. Of those 673 men only 195 rode back. Victoria, 'trembled with emotion, as well as pride, in reading the recital of the heroism of those brave men.'[31]

As the war continued the Queen worried about the loss of life in battle and the 'privations' that the soldiers were 'enduring', but whilst 'my heart bleeds for the many fallen … I consider that there is no finer death for a man than on the battlefield'.[32] The winter of the first year of the war was bitter: the troops sat out a terrible four months of raging storms and snow with supplies lost and horses killed. Cholera and dysentery struck and between November 1854 and the end of February 1855, nearly 9,000 British troops perished and almost twice that number were wounded or seriously ill. But it wasn't just the weather. The reports by W.H. Russell, the first-ever accredited war correspondent, told the readers of *The Times* of mismanagement and incompetence on a grand scale: of filthy, ill-equipped hospitals at Scutari, endless delays in receiving supplies and when the supplies did arrive, they were unusable, all left-footed

ABOVE *A porcelain pot lid depicting Queen Victoria, the Emperor Napoleon III and the Sultan of Turkey, Abdul-ul-Mejid. Its manufacture was evidence of the pro-Turkish, anti-Russian sentiment that swept Britain in 1854 when France and Russia were in dispute over the 'sick old man of Europe', the Ottoman Empire.*

BELOW *'Portrait of the Celebrated Miss-Management'. An attack on the British government for its failures in the Crimean War when corruption and incompetence meant the British army froze in the winter of 1854–55: between November 1854 and February 1855 nearly 9,000 British soldiers perished in hospital, and some 14,000 lay injured.*

boots for example, or boots for the snow and mud that had been soled and heeled with paper.

There was an immediate charitable response at home: an appeal was launched to aid the hospitals which raised £25,000 and Florence Nightingale was sent out to Scutari to take charge of the hospital there. The Queen, her daughters and the ladies of the royal household set an example by knitting socks and mittens and comforters for the frozen troops. And on 23 January 1855 a Radical, J.A. Roebuck, called for a Parliamentary committee to inquire into the mismanagement of the war. On 31 January the Government was defeated by a vote of 305 votes to 148. The Government resigned and the Queen, reluctantly, and after trying other possibilities, appointed Palmerston Prime Minister.

As the war dragged on seemingly inconclusively but with devastating loss of life, the Anglo-French alliance began to strain. At one point Napoleon III, who was losing 3,000 men a month, proposed going to war in person. The idea appealed to no one, least of all the French troops. It was suggested that the Queen should invite the Emperor and Empress to Britain in 1855, to dissuade Napoleon from his foolhardy scheme and to strengthen the alliance.

The visit was a spectacular personal success: the Queen was won over by the Emperor who afforded her the opportunity to 'converse with a man of the world on a footing of equality', and whose mien 'was of a character to flatter her vanity without alarming her virtue and modesty, she enjoyed the novelty of it without scruple of fear'. He was charming, sat a horse well, and the Queen received a *frisson* when she thought 'of a granddaughter of George III dancing with the nephew of our great enemy the Emperor Napoleon, now my most firm ally, in the Waterloo Gallery'.[33]

ABOVE *'Queen Victoria's first Visit to her Wounded Soldiers', by Jerry Barrett, 1856. An eye-witness account of a visit paid by Queen Victoria to the Brompton Hospital, Chatham, on 3 March 1855 to see some of the disabled soldiers who had returned from the Crimea. She was accompanied by Prince Albert (left) and the Prince of Wales and Prince Alfred. The injured soldiers are James Higgins, of the 7th Fusilier Guards, who lost a foot at Alma, and Private John McCabe of the 5th Dragoon Guards, who took part in the cavalry charge at Balaclava and was slashed by sabres. 'I feel a pride to have such Troops, which is only equalled by my grief for their suffering', wrote Queen Victoria at the time.*

ABOVE *Queen Victoria and Prince Albert, a photograph by Roger Fenton, 30 June 1854. Earlier that year Albert had been the subject of press vilification, accusing him of intervening on behalf of Russia in the Turko-Russian dispute. Victoria was incensed. 'The stupidest trash is babbled to the public, so stupid that you would not give it to the pigs to litter in.' In March the Crimean War broke out and Fenton, carrying a letter of introduction from Albert, became one of the first war photographers.*

For the Empress Eugénie, Victoria had nothing but praise and both she and Albert 'admired [Eugénie's] toilette extremely'. This was particularly generous of Victoria since, first, Albert rarely took any notice of any woman and secondly, the Queen's own dress sense was the despair of those who minded about such things. She 'hated being troubled about dress' and swathed her tea-cosy shape in unfashionable clothes and in unappealing colours. Her capacious poke bonnets, which she wore regardless of fashion, would have been suitable to a dowager of sixty when the Queen was in her early thirties, and on too many occasions she carried a large handbag. 'A voluminous object which she carried on her arm', General Canrobert noted when Victoria visited Paris later in the year; 'it was an enormous reticule – like those of our grandmothers – made of white satin or silk, on which was embroidered a fat poodle in gold'. The kindest conclusion was that one of her daughters had made it and that's why she loyally clutched it. The General recalled when he had first seen Victoria in Paris:

> In spite of the great heat, she had on a massive bonnet of white silk with streamers behind and a tuft of marabou feathers on top … Her dress was white and flounced; but she had a mantle and sunshade of a crude green that did not go with the rest of her costume.[34]

Whereas, on her visit to England, Eugénie 'looked lovely in a pale green dress, trimmed with Brussels lace, a shawl to match and a white bonnet.' In August that same year Victoria and Albert paid a return visit to France, accompanied by Vicky and Bertie. Again it was an outstanding success.

But still the war dragged on. Victoria visited the wounded soldiers and was stricken by the sight of

> such fine, powerful frames laid low and prostrate with wounds and sickness on beds of suffering and maimed in the pride of life [it] is indescribably touching to us <u>women</u> who are born to suffer and can bear pain more easily, so different to men and soldiers accustomed to activity and hardship, whom it is particularly sad and pitiable to see in such a condition.[35]

In May that year the Queen presented medals for gallantry to the soldiers of the Crimean War at a ceremony that was 'the first of the kind ever witnessed in England'.

> From the highest Prince of the Blood to the lowest Private, all received the same distinction for the bravest conduct in the severest actions, and the rough hand of the brave and honest private soldier came for the first time in contact with that of their Sovereign and their Queen! … They were so touched, so pleased; many I hear, cried – and they won't hear of giving up their Medals, to have their names engraved upon them, for fear they should

<u>not</u> receive the <u>identical one</u> put into <u>their hands by me</u>, which is quite touching. Several came by in a sadly mutilated state. None created more interest or is more gallant than young Sir Thomas Troubridge, who had, at Inkerman, <u>one leg</u> and the <u>other foot</u> carried away by a round shot, and continued commanding his battery till the battle was won … He was dragged by in a bath chair, and when I gave him his medal I told him I should make him one of my Aides-de-camp for his very gallant conduct.[36]

In September 1855 the French and British attacked fortresses guarding Sebastopol. The French assault, though very heavy in terms of lives lost, was successful. The British attack on Redan was not. Nevertheless the Russians anticipating its fall, razed Sebastopol to the ground and evacuated their troops after a siege that had lasted sixteen days short of a year. The peace treaty, which was signed in Paris on 30 March 1856 did not leave Russia harshly treated, nor the Allies gloating over their gains after a long war of carnage and attrition.

Prussia had declined to join the Allies in the Crimea – much to the consternation of Victoria – and of Albert who drafted the admonition she had sent in 1854:

> I have, hitherto, looked upon Prussia as one of the Great Powers which, since the peace of 1815, have been guarantors of treaties, guardians of civilisations, defenders of the right, the real arbiters of Nations … if you abdicate these obligations, you have also abdicated that position for Prussia. And should such an example find imitators, then the civilisation of Europe would be delivered up to the play of winds; right will no longer find a champion, the oppressed will find no longer an umpire …[37]

Albert had no intention of that happening. He admired the charms of the Empress Eugénie, enjoyed the fine sights of Paris, Bertie might tell the Empress 'you have a nice country. I would like to be your son',[38] but he neither liked the French nor trusted their Emperor. Albert's country was Germany and in his view, Germany was Britain's natural ally against the pretensions of France. At the end of the Crimean War the connection had to be re-established. And Albert had a powerful diplomatic tool: his daughter Vicky.

BELOW *Princess Eugénie, the wife of Napoleon III, painted by Franz Xaver Winterhalter in 1857. As part of the diplomatic initiatives to try to resolve the Crimean War, the French Emperor was invited to Britain in April 1855. It was the first time that Victoria had met the usurper of Louis-Philippe, and she was enchanted, as she – and Albert – were by his stunningly beautiful Spanish wife: She is 'quite delightful. Winterhalter's pictures of her are very like'.*

CHAPTER SIX

'AN INCONSOLABLE LOSS'

AT THE START OF 1858 VICTORIA had been Queen for twenty years and married for nearly eighteen. Her last child, Beatrice Mary Victoria Feodora, always known as 'Baby', had been born the previous April, whilst on 25 January her oldest, Vicky, the Princess Royal was married.

Vicky's husband was Prince Frederick William, the oldest son of the heir to the throne of Prussia. The Prince had paid a visit with his mother, Princess Augusta, to the Great Exhibition in 1851 and had gallantly squired Vicky – and her brothers and sisters – around the exhibits. In September 1855 he had paid another visit, this time to Scotland to stay with the royal family, who were holidaying at Balmoral. He was twenty-four: the Princess Royal was fourteen, but there was no doubt about the purpose of the visit.

Victoria and Albert had a view of the future of Europe, at present torn apart by war: they also had the future of their large family to plan. The two were inevitably entwined. 'A useful alliance', Vicky recognised, 'was the real reason for this marriage'. Six days after his arrival

> Fritz Wilhelm said he was anxious to speak of a subject which he knew his parents had never broached to us – which was to belong to our Family; that this had long been his wish, that he had the entire concurrence and approval not only of his parents but of the King [of Prussia] – and finding Vicky so allerliebst, he could delay no longer in making this proposal. I need not tell you [Leopold] with what joy we accepted him for our part; but the child herself is to know nothing till after her confirmation, which is to take place next Easter, when he will probably come over, and, as he wishes himself, make her the proposal, which, however, I have little – indeed no – doubt she will gladly accept. He is a dear, excellent, charming young man, whom we shall give our dear child to with perfect confidence.[1]

Lord Palmerston, the Prime Minister, was informed, as was Lord Clarendon, the Foreign Secretary, though the intention was not to inform Vicky at this stage. The marriage would not take place for another two years, after her seventeenth birthday, for 'she is still half a child and has to develop herself both morally and physically before their marriage takes place'.[2]

Although 'we were uncertain, on account of her extreme youth, whether he [Fritz] should speak to her himself or wait till he came back', it was difficult to conceal a matter of such moment from one of the people principally involved. Albert, perhaps mindful of his difficulties in waiting for a firm answer from Victoria when he had been a not dissimilar situation, thought that Vicky's feelings should be ascertained before her suitor left. So the Queen, her daughter and the Prussian Prince took 'a ride up Craig-na-Ban this afternoon [Fritz] picked a piece of white heather (the emblem of 'good luck'), which he gave to her; and this enabled him to make an allusion to his hopes and wishes …'.[3] As they dismounted, Fritz gave the Queen 'a wink implying that he had said something to Vicky and she was extremely agitated and nervous'. Back at Balmoral, Victoria asked her daughter how she felt about Fritz, and told her that 'if she had not liked him, we should never have forced her to this step, for which she expressed great gratitude'.[4]

The betrothal was made public as arranged, after Vicky's confirmation in April 1856. The wedding date was fixed for the end of January 1858. Victoria fretted about her daughter's 'extreme youth' and the fact that she would be going to 'a strange country to live among strangers'. Albert set aside time to instruct his daughter in the things that he considered a future Queen of Prussia should know, and the press sniped about Prussia being a second-rate power and an ally of Russia.

'It was the second most eventful day of my life', wrote Queen Victoria, on 25 January 1858, the occasion of the wedding of Vicky and Fritz at St James's Palace, 'I felt almost as if it were I that were being married again, only much more nervous'. The wedding was a grand affair with a cavalcade of twenty coaches carrying the English and Prussian royal wedding party. The Prince Consort – as he was now officially called since the Queen had finally conferred that title on him by Letters Patent the previous June – was dressed in the uniform of a Field Marshal, as was the King of the Belgians.

The groom looked pale as he awaited his bride at the altar, but both were composed as they clearly enunciated their vows and the Queen was moved both by 'our darling Flower's' composure and the recall of her own wedding when she had 'proudly, tenderly, most lovingly', knelt with Albert on the same spot as her young daughter now knelt with *her* German Prince.

When the party got back to Buckingham Palace for the wedding breakfast, the bride and groom initiated another royal custom by appearing on the balcony and waving to the cheering crowds.

The couple honeymooned briefly at Windsor, and on 1 February set off for Prussia. Victoria had been dreading the parting. There had been occasions when she had felt intimidated by her daughter's remarkable intelligence, and shut out from the companionship Vicky enjoyed with her father, whose favourite child she clearly was, and she looked forward to the chance of spending more time alone with 'her beloved angel'. But the day that Vicky left Gravesend for her new home was 'a dreadful day'.

BELOW *29 September 1855. 'Our dear Victoria was this day engaged to Prince Frederick William of Prussia, who had been on a visit to us [at Balmoral] since the 14th.' The engagement was to be kept a secret because of the 'extreme youth' of the Princess who was only fourteen at the time: Prince Frederick (known as Fritz) was twenty-four. In this photograph the Prussian suitor stands second from left, whilst Vicky, the Princess Royal, is on the far right.*

The separation was <u>awful</u>, and the poor child was <u>quite</u> broken-hearted, particularly at parting from her dearest, beloved papa, whom she <u>idolises</u>. ... But I have great confidence in her good sense, clever head, kind and good heart, in Fritz's excellent character and devotion to her.[5]

Victoria sat down – 'an hour is already past since you left' – to write the first of the multitude of letters sent to Vicky over the following decades. By May the Queen had news that Vicky was pregnant. She was not pleased,

LEFT *The marriage of the Princess Royal to Prince Frederick of Prussia which took place in the Chapel Royal, St James's Palace on 25 January 1858. The Queen stands with her younger children, Prince Albert and Prince Leopold of the Belgians. The painting is by John Gilbert. Princess Alice 'cried dreadfully', the Queen felt 'much more nervous' than on her own wedding, but fortunately Vicky was 'composed' even though she was only seventeen years old.*

feeling that 'the two first years of my married life [had been] utterly spoilt by this occupation! I could enjoy nothing … if I had waited a year as I hope you will, it would have been very different'.[6] However, when Vicky's confinement came, the Queen grieved that she could not be 'where every other mother is – and I ought to be and can't at her daughter's bedside', but she sent the royal physician Dr Martin to deliver her first grandchild. It was a difficult birth, and for a time there was fear for the life of mother and baby. The infant's arm was wrenched from its socket during the delivery and was to hang paralysed and useless for the rest of the life of Frederick William Victor Albert who was to grow up to be Kaiser Wilhelm of Germany and lead his country to war with Britain in 1914.

During much of the late 1850s Victoria and Albert were necessarily preoccupied with settling the futures of their children. The most pressing of course was Bertie, the heir to the throne, of whom his parents despaired. 'Unfortunately he takes no interest in anything but clothes, and again clothes. Even when out shooting he is more occupied with his trousers than with the game!',[7] his father wrote to Vicky on the eve of the Prince of Wales's visit to his sister in Berlin. Most of that year Bertie took a somewhat truncated 'grand tour' of Europe before going up to Oxford in the autumn of 1859. But as Bertie had been frivolous on the Continent in his father's view, so he was at Oxford, where, for the first time in his life, he was able to enjoy the company of young men of his own age. In the vacation in 1860 he undertook his first ambassadorial role going to Canada, as a mark of gratitude for the regiment that Canada had sent to help Britain during the Crimean War. The visit was an outstanding success, a triumph that was repeated when Bertie crossed into the United States, not this time as a representative of the Queen but as a private tourist, 'Baron Renfrew'. Again he 'created the most favourable impression'.[8] It seemed that whenever the Prince of Wales was away from his

ENGLAND'S HOPE

ABOVE *A* carte-de-visite *of the Prince of Wales. 'I hope and pray he may be like his dearest Papa', wrote Victoria soon after his birth, and the project to turn Bertie into a replica Albert was all-consuming to both parents. But it was not to be, even though they followed Stockmar's precepts: 'Education must be directed to the regulation of a child's natural Instincts, to give them the right direction and above all to keep its Mind pure'.*

parents and their expectations, which were never to coincide with his particular attributes, he seemed perfectly capable of demonstrating the 'good breeding' appropriate to his station.

The question of who the Prince of Wales would marry was a vexed one. Vicky's help was enlisted to draw up a suitable list of royal princesses – they had to be Protestants, of course, which restricted the field considerably. None of the possible candidates appealed to Bertie. Reluctantly his sister produced another likeness, that of Princess Alexandra of Denmark. 'Alix' was considered to be 'outrageously beautiful', but the situation between Denmark and Prussia over the duchies of Schleswig and Holstein made the match politically sensitive, and in addition there were rumours that the Danish court had more fun than the Prince Consort thought was proper. But Alexandra was a Protestant – and she was beautiful. Moreover it was known that the Tsar was considering the Princess as a bride for his heir. 'We dare not let her slip away', Albert warned Vicky, who, on the death of King Frederick William IV of Prussia, had become the Crown Princess. Vicky arranged a meeting between the nineteen-year-old Prince and the sixteen-year-old Princess and it seemed that:

Alix has made an impression on Bertie, though in his own funny, undemonstrative way, he said that he had never seen a young lady who pleased him so much. At first I think he was disappointed about her beauty and did not think her as pretty as he expected.

However, 'after a quarter of an hour' Bertie thought her lovely 'but said her nose was too long and her forehead too low'.[9] In any case, much to the disappointment of his Mamma and his sister, Bertie was unwilling to commit himself to settling down, for he was not yet out of his teens and hankered after a career in the army.

This was not permitted to him, but he had been sent on a military training course at the Curragh barracks near Dublin. He had been attached to the 1st Grenadier Guards and the idea had been that he would learn a soldier's trade. Again he had not been allowed to live with the other officers, as he had not been permitted to live in college at Oxford, and again he was to confound his parents expectations, this time in a particularly spectacular way.

When the Queen and the Prince Consort arrived in Ireland at the end of August 1861, they found that their son had not progressed through the ranks as they had hoped, and was not ready to take command of a battalion. Worse, though they did not know it at the time, the Prince had been the victim of a mess party prank, when some fellow officers, amused at the sheltered life the Prince of Wales led, smuggled into his bed a young actress, Nellie Clifden. The Prince was rather taken with Nellie, and when he returned to Windsor, she went too.

When the story came to the ears of Prince Albert he was mortified and sent a long missive to his son about the matter which has 'caused me the greatest pain I have yet felt in this life'[10] and when the Queen heard the news she felt she 'never can or should look at [that boy] without a shudder'. The Prince of Wales was unmarried, he was young, and the aristocratic conventions of the time were that young men needed sexual experience before marriage and that all young blades sowed a few wild oats before settling down. But that is not how Prince Albert saw it. He described his son as 'depraved' and projected a salutary scenario in which his eldest son would be ridiculed by society, the actress – who he said was already being referred to as 'the Princess of Wales' – would probably get pregnant and if the Prince of Wales tried to deny paternity of the child she would take him to court and 'disgusting details of your profligacy' would be revealed in the witness box.

The vehemence of Prince Albert's feelings was partly, no doubt, due to the disgust he had felt about his own father's dissoluteness, which had induced in him a fear of any sexual license outside the marriage bed that was extreme in its intolerance. It was also partly due to the cumulative disappointment he felt with his son's behaviour, which he always sought to condemn and reform, never to understand, and a feeling that Bertie was the legatee of Victoria's disgraceful uncles. He feared that Bertie would return the monarchy to the state of contempt in which it had been held before the efforts of he and Victoria had made it a revered and popular institution. It was also because Albert was, by the autumn of 1861, a very sick – indeed a dying – man.

Victoria's mother had died earlier that year, on 16 March 1861. Victoria had been distraught, as if the years of conflict and distance had never happened. She had written to Leopold, her mother's brother on 16 March 1861:

> On this most dreadful day of my life, does your poor broken-hearted child write … <u>She</u> is gone! That <u>precious, dearly beloved tender</u> Mother – whom I was never parted from but for a few months – without whom <u>I</u> can't <u>imagine life</u> has been taken from us! It is <u>too</u> dreadful! … the watching that precious life going out as fearful … Dearest Albert is dreadfully overcome – and well he may be, for <u>she</u> adored him …

It was not until 9 April that Victoria had felt well enough to leave her room for lunch with her family. She continued to take her other meals in her room and suffered frequent outbursts of uncontrollable crying. '… to open her drawers and presses, and to look at all her dear jewels and trinkets in order to identify everything … is like a sacrilege, and I feel as if my heart is being torn asunder!'

BELOW *A* Punch *cartoon showing the widening gulf between the future king and his father, the Prince Consort. The upright, industrious, repressed Albert was incensed by the louche indolence of Bertie, shown here smoking and holding a hand of cards. He tried to impose a rigid regime on his son. 'The only use for Oxford is that it is a place for <u>study</u>', Albert insisted in vain - and perhaps with a hint of envy.*

Albert had been unwell throughout the year. He suffered from toothache – probably caused by an abscess – and aches, pains and fevers. He was working obsessionally hard and seemed driven, rising early and starting work straight away, taking endless notes of all he read and refusing all interruptions. In addition, his son's 'escapade' haunted him and made him unable to sleep. Victoria wrote to her daughter on 27 November, after Albert had been to Cambridge to talk with Bertie as they walked in the rain and cold,

> Dearest Papa … is not well … with a cold and neuralgia – a great depression which has been worse these last five days – but I hope will be much better tomorrow. The sad part is – that this loss of rest at night (worse than he has ever had before) was caused by a great sorrow and worry which upset us both greatly – but him especially – and it broke him quite down I never saw him so low.

Despite his ill-health Albert continued to carry out his official duties. At the end of November 1861, an issue erupted which engaged his attention. On the outbreak of the American Civil War, the British Government had declared its neutrality. However, the Confederate South was anxious for European recognition and two envoys were despatched to Europe. They travelled on a British mail steamer, the *Trent*. On its voyage the *Trent* was intercepted, shots were fired across her bows, and the Southern envoys were taken off. Palmerston, who was sympathetic to the South, drafted a strongly worded despatch to Washington within days of the *Trent*'s arrival in Southampton and the story being known, stating that

> What had been done is a violation of international law, and of the rights of Great Britain and that your Majesty's Government trust that the act will be disavowed and the prisoners set free and restored to British Protection;[11]

and that if this was not done, the British Ambassador to the United States would be recalled forthwith.

Prince Albert, whose support inclined to the North, recognised that the British flag had been insulted and that the Government could not permit this, nevertheless he was disturbed by the bellicose tone of Palmerston's note, and concerned that Britain might find herself at war with the United States – which was certainly the mood of the country after the numerous difficulties that had existed in Anglo-American relations over recent years. He thought the wisest course was to assume that the incident had taken place without the knowledge of President Lincoln, and therefore an apology would suffice. Though he was so weak that he could hardly hold his pen, the Prince drafted a memorandum that he requested the Queen to send to Palmerston moderating his despatch in accordance with the belief that this had been an over-zealous Federal Officer acting on his own initiative rather than a 'wanton insult' by the United States Government. Palmerston conceded and the amended note was despatched and the possible threat of war averted. It was the Prince Consort's last public act.

By now Albert was very weak, and hardly able to eat. His doctors, Sir James Clark and Dr William Jenner – despite the fact that Jenner 'is the <u>first fever</u> Doctor in Europe, one may say' – still seemed to think that he was suffering from a fever that would soon run its course.[12] The Queen, though desperately concerned, seemed content to accept this diagnosis and curtly turned down Palmerston's suggestion of seeking a second opinion.[13]

> Her Majesty would be very very unwilling to cause unnecessary alarm, where no cause exists for it, by calling in a medical man who does not upon ordinary occasions attend at the Palace.[14]

The Prince grew weaker daily, he was restless and in great discomfort and could only manage to sip Seltzer water and eat a little jelly. Occasionally he rallied, talking quietly, being read to from Sir Walter Scott, gazing at a copy of Raphael's *Madonna* painted on porcelain that hung on the wall, or enjoying the chatterings of 'Baby'. His doctors gave him drops of ether and Victoria and Princess Alice, who was now eighteen, kept a vigil at his bedside.

On the morning of 7 December Dr Jenner told the Queen that the doctors were now sure that they knew what ailed the Prince. A characteristic rash on the lower part of the stomach indicated 'gastric and bowel fever' – that is typhoid fever. Victoria did not seem to realise how serious this was, continuing to talk in terms of a long, rather than a terminal illness and losing 'my guide, my support, my all, <u>for a time</u>'. She was delighted when Albert seemed to rally the next day and asked to hear some music. A piano was moved into the next room and Alice played one of his favourite Lutheran hymns, *Ein Feste Burg Ist Unser Gott* (A Strong Fortress is Our God), for her father who was very touched. Occasionally he was able to hold Victoria's hand, or stroke her face, and call her pet names.

Gradually the Prince deteriorated, his breathing grew rapid and rasping, his pulse weakened, and his mind would wander. His doctors grew more anxious. At half-past five in the evening of 14 December 1861, the Prince rallied briefly, kissed his wife, and then 'seemed to wander and to doze'. Bertie, Alice, Helena, Louise and Arthur filed in to say good-bye to their father, but he did not respond to their touch. Vicky was in Berlin, pregnant with her third child; Leopold was convalescing in the South of France; Affie was on a naval exercise, and Beatrice was considered too young for such a tragic occasion.

> Two or three long but perfectly gentle breaths were drawn, the hand clasping mine, & (oh! it turns me sick to write it) <u>all all</u> was over … I stood kissing his dear heavenly forehead & called out in a bitter agonising cry:

ABOVE *A life-size white marble statue of the Duchess of Kent by William Theed for the Duchess's mausoleum at Frogmore. Victoria's mother died on 16 March 1861 aged seventy-five. The Queen was desolate, despite her youthful difficulties with the Duchess: 'This is a life of sorrow … except Albert (who I very often don't see but little in the day) I have <u>no human</u> being except our children and that is not the same … a <u>woman</u> requires a <u>woman's</u> society and sympathy sometimes'.*

ABOVE *Prince Albert during his final illness depicted in his dressing-gown by Thorburn. In his hand the Prince Consort holds a draft of the memorandum he wrote about the Trent affair on 1 December 1861, even though he was 'so weak' that he could hardly hold a pen. Less than a fortnight later he was dead.*

'Oh! my dear Darling!' & then dropped on my knees in mute, distracted despair, unable to utter a word or shed a tear.[15]

Prince Albert died at a quarter to eleven that night in the Blue Room at Windsor Castle where William IV had died.

The poor fatherless baby of eight months is now an utterly broken-hearted and crushed widow of forty-two! My <u>life</u> as a <u>happy</u> one is <u>ended</u>! the world is gone for <u>me</u>! If I <u>must live</u> on … it is henceforth for our poor fatherless children − for my unhappy country, which has lost <u>all</u> in losing him − and in <u>only</u> doing what I know and <u>feel</u> he would wish, for he is near me − his spirit will guide and inspire me! But oh! to be cut off in the prime of life − to see our pure, happy, quiet domestic life which <u>alone</u> enabled me to bear my <u>much</u> disliked position, CUT OFF at forty-two − when I <u>had</u> hoped with such instinctive certainty that God never <u>would</u> part us and would let us grow old together − is <u>too awful,</u> too cruel![16]

The bell atop St Paul's Cathedral tolled out just before midnight to announce the Prince's death and all the next day, Sunday, the bells signalled a death, and in services the name of the Prince Consort was omitted from the prayer for the royal family: it was the first many had heard of his death. On Monday, newspaper placards which had been shrill with talk of war, became sombre with the announcement of death. People queued up throughout the day to sign the book of condolences at Buckingham Palace in 'a room hung with black, & lighted with wax'. Many small shops closed as a mark of respect, and the larger department stores were draped in black. The Queen's household went into deep mourning for a year, her communications were forthwith written on paper with a black border three-quarters of an inch thick, and tears were wiped away with handkerchiefs similarly edged. The Queen decreed that the Blue Room, where her 'beloved angel' had died, should be left as a memorial to Albert, scattered with his likenesses and his dressing-room should be kept as if it were still in use by him, with clean towels and fresh water for shaving placed there daily. Then the inconsolable royal widow, who had relied on her husband's guidance on foreign policy, as on the choice of bonnets, set off, 'with a desolate look [on] her young face in Her <u>Widow's</u> cap',[17] to Osborne, to mourn and to confront her future − in what she saw as a 'life in death'.

When the Duchess of Kent had died, Disraeli had spoken of the Queen's bereavement in the House of Commons. His words seemed even more appropriate at this, her even greater loss.

It is generally supposed that the anguish of affection is scarcely compatible with the pomp of power, but that is not so in the present instance. She who reigns over us has elected, amid all the splendour of empire, to establish her life on the principle of domestic love. It is this, it is the remembrance and consciousness of this, which now sincerely saddens the public spirit, and permits a nation to bear its heart-felt sympathy to the foot of a bereaved throne, and to whisper solace to a royal heart.[18]

The sympathy and respect that her ministers felt for Victoria at this time was real; it was also tinged with anxiety. The grieving widow was the Queen of Great Britain. What if Disraeli's tribute was truer than he realised? 'With Prince Albert we have buried our Sovereign. The German Prince has governed England for twenty-one years with a wisdom and energy such as none of our Kings have ever shown.'[19] It was to be Disraeli who helped Victoria back to her role as sovereign, but that was in the future. In the mean time her energies were to be expended not on the business of governance but on the remembrance of Albert.

ABOVE *The dedication to Prince Albert in a new edition of Tennyson's poem* The Idylls of the King *which was published in February 1862. Albert had much admired this work, but Victoria thought a verse from another poem,* In Memoriam *spoke to her condition: 'O sorrow, wilt thou live with me/No casual mistress but a wife,/My bosom-friend and half of life; As I confess it needs must be;'*

She started an *album consolatium*, a commonplace book of mourning, in which she copied comforting or stirring poems and letters on her state, and she fitfully dictated reminiscences of

> our life in the most minute and detailed manner I can. At 7am the wardrobe maid came in and opened the shutters and generally also the window. Almost always the Prince got up then. He slept in long white drawers, which enclosed his feet as well as his legs, like the sleeping suit worn by small babies … He then went to his room – sitting-room, where in winter a fire was made and his green German lamp lit, he brought the original one from Germany, & we always have 2 on our 2 tables which everywhere stand side by side in my room (& Shall ever do so) and wrote letters, read etc. and at a little after 8, sometimes a little sooner or later, he came in to tell me to get up … Formerly he used to be ready frequently before me … and would either stop in my sitting-room next door to read some of the endless numbers of despatches which I placed on his side … Baby generally went into his dressing-room (oh! that poor dear dressing-room so full of <u>dear</u> and <u>sad</u> recollections) and stopped with him till he followed with her at his hand coming along the passage with his dear heavenly face … Poor darling little Beatrice used to be so delighted to see him dress and when she arrived and he was dressed she made dearest Albert laugh so, by saying 'What a pity!'[20]

Victoria vowed that never again would she wear a *décolleté* dress since her beloved was no longer there to admire her shoulders.

With the flesh and blood man gone, the Queen set about peopling the land with his marmoreal image. For a time the building of memorials to Albert seemed her only interest: their unveiling the only reason she would leave the seclusion of her home. Lord Clarendon found himself on a committee charged with deciding on an appropriate memorial for the Prince Consort. Victoria had suggested an obelisk, and Clarendon thought himself no better equipped to make such a decision than he was 'for leading the orchestra at the Opera House'. But he did consider that when it came to her choice of a likeness, the Queen had 'no more notion of what is right and pure in art than she has in Chinese grammar', and predicted a veritable crop of 'the late Consort in robes of The Garter upon some curious and non-descript animal that will be called a horse, & Albert Baths and Washhouses' throughout the provinces.[21]

The memorials 'hewn in granite, bronze or marble' proliferated: among the many planned there was the statue, now known as the Albert Memorial, by Joseph Durham, of Albert, pensive, studying the catalogue of the Great Exhibition, in 'Albertropolis', South Kensington, situated in front of what would later be the Albert Hall, whilst the first municipal tribute was an equestrian statue by Thomas Thornycroft, unveiled in Wolverhampton in November 1866. Marble busts and figures were commissioned to join those already *in situ* in the royal residences and they appeared in posed portraits and daguerreotypes, poised exactly where the Prince Consort would have stood had he been still living. Indeed, when the Prince of Wales was to be married in 1863 he and his bride were taken by the Queen to stand in front of Albert's tomb effigy at Frogmore, Windsor, to receive 'his blessing'.

As far as the Queen was concerned the Mausoleum at Frogmore was the most important – and comforting – memorial to her departed 'angel'. She laid the foundation stone on 15 March 1862. The tomb was to be of granite with a likeness of Albert in white marble by Baron Carlo Marochetti reclining on top. At the same time as the Prince Consort's effigy was being carved, one was being made to the Queen's measurements and stored until the day came that it could lie alongside.

Understandably, the shock of her husband's death had numbed Victoria. She felt alone, unsure and, without his experienced guidance and support, totally unable to cope with the demands of her role. During an essential Privy Council meeting on 6 January the Queen sat in the next room as her approval was read out; she could not face seeing her Prime Minister until a month after Albert's death, and refused to see her Ministers other than separately. 'She does not seem to improve and her only relief in thinking about her desolate future is Her conviction that She shall and must die soon' one of them noted. Some Ministers thought that the best thing for her

> is the responsibility of her position and the mass of business wh[ich] She
> cannot escape and wh[ich] during a certain portion of the day compels her
> to think of something other than her all embracing sorrow.[22]

In fact Victoria was in a fragile state for three years after Albert's death. She was anxious at her own mental state (as the public came to be) and thus self-protective against the pressures she felt her Government was putting on her.

The most pressing concern, as Palmerston reminded her when he crossed the Solent for an audience at the end of January 1862, was to get the Prince of Wales married. It was always possible that Victoria might abdicate in favour of Bertie and the sooner some stability was brought into his rackety life, the better. However, first there was the marriage of Princess Alice, the second daughter, who had been so stalwart through the months of Albert's illness. She had become engaged to Prince Louis of Hesse-Darmstadt in June 1860. The wedding took place in 1862 in the dining room at Osborne – with Albert 'present' in the Winterhalter painting of the royal family that dominated the room. The bride was in mourning, her trousseau was black and her mother sat apart throughout the ceremony. As Victoria wrote to Vicky it 'was more like a funeral' than a wedding.[23]

The Prince of Wales was now nearly twenty-one, and, thanks to his father's administrative acumen, a wealthy man. Since the Duchy of Cornwall had been efficiently managed it had turned in a handsome profit and Bertie had acquired Sandringham, an estate in Norfolk, as a country residence. His father had planned the Prince's future before he died: a visit to the Holy Land and on his return, marriage to Princess Alexandra of Denmark.

The wedding took place at St George's Chapel, Windsor, on 5 March 1863. It was a grand affair but chaotic: Palmerston was obliged to travel in a third-class compartment of the special train, along with the Duchess of Westminster, who was wearing jewelry worth half a million pounds, and Disraeli, who couldn't find a seat and was obliged to perch on the knee of his perpetually uncomplaining wife, Mary Anne, all the way back to London. The Princess Royal's oldest son, Frederick William, behaved rather badly, throwing his mother's muff out of the carriage, biting the knees of his uncles when they reprimanded him and addressing his grandmama as 'duck'. The Queen stayed majestically aloof for the occasion. Clad all in black she watched the ceremony from Catherine of Aragon's closet high above the altar, and declined to attend the wedding breakfast. After a solitary lunch, she went to the Mausoleum and knelt beside Albert's tomb 'and prayed by that beloved resting-place feeling soothed and calm'.

But, however aloof she might try to keep from events, Victoria's growing web of dynastic connections throughout Europe drew her in. Shortly after the wedding the Schleswig-Holstein problem flared up again. It was a complicated one that Palmerston said only three people had ever understood. In essence it was a matter of rivalry between

BELOW *The unveiling of the Prince Consort's statue in the Markplatz at Coburg on 26 August 1865, the anniversary of Albert's birth. All the royal children made the journey and Victoria wrote that it was 'the most beautiful ceremony I ever saw. Nothing ever was better done, and nothing was <u>more</u> felt ... such a crowd of people but they behaved so beautifully and showed <u>such loyalty</u> and sympathy. It was quite touching ... The Burgomeister [gave] a beautiful address. Then the statue was uncovered, and such a cheer raised it sent a thrill through us.'*

Prussia and Denmark over Schleswig-Holstein which had been placed under Danish suzerainty in 1852. When the King of Denmark died and was succeeded by Princess Alexandra's father, Prince Christian, in 1863 both duchies demanded the right of self-determination. It was Victoria's first major foreign policy conundrum on her own – and one in which the positions of Vicky and Princess Alexandra made her intimately and agonisingly involved. She had vowed to carry on the policies of the Prince Consort: 'his wishes, his plans ... his views about every thing are to be my laws! And no human power will make me swerve from what he decided and wished.'[24]

She had done just this in the case of Bertie's marriage. But what would Albert – who after all was one of the trinity who understood the issue – have done about Schleswig-Holstein? Support Prussia Victoria decided. However, in addition to the distress of her now pregnant daughter-in-law, British public opinion was with the underdog, Denmark, as was that of the Government, which was also wary of Prussian expansionism. Palmerston admonished the Queen for unconstitutional behaviour: 'an impression is beginning to be created that Your Majesty has expressed personal opinions on the affairs of Denmark and Germany.' Meanwhile Princess Alexandra, who had cried herself to sleep nightly at the thought of the plight of her country, gave birth to a tiny, two-month premature baby, who was named Albert Victor.

In 1864 the Prussian armies occupied both Schleswig and Holstein and Palmerston considered sending a gunboat to Copenhagen in case the Prussian army marched on. Victoria exerted great efforts to ensure that 'England stays neutral' – that is, in the circumstances, condone Prussia's aggressive action. An armistice in April 1864 brought the war to an end, and Victoria congratulated herself on the success of her Albertian policy of 'neutrality'. However, when conflict flared up again between Prussia and France in 1870, British neutrality meant, that despite Victoria's urgings for peace, the country had little influence over European events: 'for the present they must rest on their oars, excepting as to proclamations of neutrality', Earl Granville, the Foreign Secretary, pronounced. The Franco-Prussian war erupted following France's objection to a Prussian candidate for the Spanish succession. King William IV of Prussia, Vicky's father-in-law, was prepared to be conciliatory over the matter, but his Chancellor, Otto von Bismarck was not. He wanted war and manoeuvered to ensure that France appeared to be the aggressor in the conflict that broke out on 19 July 1870. On 2 September, Napoleon III was defeated at Sedan; a republic was proclaimed and the Prussians laid siege to Paris until the end of January 1871. Meanwhile the southern states of Bavaria, Baden and Württemberg, seized with nationalist fervour, joined the German Confederation. Bismarck's dream of a united Germany under Prussian hegemony was realised. William IV of Prussia was proclaimed Emperor of Germany at the Palace of Versailles on 18 January 1871.

Victoria had been horrified at the prospect of war: it was clear that her son-in-law was anxious that the matter should be settled amicably, whilst to the Crown Princess it seemed liked 'a horrid dream'.[25] Victoria was overwhelmed with … the terrible anxiety and sorrow which this horrible war will bring with it. The Queen hardly knows how she will bear it! Her children's home threatened, their husbands' lives in danger, and the country she loves best next to her own – as it is her second home, being her beloved husband's and one to which she and all her family are bound by the closest ties – in peril of the gravest kind, insulted and attacked, and she unable to help them or come to their assistance. Can there be a more cruel position than the unhappy Queen's?[26]

With two sons-in-law in the field – Fritz and Alice's husband – her oldest son, the pro-French Prince of Wales, publicly wishing to see Prussia beaten, and the exiled Empress of France seeking sanctuary in England, the European war was mirrored in microcosm in Victoria's own family: 'These divided interests in royal families are quite unbearable. Human nature is not made for such fearful trials, especially not mothers' and wives' hearts.'[27] When German unity was proclaimed Victoria, whilst convinced that 'a powerful Germany can never be dangerous to England, quite the reverse',[28] had occasion to remind her daughter that the British people's 'sympathies, strange to say … have become very pro-French'.[29] The Queen's popularity was not helped by what was perceived as her pro-Prussian stance.

A long mourning period was considered appropriate in mid-nineteenth century England, and for the first year of her seclusion the Queen largely had the sympathy and understanding of the nation in her incapacity, and the complicity of her Government, which shielded her from all but the most essential business. But as the years went by and Victoria continued to act as a recluse – she did not so much as appear in public for two years after Albert's death – demands grew for her to resume her role as a monarch.

The press talked of 'the luxury of indulging in sorrow' and even though in November 1863 William Gladstone, the then Liberal Chancellor of the Exchequer, thought he detected 'the old voice of business', when talking with the Queen, he was mistaken. Indeed on 6 April 1864, following what she thought was an undue clamour for her to return to public life, the Queen had written a letter to the editor of *The Times* which was published anonymously, though there was no doubt who the author writing from 'the Court' was:

> An erroneous idea seems generally to prevail and has latterly found frequent expression in the newspapers, that the Queen is about to resume the place in society which she occupied before her great affliction; that is, that she is about to appear as before at Court balls, concerts, &c. This idea cannot be too explicitly contradicted.

She conceded that she would appear in public whenever 'any real object is to be attained' by her doing so, but there were 'higher duties' than those of 'mere representation'. The communication concluded firmly: 'More than that the Queen <u>cannot</u> do, and more the kindness and good feeling of her people will surely not exact from her'.

THE ROYAL WINDSOR PAIR.!

ABOVE *A depiction of the Prince of Wales and his bride, Princess Alexandra of Denmark. The marriage, on 5 March 1863, was a great relief to the Queen who regarded her new daughter-in-law as 'a jewel dropped from the skies' and hoped that Alix would prove to be her troublesome oldest son's 'SALVATION', and that he would, despite the portents, make a 'steady husband'.*

Earlier, a handbill had appeared on the railings of Buckingham Palace: 'These extensive premises to be let or sold, the late occupant having retired from business'.[30] It was amusing but accurate and the gossip was getting more barbed: it was becoming obvious to her Ministers that the Queen had forgotten that she had a public responsibility as well as a personal inclination. One referred to her as 'the royal malingerer' because she refused to deviate from her pattern of holidays at Osborne or Balmoral, regardless of the importance of Government business. Meanwhile, to her Foreign Secretary she continued to entertain 'absurdly high notions of her prerogative and the amount of control she ought to exercise over public business: wishes to be able to form a judgment independent of her ministers, but cannot do it without help'.[31] It was said that there was 'general discontent' among the London tradesmen 'they believe the Queen to be insane, and that she will never live in London again'.[32] But the Queen remained out of the public eye. Apart from occasional diplomatic receptions, and excursions such as laying the foundation stone for the new St Thomas's Hospital in 1868 (a project of Florence Nightingale's) Victoria consistently pleaded delicate health for her non-appearances. She consistently refused to open Parliamentary sessions: and did so only seven times in the last thirty-nine years of her reign.[33]

> The Queen must say that she does feel <u>very</u> <u>bitterly</u> the want of feeling of those who <u>ask</u> the Queen to go to open Parliament. That the public should wish to see her she fully understands, and has <u>no</u> wish to prevent − quite the contrary: but why this wish should be of so <u>unreasonable</u> and unfeeling a nature as to <u>long</u> to <u>witness</u> the spectacle of a poor widow, nervous and shrinking, dragged in <u>deep mourning</u> ALONE <u>in</u> STATE as a <u>Show</u> where she used to go supported by her husband to be gazed at, without delicacy of feeling, is a thing <u>she cannot</u> understand, and would never wish her bitterest foe to be exposed to![34]

She made exceptions, however, when she needed to apply to Parliament for funds. In February 1866 she did so for the first time since Albert's death: Prince Alfred was about to come of age and required an annuity, and Princess Helena, known as Lenchen, was to be married to the impecunious and balding Prince Christian of Schleswig-Holstein in July and therefore was also in need of an annuity − and a dowry.

In February 1870 the Queen again opened Parliament, still dressed entirely in black but with a 'new small diamond crown, over a veil, on my head'. This time she requested an annuity of £15,000 for Prince Arthur and an annuity and a dowry for Princess Louise, who was about to marry a wealthy subject, the Marquis of Lorne, heir to the Duke of Argyll.

One alternative the Queen might have considered was to pass the 'royal business' on and abdicate in favour of the Prince of Wales. But this was something she did not contemplate. Bertie's marriage had not meant that he was given more responsibility. Indeed the control his mother continued to exert on her son was noticeable. She disapproved of him smoking; she disapproved of his interest in horse-racing; she disapproved of his friends, men from the new money, like the grocer Thomas Lipton, rather than from old landed families. She rejected the idea that he might take on official roles – he was far 'too young and inexperienced'; yet she turned down any opportunities that might come his way to gain experience by deputising for her on occasions.

'Much talk in London about the extraordinary way in which the Queen undertakes to direct the Prince and Princess in every detail of their lives', noted Lord Stanley:

> They may not dine out, except at houses named by her: nor ask anyone to dine with them, except with previous approval or unless the name of that person is on a list previously prepared: and the Princess, after riding once or twice in the Park, was forbidden to do so again. In addition, a daily and minute report of what passes at Marlborough House is sent to the Queen.[35]

In June 1870, in response to yet another dictat about his attendance at the races, Bertie replied wearily:

> I am always most anxious to meet your wishes, dear Mama, in every respect, and always regret if we are not quite *d'accord* – but as I am past twenty-eight and have some considerable knowledge of the world and society, you will, I am sure, at least I trust, allow me to use my own discretion in matters of this kind …[36]

But to Vicky, the Queen bewailed: 'Oh! what will become of the poor country if I die! I foresee, if B. succeeds, nothing but misery …'. It was a view the Government seemed to share. 'The Queen is invisible', wrote Gladstone in December 1870, 'and the Prince of Wales is not respected'.

It was clear that, as Stanley put it, 'people find out that they can do as well without a Court, etc'.[37] They failed to see why they should pay to support a vacant throne – a cost that annually probably came to a figure in excess of a half a million pounds – though in fact the Queen had been quite seriously ill throughout the summer of 1871 whilst in Scotland. 'Never since a girl, when I had typhoid fever at Ramsgate in '35, have I felt so ill', she wrote in her journal for 22 August 1871. Her illness muted criticism of her inactivity. The Prince of Wales wrote from army camp in early September:

> I read all the articles in the newspapers you mention, and was sure you would be gratified by them. If the papers were severe in July, and last month, it was merely the anxiety expressed by public opinion at large to see more of you, and to express their feelings of loyalty and attachment to you. The people are really loyal; but it is feared in these Radical days that, if the Sovereign is not more amongst them, and not more seen in London, the loyalty and attachment to the Crown will decrease, which would be naturally much to be deplored …[38]

Fanned by news from France of Napoleon III's overthrow, republican sentiment was growing in Britain. A pamphlet circulated asking 'What does She do with it?', meaning the £385,000 a year granted by Parliament for the upkeep of Buckingham Palace, Windsor Castle and the royal yacht. When the Prince and Princess of Wales' third son was born, in April 1871, *Reynold's Newspaper* headlined the announcement 'Another Inauspicious Event' and when the infant died the next day it took much satisfaction in headlining that news 'A Happy Release' – for the tax-payers that was. Republican clubs sprung up in London boroughs, and several cities around the country. Sir Charles Dilke, Liberal MP for Chelsea, launched a pointed attack on the cost of the monarchy to the nation and the paltry return it got for its close on a million pounds investment.

The Queen was distressed, not only by Dilke's attack, but by the failure, as she saw it, of Gladstone, who was now Prime Minister, to 'take an opportunity of reprobating in very strongest terms such language'. She did not 'for a moment doubt the sentiments of the Cabinet on the subject, and only wishes that they should be expressed'; for

> these revolutionary theories are allowed to produce what effect they may in the minds of the working classes. Gross mis-statements and fabrications, injurious to the credit of the Queen, and injurious to the Monarchy, remain unnoticed and uncontradicted; some of which, such as the Queen never having paid Income Tax ... and could at once be contradicted by any official person ... Mr Gladstone may feel sure that a large section of his supporters ... look to him and his colleagues for some very decided expression of their condemnation of such opinions.[39]

Gladstone scrupulously defended his colleagues against the ire of the Queen, maintaining the right of any Englishman to speak out 'without any limit at all on matters relating to the institution under which we live'. But he also indicated that the situation was more serious than the Queen seemed to realise and this was no time for getting on the royal high horse since he regarded it as a fact of extreme gravity, giving much pause for reflection, that any public man, even of the moderate weight of Sir Charles Dilke, should have propounded these views to a large public meeting in Newcastle and should have received a vote of thanks for his speech.

BELOW *A comment on Victoria's alleged dereliction of duty in the years after Albert's death, when she spent long periods at Osborne or Balmoral, and declined to undertake her official duties, only appearing in public infrequently. The constitutionalist, Walter Bagehot remarked, 'the Queen has been so little seen in public, and it is the essence of the showy parts of the constitution to acquire importance and popularity by being seen'.*

EPISODE DURING A BRIEF VISIT TO LONDON.

AUGUST PERSONAGE: "What is that large empty building there?"
FOOTMAN: "Please, your Majesty, that's Buckingham Palace?"

Gladstone pointed out that though Dilke's supporters were

> a small minority, as he hopes in the country … a few years ago that
> minority (as far as he knows) did not exist. The causes that have brought it
> into existence, may lead to its growth. Its existence is not only matter of
> grief and pain to Mr Gladstone and his colleagues, but it is also matter of
> grave public importance … with regard to the Civil List Mr Gladstone
> would remind your Majesty that, for the whole of the arrangements
> connected with it, Ministers are responsible. Were any of them to enter into
> an argument with Sir Charles Dilke, Mr Gladstone has the fear that the
> effect might be to widen, and, so to speak, establish the controversy …[40]

However, within weeks of Dilke's attack, news came that Bertie had
contracted typhoid fever whilst visiting Scarborough, a town notorious at the
time for its poor sanitation, almost a decade after Prince Albert had died of
the same fever. 'This fearful fever, and at this time of year!' the Queen wrote
in her journal on 22 November. The crisis came on 13 December – the eve
of Albert's death – and the family 'and I believe the whole country [was
filled] with anxious forebodings and the greatest alarm'. But this time as the
Queen and Princess Alice sat with Princess Alexandra at the Prince's bedside,
the fever began to subside.

Public interest in the Prince's illness was acute and relief at his recovery
sincere. A service of thanksgiving was held in St Paul's Cathedral on 27
February 1872 though 'Bertie was very lame and did not look at all well'.
That evening the Queen 'had no time to describe at length the … astounding
affectionate loyalty shown. The deafening cheers never ceased the whole way
… it was a most affecting day, and many times I repressed my tears.' The
scene suggested that republican sentiment was, by the 1870s, pallid and
lacked focus and that there remained a reserve of public goodwill towards the
institution of monarchy which it was still possible for the Queen to tap.

Though the Queen had refused to participate in most public events after
Albert's death, since the mid-1860s, she had, in fact, slowly been finding life
as a widow more bearable. One reason for her growing equilibrium was the
relationship that had developed between the Queen and her Scottish servant,
John Brown. He was one of the royal gillies at Balmoral, and in the more
relaxed atmosphere that pertained there, sovereign-servant relationships were
less formal and more open than at court. One of the Queen's ladies-in-
waiting had written of dancing lessons in Scotland:

> The Queen came the other day and joined the reel … HM comes in for
> her share of praise, advice, encouragement and, where it is necessary,
> reprobation, just like other people – 'Now gently, me deare, try and dance
> like a lady'. This is what we imagine he says to his Sovereign in private.[41]

Brown had been a favourite of Albert's and it was the Prince Consort who
had charged him with tasks that included looking after the Queen's safety. In
the autumn of 1864, the Queen's physician, Dr Jenner, considered that it
would do the Queen's health and nervous disposition good if she continued

BELOW *A commemorative silk
bookmark for Princess Louise's
marriage. The Queen defended
Louise's choice of a subject: 'small
foreign Princes (without any money)
are very unpopular here … one
naturally turns towards those in
one's own country, who possess
large fortunes and rank certainly
equally to small German Princes'.*

riding through the winter. The Queen insisted on a groom she already knew and trusted and John Brown was called from Balmoral.

By the next year Brown was becoming important to the Queen: he was to remain with her throughout the year supervising her horses, carriages and dogs, and as 'the Queen's Highland Servant' he would take orders from her alone. The Queen wrote to Vicky that Brown had become 'entirely and permanently' her personal 'out of doors servant'.

> He comes to my room after breakfast and luncheon to get his orders – and everything is always right; he is so quiet, has such an excellent head and memory, and is besides so devoted, and attached and clever and so wonderfully able to interpret one's wishes. He is a real treasure to me now, and I only wish higher people had his sense and discretion and that I had as good a maid … I feel I have here and always in the house a good devoted soul … whose only object and interest is my service, and God knows how much I want to be taken care of.[42]

ABOVE AND BELOW *In December 1871, almost ten years to the day that his father had died, the Prince of Wales fell ill of typhoid fever and for several days his life hung in the balance. The Crown Princess wrote 'I cannot fancy him ill – he who is always so gay and strong and active, so full of life and vigour'. On 27 February 1872 a service of thanksgiving was held for his recovery. 'It was a day of triumph,' reported his mother, 'Millions must have been out and … the cheering [was] deafening. It was the first time since Bertie was a boy that he had ever been with me on a great public occasion'.*

Predictably Brown's role in 'taking care of' the Queen led to difficulties. He was a straightforward Highlander – a 'child of nature', the Queen's equerry, Sir Henry Ponsonby called him – with an intense loyalty to his employer. His direct manner of address – he was often heard to call the Queen 'wumman' – contrasted with, and thus offended, court etiquette particularly the etiquette of the courts of Victoria's children.

Since very little was known, and much was speculated on, about the Queen's seclusion, gossip and rumour soon spread about her relationship with John Brown. Lord Stanley thought it was hardly surprising:

> She is really doing all in her power to create suspicions which I am persuaded have no foundation. Long solitary rides, in secluded parts of the park; constant attendance upon her in her room: private messages sent by him to persons of rank: avoidance of observation while he is leading her pony or driving her little carriage: everything shows that she has selected this man for a kind of friendship that is unwise and unbecoming in her position. The Princesses – perhaps wisely – make a joke of the matter, and talk of him as 'mama's lover'.[43]

Stories circulated that Brown was the Queen's 'medium' for getting in touch with her 'beloved' angel on 'the other side'; that the pair were secretly married (on occasion crowds would shout 'Mrs Brown' to the Queen; just as, thirty years earlier they had dubbed her 'Mrs Melbourne'); that the Queen's visit to Switzerland, with John Brown in attendance in 1868, was so that she could give birth to his child in Lausanne. More damagingly, it was suggested that the Queen had, as it were, an *eminence brun*, that in her lassitude she had devolved power to Brown, that like Albert he had taken up the reins of state. In the vacuum left by the Queen's withdrawal from public life flooded rumour and innuendo. 'There is nothing in this', declared Lord Stanley, 'except a fancy for a good-looking and intelligent dependent … eccentricity, solitude and the impossibility of hearing an honest opinion are explanation sufficient'.[44]

John Brown, who liked the drink rather too much – on occasions he had to be excused his duties, being 'bashful' as the euphemism was, and he and the Queen preferred whisky on their picnics to tea – died of erysipelas, a painful skin condition known as 'St Anthony's Fire' – on 29 March 1883. The Queen was heartbroken: 'he became my best and truest friend, – as I was his', she said simply. 'The shock, – the blow, the blank, the constant missing at every turn of the one strong, powerful reliable arm and head almost stunned me and I am truly overwhelmed', she wrote to Vicky.[45]

The Queen mourned in the same language she used when Albert died; her children replied politely, regretting the loss of a faithful servant. In that chasm, there is some indication of the relationship Victoria had with John Brown, and also a part explanation of why she had formed such a warm attachment to him. A scrapbook was started in tribute, a monument was commissioned for Balmoral and Tennyson requested to compose its inscription:

> Friend more than Servant, Loyal, Truthful, Brave, Self less than Duty, even to the Grave.

Brown's room at Windsor was left as he had left it when he died. At the Queen's command, a fresh flower was placed on the pillow every day until *she* died. *The Times* carried a full-column obituary – unusual in the case of a servant – and on the grave in the churchyard at Crathie, which became an essential carriage-stop for all trippers to the area, the epitaph, read:

> That friend on whose fidelity you count, that friend given to you by circumstance over which you have no control, was God's own gift.

By the time John Brown died, however, Victoria was once more fully immersed in the affairs of state. Her 'missing years' had ended and she had emerged from her self-imposed semi-abdication thanks, in no small measure, to another 'loyal servant', but of a very different order: her Conservative Prime Minister, Benjamin Disraeli.

BELOW *A photograph of John Brown in highland dress 'I have not, I think', wrote Victoria ingenuously to her oldest daughter in April 1865, 'told you that I have taken good J. Brown entirely and permanently as my personal servant … he is one in a thousand for he has the feelings and qualities which the highest Prince might be proud of.' Vicky replied guardedly: 'I am so glad you have made an arrangement with John Brown that suits you and that you find comfortable'.*

CHAPTER SEVEN

'DIZZY & THE GRAND OLD MAN'

I HOPE MR DISRAELI WILL FILL his important place well, and that you think him up to it. He is vain and ambitious is he not? He must feel very proud of having risen to his present position which he owes to his talents, and to the dearth of clever men in the Tory party I suppose?

wrote the Crown Princess of Prussia to Queen Victoria on 29 February 1868. Her letter crossed with one the Queen wrote to her on the same day:

> I think the present man will do well, and will be particularly loyal and anxious to please me in every way. He is very peculiar, but very clever and sensible and very conciliatory.[1]

Both assessments were entirely correct – though it had been a gradual change of heart for Victoria who in the political crisis of 1851, when Lord Derby was unable to form a Conservative government, had written 'I do not approve of Mr. D' and was only prepared to accept Disraeli as Leader of the House of Commons if Derby would guarantee that 'he will be temperate'.[2]

Benjamin Disraeli had 'climbed to the top of the greasy pole' to succeed the ailing Derby as Prime Minister after a long political career. The son of the writer Isaac D'Israeli, he was baptised a Christian but was profoundly influenced by his Jewish heritage. He had entered Parliament in 1837 after several unsuccessful attempts to do so, and first came to the notice of his fellow politicians during the Corn Law debates in 1846 when, with brilliant and wounding invective, he opposed the Free Trade policies of Peel. Denied a seat in Peel's Cabinet of 1841, the alienated Disraeli had become the leader of the Young England movement, a grouping of younger Conservative dissidents who believed in an imaginary lost world of aristocratic, paternalistic, feudal influence, where wealth and aristocratic position carried duties as well as bestowing privileges. It was a profoundly romantic approach that united landowners, intellectuals and discontented workers against the brutalisation of rapid industrialisation, and sought to mediate its more unacceptable exploitation through social legislation. The movement, which had symbolic, rather than practical political resonance, was perfectly expressed in the novels that Disraeli wrote, particularly the trilogy *Coningsby* (1844), *Sybil* (1845) and *Tancred* (1847). Disraeli's Burkean ideology, that the nation was an organism where well-being depended on the preservation of a balanced hierarchy between crown, church and aristocracy, suggested a continuing role for the landowning class in a way that appealed to Victoria, as did his forward foreign policy and Imperial ambitions and rhetoric.

For Disraeli, the Queen sat at the pinnacle of 'one nation' that was to include more and more of the globe, and he had no inhibitions in telling her this. He was an outsider in the corridors of power, a chronicler and devotee of the hierarchy, rather than a member of any of its layers. Vicky wrote to her mother, perhaps half in self-persuasion:

LEFT '*The Fall of the Rebels*'. *Gladstone goes down defiantly clutching his tattered Home Rule Bill, which was defeated in the House of Commons on 8 June 1886 by 343 votes to 313, a majority of 30. The Queen who could not 'help feeling relieved' at the defeat which she thought 'is best for the interests of the country', leads the vanquishing angels who include Benjamin Disraeli, Lord Salisbury, Randolph Churchill, Lord Hartington and Joseph Chamberlain, who clutches his own 'scheme for Ireland'.*

ABOVE *'Benjamin D' a skit on Disraeli, the surprising, polymath Prime Minister. His political ally, friend and literary executor, Lord Stanley (later the 15th Earl of Derby) recalled dining with Disraeli: 'I found him less interested in politics than literature … he talked of retiring from affairs, of writing an epic poem, and a life of Christ from the national point of view - mere talk, but characteristic'.*

> It is absurd to have an aristocratic prejudice against Mr Disraeli – on account of his being a Jew and an adventurer. A person that rises to a high place by his abilities has surely as good a right as anyone to be your Prime Minister.[3]

Yet much of Disraeli's success depended on his superb parliamentary skills and abilities of political management. He flattered the Queen 'with a trowel', he conciliated her, he persuaded her. He also believed that he managed her with a consummate skill: 'I never deny; I never contradict; I sometimes forget'.[4] These were things that his Liberal opposite number, William Ewart Gladstone, with his ponderous addresses, convoluted logic and sententious morality, signally failed to do. But prejudice lived on: the Conservative Lord Salisbury in 1868 noted 'matters seem very critical – a woman on the throne, and a Jew Adventurer [who] has found out the secret of getting round her'.[5]

When Disraeli went to Osborne to kiss hands in February 1868, the Queen was enchanted: 'He is full of poetry, romance & chivalry. When he knelt down to kiss my hand wh[ich] he took in both his – he said: "In loving loyalty and faith".' And he continued for the rest of his life, in office and out, to write to Victoria with the pen of a novelist and a confidante – 'she never had such letters in her life', wrote one of her ladies, 'and she never before knew *everything*'[6] – and he treated her as a woman who was lonely for sentiment and intimate friendship. 'Gladstone treats the Queen like a public department', Disraeli suggested, 'I treat her like a woman.'[7]

It was a brief pleasure. On 4 December 1868, 'Mr. Disraeli came down to Windsor … and tended his resignation to the Queen. It was accepted and Her Majesty at once wrote to Mr Gladstone …'.[8] The general election, fought with an electorate swelled by the urban workers enfranchised by the 1867 Reform Act introduced by Disraeli, had swept the Conservatives from office in a Liberal landslide.

Gladstone and Queen Victoria clashed less during his first ministry than they would later. She resented his attempts to get her to resume her official duties and his efforts to deal with the other 'Royalty question': what was to be done with the Prince of Wales? In the early 1870s the relief at the Prince's recovery from typhoid wore off and the issue became urgent again:

> … there is a strong and increasing feeling that to lead an idle life would be very calamitous and that [the Liberal Government] urgently hoped that he would have some occupation.[9]

Gladstone thought the answer might be greater involvement in the interests of his late father, art and science, but this did not seem very plausible for a young man whose only reading matter was reputed to be the racing results. A solution first tentatively expressed by Disraeli was revived. In February 1872 the Cabinet 'were coming to the conclusion that employment in Ireland was the best if not the only mode of settling the difficulty'.[10] But this was not the answer either. Sir Henry Ponsonby, who had been promoted to be the Queen's Private Secretary in 1870, reported in March 1872:

It appears that the Prince of Wales dislikes any suggestion about Ireland, and would positively refuse to go there officially in any capacity unless urged to do so by your Majesty.

Rather, he

> wished to be attached to different offices of the Government so that he might be taught the business of the different departments. The idea may be very good but it is at present somewhat vague ...[11]

As far as the Queen was concerned, the idea was a non-starter and Ponsonby thought that it was 'impossible he should see state papers and criticise and object'.[12] The Prince himself suggested a military career, but the Queen was dismissive and in 1873 prevented him from becoming a colonel in a Russian regiment which 'he took very badly because he dearly loved uniforms'.

The notion of sending Bertie to Ireland was indicative of the growing importance of Irish affairs in British politics. Home Rule agitation was growing and in by-elections in Kerry and Galway, Home Rule candidates were elected. It was mooted that the Queen should acquire an Irish home to balance Balmoral. In early 1872 she was shot at, as she rode in her carriage in London, by a man purporting to be wishing to deliver a letter from the Fenians and later in the summer a statue of the Prince Consort in Dublin was damaged by explosives. That year the British consul in Ireland suggested that the Queen should pay a visit there, though he recognised that

> there is much in these outrages which discourage a Royal state visit to Dublin; at the same time ... the last two Royal visits notwithstanding the subsequent drawbacks, have had a real and genuine good effect. They drew out the loyalty of a large body of citizens, and encouraged very materially those who oppose Fenianism and rowdyism.... The people require to see the person, or the nearest representative of the person to whom they are bound to give allegiance, and when they do get the opportunity their good feelings and loyalty are drawn out and developed ... Lord Spencer would earnestly continue to urge a continuance of Royal visits, as one of the most effectual means of winning the Irish to love for the Throne and English rule. Nothing would be as effective as a Royal residence ... The mainspring of all Irish discontent is the long-standing feeling of oppression and injustice, of which ... England in many cases was guilty towards Ireland in former days. It will take many years to remove altogether this feeling, but ... it will eventually be done by

THE CHAMPIONS.

ABOVE *'The Champions'. Secure in the support of the Queen, under whose standard he stands, Disraeli constantly hammered Gladstone and his Liberal government for its alleged weak foreign policy, its neglect of the navy and the folly of its army reforms. 'You behold a range of exhausted volcanoes', he accused Gladstone during a three-and-a-quarter hour long speech at Manchester Free Trade Hall on 3 April 1872.*

patient dealing and careful attention to the wants of the Irish, and even by concession to some of their sentimental views as to personal neglect etc.[13]

Ireland was increasingly to dominate Gladstone's political thinking and actions: it was an Irish matter that brought the defeat of his government in March 1873 when, as the Queen wrote to Vicky,

I am in the midst of a Ministerial crisis … You will have seen how very great the opposition to and dislike of this Irish university bill has become. The adverse vote … led to Mr Gladstone's resignation … Good Mr G. is not judicious and this mission to redeem Ireland – which has signally failed – has been the cause of the defeat.[14]

But Disraeli declined to form a government and Gladstone withdrew his resignation. The Liberal government limped on until a general election in February 1874 when the Queen was able to rejoice:

We have a large Conservative majority and the change of ministry will take place very shortly!! Mr Gladstone has contrived to alienate and frighten the country. Since '46, under the great, good and wise Sir Robert Peel – there has not been a Conservative majority!! It shows a healthy state of the country.[15]

The Conservatives had won the election less on a programme of their own intentions than by their assault on a tired, discredited and fissiparous Liberal party. Thus when Disraeli took office with no clear electoral programme, the Queen's Ministers recognised that the Queen's wishes might become her Prime Minister's command. Sir Henry Ponsonby thought that whilst

Dizzy … has got the length of her [Victoria's] foot exactly and knows how to be sympathetic … I know that his sympathy is expressed with h[i]s tongue in his cheek. But are not her woes told in the same manner?

The Keeper of the Privy Purse, Sir Thomas Biddulph, considered that: 'Dizzy is a perfect slave to the Queen and that she is always at him about something that we know nothing about. If so I pity him …'[16]

The first such measure was a fierce piece of legislation that sought to ban papist practices which, in Victoria's opinion, were undermining the integrity of the Anglican church with their rococo rituals. She urged the Public Worship Bill on Disraeli whose 'tact and temper for which he [Disraeli] is so remarkable' helped get the Bill through both Houses of Parliament.

The second measure was the Royal Titles Bill. The Queen had originally suggested it to Ponsonby in 1873 (India had been transferred from the East India Company to the British crown in 1858). Her son Prince Alfred, the Duke of Edinburgh, had married the daughter of the Tsar of Russia, Princess Marie, in St Petersburg in January 1874, and Marie's father insisted that she should be addressed in the imperial manner; her daughter-in-law was an Empress and indeed so was Victoria

an Empress and in common conversation am sometimes called Empress of India. Why have I never officially assumed this title? I feel I ought to do so and wish to have some preliminary enquiries made.[17]

ABOVE *The* carte-de-visite *of Benjamin Disraeli, Earl of Beaconsfield (top) and William Ewart Gladstone (bottom), Queen Victoria's alternating premiers.*

It was not a measure that would get through a Liberal-dominated Commons, but in fact the proposal ran into opposition with a Conservative majority when it came before the House in January 1876. Disraeli had not prepared the Queen for any opposition and she was hurt and angry at what she regarded as unnecessary factionalism. Disraeli comforted his 'faery Queen' (as he referred to her) in her wish to be 'faery Empress' and assured her:

> Mr Disraeli has long perceived that, though seated on a lofty throne, and gifted with an intelligence not unequal to the great occasion, the fact of empire, and the fitness for its rule, are combined in the instance of your Majesty, with a heart of extreme sensibility.[18]

The objection was that the title Empress would take precedence over that of Queen. Victoria herself sought to clarify the position:

> There seems a very strange misapprehension on the part of some people, which is producing a mischievous effect; viz. that there is to be an alteration in the Queen's and Royal family's ordinary appellation. Now this is utterly false. The Queen will always be called 'the Queen' and her children 'their Royal Highnesses,' and no difference whatever is to be made except OFFICIALLY ADDING after Queen of Great Britain, 'Empress of India', the name which is best understood in the East, but which Great Britain (which is an Empire) never has acknowledged to be higher than Queen or King.[19]

BELOW *A Queen among saints. Victoria depicted in a stained glass window in the Church of St Peter in Fakenham, Norfolk. The halo of Christ and St Peter is paralleled by Victoria's earthly crown, and she holds her orb of office to their Holy Lamb and Bible.*

The Bill was finally successful despite 'clamour and intimidation and misrepresentation'. On 1 January 1877 Victoria was declared Queen-Empress in a glittering ceremony in Delhi which she did not attend, though she threw a celebratory dinner at Windsor where she wore an excess of jewels that had been gifts from Indian princes. Thereafter, she did not always reserve the title for use east of Suez; she signed herself V.R. & I (Victoria Regina et Imperatrix) on many occasions when it was neither strictly necessary nor protocol, and indeed Disraeli toasted Victoria at her own dining table as 'Empress of India'.

By this time Britain had secured the shortest route – through the Suez Canal – to India. In November 1875 Britain had acquired a major shareholding in the Canal Company when Disraeli had purchased the holdings of the nearly bankrupt Khedive of Egypt. Disraeli had presented the purchase as another Imperial gift: 'It is just settled', he had written to the Queen on 24 November 1875, 'you have it, Madam. The French Government has been out-generalled'. This acquisition – though somewhat exaggerated by Disraeli – appealed to the Queen's

ABOVE *An Indian matchbox depicting the Empress Victoria.*

BELOW *The Prince of Wales tiger-shooting. In October 1875 Bertie set off on an expedition to India with a large party that included three chefs, a piper, a botanist, a taxidermist, a clerk from the India Office, the Prince's French poodle, but not the Princess of Wales. The imperial adventure cost some £280,000.*

sense that Britain needed to regain a presence on the world stage and pursue a more 'forward' strategy rather than the inactive, conciliatory tendencies that had been Gladstone's preference.

The decline of France and the rise of the *Dreikaiserbund*, the alliance between the Emperors of Austria, Germany and Russia had shifted the balance of power in Europe and marginalised Britain. Disraeli's foreign policy aim – he had a sketchy and rather out-of-date understanding of foreign affairs, or even the map of Europe – was to sunder the League of the Three Emperors and reassert Britain's voice in European affairs. The revival of the 'Eastern Question' was the opportunity.

In 1875 rebellion broke out in a number of Turkish provinces. Turkey, for so long the 'sick man of Europe', seemed likely to expire. British foreign policy had been that he must be propped up for as long as possible, primarily as a bulwark against Russian expansionism and any threat to the passage to India, despite the fact that the Suez Canal had now rendered this a chimera. It was an outdated policy and it was one that was hard to justify morally since not only was Turkey weak and disintegrating, but the Turkish government was also cruel and barbaric in the treatment of its subject peoples. Whilst Disraeli read the situation between Turkey and its Balkan possessions as being the same as that pertaining to Britain with Ireland's growing struggle for Home Rule, there was growing disquiet at Turkish misrule. This disquiet was fanned by stories of reprisals committed against the Bulgarian peasantry by the Bashi-Bazouk, irregular Turkish troops; it was alleged in the British press that 25,000 people had been slaughtered. Disraeli, who had refused to sign a note from the *Dreikaiserbund* earlier in the summer condemning the atrocities, played down the seriousness of the Turkish massacre.

However, during the summer recess Gladstone published a pamphlet *The Bulgarian Horrors and the Question of the East*. In less than a month 200,000 copies had been sold and the country was divided between those who supported Russia (in its attempts to regulate Turkey) and the pro Turks. The Queen was resolutely – and a late convert – pro Turk, as were all her family except the Duke of Edinburgh, having recently married a Russian princess: 'Affie is I am afraid quite Russian. I have had to warn him strongly'. She was particularly incensed by Gladstone's agitation and whilst she had never liked the Liberal statesman, her violent opposition to him dated from this time and she came increasingly to explain his policies as being a result of insanity:

The Eastern Question becomes more and more troublesome and those people here (with the incomprehensible Mr Gladstone, that most mischievous – though I believe unintentionally so – of men at their head) have gone mad and will not reflect on the great danger of furthering Russia!![20]

A conference was convened at Constantinople in late December 1876 with the six great powers – Russia, Germany, Austria, France, Britain and Turkey – meeting to consider the future of Turkey. It broke up inconclusively on 20 January 1877 and on 24 April Russia declared war on Turkey. The mood in the music halls was militant:

> We don't want to fight but by jingo if we do
> We've got the ships, we've got the men, we've got the money too
> And while Britons shall be true
> The Russians shall not have Constantinople.

The Queen was also impatient for British intervention. She bombarded Disraeli with her opinions: 'the Queen writes every day and telegraphs every hour', and wrote to Vicky on 19 June:

> You say that you hope we shall keep out of the war and God knows I hope and pray and think we shall – as to fighting. But I am sure you would not wish Great Britain to eat humble pie to these horrible, deceitful, cruel Russians? I will not be the Sovereign to submit to that!

She found Parliament's 'lack of patriotism' and the limits of her influence, extremely frustrating: 'It is a miserable thing to be a constitutional Queen and to be unable to do what is right. I would gladly throw all up and retire into quiet'.[21]

Disraeli continued to keep the balance between a bellicose monarch 'badgering for war' and threatening to abdicate if Britain did not 'hold firm' against Russian expansion, and a neutralist-inclined Cabinet, by wringing from his Ministers a reluctant agreement that if the Russians occupied Constantinople, Britain would intervene. On three occasions in February 1878 the British fleet set off for Constantinople, only to be withdrawn. The Turks, unable to count on British support signed a secret peace treaty, the Treaty of San Stefano, with Russia in which they acquiesced to greater Russian influence in Europe at the expense of Turkey. A Congress was held in Berlin in June 1878, under the chairmanship of Bismarck, to ratify the gains and Disraeli insisted on going despite being frail and ill. His diplomacy was successful though the Queen was sorry that

> Russia had got anything at all and 'must own to disbelieving any <u>permanent</u> settlement of Peace until we have

BELOW *Disraeli contemplates the Sphinx as he holds the key to the Suez Canal,* Punch, *11 December 1875. The Canal cut the travelling time to India by several weeks: in the event of Russian aggression or another Indian mutiny, British reinforcement could be rushed to the subcontinent. Disraeli's purchase of shares in the canal in 1875 prevented it becoming wholly French-owned, and refigured British India: 'India is any number of cyphers; but the canal is the unit that makes those cyphers valuable'.*

PUNCH, OR THE LONDON CHARIVARI.—December 11, 1875.

"MOSÉ IN EGITTO!!!"

ABOVE *'Bashi-bazouks burning a village.' An engraving from the* Illustrated London News, *19 August 1896. 'Much indignation is still felt at the reported atrocities which the Circassians and Bashi-bazouks have perpetuated in Bulgaria since the suppression of the local insurrection there in June … The Bashi-bazouks are the irregular cavalry attached to the Turkish Army, mostly half savage koords from Asia. Their style of equipment and general appearance may be seen from Mr. Simpson's drawing; he saw much of them in the Crimean War.'*

fought and beaten the Russians and that we shall truly have only put off the evil hour. But truly happy shall she be if she is mistaken …[22]

When Disraeli returned to London to which he had brought 'peace with honour' (and the control of Cyprus, which was to be used as a base to defend Britain's East Mediterranean trade routes in return for a pledge to defend Turkey) a 'large crowd from Charing Cross to Downing Street gave Lord Beaconsfield [Disraeli had received a peerage in 1876] a hearty reception' and Ponsonby rushed forward with a huge bouquet from the Queen for her returning Prime Minister.

In April 1880 the Queen travelled to Darmstadt for the confirmation of two of her granddaughters, Princesses Victoria and Ella of Hesse. It was a poignant visit for their mother, the constant Princess Alice, had died of diphtheria, caught whilst nursing her sick children, on 14 December 1878. Whilst she was visiting the family Victoria received a telegram: the Conservatives had been defeated in the election. Gladstone, deserving now the epithet 'the People's William', had been on a moral crusade raging against the frippery and immorality of the Conservatives' vainglorious Imperial policies, and he had found an accord in 'the nation'.

Victoria shot a note off to Ponsonby who was in Germany with her:

… the gr[ea]t alarm in the country is Mr Gladstone, the Queen perceives, & she will sooner <u>abdicate</u> than send for or have any <u>communication</u> with that <u>half-mad fire-brand</u> who w[oul]d soon ruin everything & be a <u>Dictator</u>. Others but herself <u>may submit</u> to his democratic rule, but <u>not the Queen</u>.[23]

Gladstone had resigned as leader of the Liberal Party in 1875, and the Queen continued to delude herself that though she would have to accept a Liberal government 'the question of him [Gladstone] coming into office was as improbable as if she were to send to the Archbishop of Strassbourg'. Ponsonby had to advise the Queen that:

he would prefer to see Mr Gladstone in the Cabinet rather than out of it. In the Cabinet he would be invested with responsibility, advised by his colleagues and influenced by Your Majesty. He is loyal and devoted to the Queen who can control him … Out of the Cabinet, he would have power without responsibility, he would exercise an undue influence over Ministers and he would be thrown into the arms of designing men who would make him unconsciously and unwillingly their leader.[24]

Victoria would have none of this. From 'on board *Victoria & Albert*' as she steamed home to face the constitutional crisis, she rebarbed:

… the <u>Queen cannot</u> send for Mr Gladstone – but she <u>cannot</u> leave 2 expressions of his [Ponsonby's] without <u>a remark</u>.

He says 'Mr Gladstone is <u>loyal & devoted to the Queen</u>'!!! He is <u>neither</u>; for <u>no one</u> CAN be, who spares no means ... to <u>vilify – attack</u> – accuse of <u>every</u> species of iniquity a Minister who had most difficult times and questions to deal with – and who showed a most unpardonable and disgraceful spite and personal hatred to Lord Beaconsfield who has restored England to the position she has lost under Mr Gladstone's Gov[ernmen]t.[25]

In the end of course, Gladstone, the Liberal victor, had to be sent for. He kissed hands and was observed by the Queen – ever hopeful that the Grand Old Man of British politics would not last long and the 'natural party of government' would soon be back – to be looking 'ill and haggard'. She crisply informed her incoming Prime Minister that the foreign policy which he had railed so successfully against at the polls, must not be reversed:

> There must be no democratic leaning, no attempt to change the Foreign policy ... no change in India, no hasty retreat from Afghanistan, and <u>no</u> cutting down of estimates. In short <u>no lowering</u> of the <u>high position</u> this country holds, and <u>ought always</u> to hold.[26]

The Liberals, who had pressed her during her early years of widowhood and retreat that the sovereign's duty was to open the parliamentary session, now informed her when she tried to refuse to include a statement about British withdrawal in Afghanistan in the speech from the throne that the 'Speech of the Sovereign, is only the Speech of the Ministers'.[27] Though Disraeli erroneously soothed her that this was 'a principle not known to the British Constitution. It is only a piece of Parliamentary gossip',[28] she recognised that

LEFT '*Peace with Honour*', by *Theodore Blake Wirgman. Disraeli's return from the Congress of Berlin in 1878. 'I hope to bring with me signed and sealed, a Treaty of Peace of which the Country will not be ashamed, and which will secure the tranquillity for a long time of regions in which we are deeply interested'. The Queen was ecstatic: 'He has gained a wreath of laurels which she would willingly herself offer him ... would he not accept a Marquisate or Dukedom <u>in addition</u> to the Blue Ribbon [the Order of the Garter]? And will he not allow the Queen to settle a Barony or Viscounty on his Brother or Nephew? Such a name should be perpetuated!'*

in fact 'a Constitutional Sovereign <u>at best has a most difficult</u> task, and it may become <u>almost an impossible one</u>, IF things are allowed to go on as they have done of late years'.[29]

On 19 April 1881, the frail, asthmatic, Disraeli died of bronchitis. It was reputed that he had declined a visit from the Queen on his deathbed: 'she would only ask me to take a message to Albert', he had protested. When the news was telegraphed to her, Victoria could

> scarcely see for my fast falling tears. I did <u>not</u> expect this very rapid end tho' my hopes sank yesterday very much … the loss is so <u>overwhelming</u> … never had I <u>so</u> kind and devoted a Minister and very few such devoted friends. His affectionate sympathy, his wise counsel – <u>all</u> were so invaluable even out of office. I have lost <u>so</u> many dear and valued friends but none whose loss will be more keenly felt. To England (or rather Gt Britain) and the <u>World</u> his loss is <u>immense</u>.[30]

There was to be no state funeral: Disraeli had directed that he wished to be 'buried in the same Vault in the Churchyard at Hughenden in which the remains of my late dear Wife Mary Anne Disraeli … were placed'. Protocol forbade the Queen to attend the funeral of one of her subjects. She sent two wreaths of fresh primroses, 'his favourite flowers' from Osborne, visited his grave later in the year and had a marble monument erected above the pew Disraeli used to occupy in Hughenden Church. The inscription, taken from the Book of Proverbs, concluded 'Kings love him that speaketh right'.

Gladstone was not proving a promising substitute. For one thing the Queen was '<u>seriously</u> alarmed at the <u>extreme Radicals</u> being at all cajoled by the present Government' when

> the Government <u>ought</u> to do <u>all</u> to obtain the <u>support</u> of their <u>moderate</u> <u>Whig</u> supporters <u>instead</u> of courting the support of the <u>extreme Party</u>. She <u>knows</u> that the Opposition would give them <u>every support</u>, in resisting any policy which <u>strikes</u> at the <u>root and existence</u> of the Constitution and Monarchy. The Queen herself can <u>never</u> have <u>any confidence</u> in the men who encourage <u>reform</u> for the <u>sake of the alteration and pulling down what</u> <u>exists</u> and what is <u>essential</u> to the <u>stability</u> of a Constitutional Monarchy. A <u>Democratic Monarchy</u> she will not <u>consent to belong to. Others</u> must be found <u>if</u> that is to be, and she <u>thinks</u> we are on a dangerous and doubtful slope which may become too rapid for us to stop, when it is too late. The Queen is all for <u>improvement</u> and <u>moderate reform of abuses</u>, but not merely for <u>alteration's and reform's sake</u>.[31]

Foreign affairs once more became a source of tension. There was the retreat from Afghanistan. There was the Anglo-Boer War, which broke out in the Transvaal in 1880 when the Dutch Boers refused to pay taxes to the British who had annexed their territory in 1877. Following the British defeat at Majuba Hill in 1881, Victoria insisted that 'we must not give in to Boer demands' but rather than go to war, Gladstone preferred to give the Transvaal qualified independence. Then there was Egypt.

A coup in 1882 by Arabi Pasha, the Egyptian Foreign Minister, against the government of the heavily indebted Khedive (from whom Britain had purchased shares in the Suez Canal Company) threatened British interests. 'Egypt is VITAL to us', insisted the Queen. The Prince of Wales volunteered to join the Guards expeditionary force that was sent under the command of Sir Garnet Wolseley. No one thought that this was a good idea.

In the event Prince Arthur, Duke of Connaught, whom Victoria generally regarded as the only satisfactory one of her sons, went. He was thirty-two and though his mother had a 'heavy heart' at the prospect, she agreed with her cousin, the Duke of Cambridge, Commander-in-Chief of the Army, who considered it 'most advisable that he should have the command of the Brigade of Guards, which I think would be considered as a high compliment by those distinguished and admirable troops ...'.[32]

And so 'wearing serge, quite loose, flannel shirt, high boots over breeches, and white helmet with a pugaree' and equipped with a 'canteen and spy glass' given him by his mother, Prince Arthur was in command of his brigade when the British troops seized victory at Tel-el-Kebir on 13 September 1882. The Queen and his wife 'dear Louischen' (Princess Louise of Prussia whom he had married in 1878), 'felt unbounded joy and gratitude' and a bonfire was lit in celebration at Balmoral on the same spot as the one that had flared when Sebastopol fell in 1855.[33]

The Queen was particularly anxious that, despite her relief, Prince Arthur should not be seen 'to be the first to come home', but above all, that 'there should be no undue haste in withdrawing the troops from Egypt' and she reminded Gladstone, who was all for instant withdrawal

BELOW *Queen Victoria and the Crown Princess of Prussia reviewing the British troops on their return from Egypt on 18 November 1882. 'I think much of today — so unclouded and bright — so full of emotions ... my heart was in my mouth as my darling Arthur rode past at the head of the brave men he led into action — and looking so like darling, beloved Papa. It was almost overpowering.'*

> of the <u>unfortunate result</u> of the haste with which our Troops were brought back from Zululand & South Africa, and the consequent loss of prestige wh[ich] ensued in the Transvaal. This s[houl]d be a warning to us in the <u>present instance</u>.[34]

By November 1882, most of the British troops were home from Egypt and on 21 November the Queen presented decorations at Windsor:

> First came Sir G. Wolseley, on whose breast I pinned the medal, followed by officers and men of the Navy. It was a proud moment for me, when dear Arthur came up ... and I pinned a medal [the Order of the Bath (Military Division)] on him.

Finally came

> all the Indians, on all of whom I pinned the medal, but, I fear, pricked one. Some of the Indians held out their swords for me to touch, as is their custom. I liked to be able to look at them close by, such fine men, and some of them so handsome. I stood on the fine Turkish carpet which had belonged to Arabi, and which had been taken out of his tent at Tel-el-Kebir. Arthur slept on it that memorable night ...

But Arabi's defeat was not the end of the matter. Unrest spread south to the Sudan, which Egypt controlled. As Britain continued to supervise the fragile Egyptian administration, this led to further British entanglement in Africa. In 1883 the forces of Mohammed Ahmed, a religious leader, known as the 'Mahdi', the Expected, almost annihilated the Egyptian army. The Queen was for intervention; her Prime Minister for evacuation. The Foreign Secretary explained that the Cabinet 'are strongly convinced that the Egyptians cannot conquer the Soudan, that it is out of the question to send British or Indian troops to recover this useless possession for Egypt'.[35]

> The Queen acquiesced, though with regret, in the abandonment of the Soudan by Egypt ... But since this policy has been adopted the Queen is very anxious that every effort should be made to save the lives of those who have been loyal to the Khedive and to secure the safety of the garrisons.[36]

On 18 January 1884 General Gordon was sent to the Sudan

> with instructions to report on the military situation in the Soudan, on measures for the security of Egyptian garrisons and of European population of Khartoum, on best mode of evacuating the interior and of securing safe and good administration of the sea coast by the Egyptian Government ... and to perform other such duties as may be entrusted to him by the Egyptian Government through Sir E. Baring.[37]

'He is a genius', wrote the Foreign Secretary of Gordon, 'and of splendid character. It is a great shame that there should be some eccentricity'. The Queen was grudgingly pleased:

> Why this was not done long ago and why the right thing is never done till it is absolutely extorted from those who are in authority, is inexplicable to the Queen.[38]

In fact Baring had been reluctant to send Gordon and insisted that there had to be 'a perfectly clear understanding with him as to what his position is to be and what line of policy he is to carry out'.[39] But once 'China' Gordon, so called for his victorious campaigns in the East, arrived in Khartoum, rather than winding up British rule, he called for more troops. On 18 March 1884, the Mahdi's troops moved in to besiege Khartoum. As far as Gladstone was concerned Gordon did not need *more* troops: his task had been to withdraw those that were there since, in his view, the followers of the Madhi 'were struggling to be free'. Victoria was fiercely partisan for Gordon. She 'trembles for General Gordon's safety. If anything befalls him, the result will be awful', and urged repeatedly that the troops he called for should be despatched immediately.[40] Over a year after Gordon had left for the Sudan reinforcement troops arrived on 28 January 1885. It was too late. Two days earlier the Mahdi's troops had stormed the garrison and speared Gordon to death.

> Dreadful news after breakfast. Khartoum fallen, Gordon's fate uncertain! [wrote the Queen in her journal on 5 February] All greatly distressed ... It is too fearful. The Government alone is to blame, by refusing to send the

expedition till it was too late. Telegraphed *en clair* [that is not in cypher, so the telegram could be intercepted and read by anyone] to Mr Gladstone … expressing how dreadfully shocked I was at the news, all the more so when one felt it might have been prevented.[41]

The Prime Minister replied in characteristic style:

> Mr Gladstone has had the honour this day to receive your Majesty's telegram *en clair*, relating to the deplorable intelligence received this day from Lord Wolseley and stating that it is too fearful to consider that the fall of Khartoum might have been prevented and many precious lives saved by earlier action.
>
> Mr Gladstone does not presume to estimate the means of judgment possessed by your Majesty, but so far as his information and his recollection at the moment go, he is not altogether able to follow the conclusion which your Majesty has been pleased to announce.[42]

He gave careful details of alternative routes the relief troops might have taken. But it was the Queen who was in tune with most of her people: Gordon was hailed as a hero who had died valiantly at heathen hands and in the music halls the G.O.M. (Grand Old Man) became the M.O.G. (Murderer of Gordon).

Victoria and Gladstone also clashed over Ireland. Victoria tended to regard the Irish problem as she regarded any mass protest, as the work of agitators that needed to be suppressed in the name of law and order. Indeed she frequently compared the loyalty of her Scottish subjects to the disloyalty of her Irish subjects, showing incomprehension at the difference in their societies. However, Victoria's intolerance of the Catholic question was confined to the converts and recusants of England, not the Catholics of Ireland, where she recognised that the majority of the population could hardly be called Dissenters, though she was sufficiently shrewd to realise that the discontent in Ireland was not likely to be settled by the disestablishment of the Irish church. And although the Irish with whom she had social intercourse were the Anglo-Irish landowning ascendancy, in 1881 she had not been opposed in principle to Gladstone's proposed Land Act which gave fixity of tenure and adjudicated fair rents. But this was the carrot. First the stick. The Queen insisted that a Coercion Bill must first be passed. Irish discontent with English rule was not assuaged: Gladstone's brother-in-law, the new Chief Secretary to Ireland, Lord Frederick Cavendish, was murdered whilst walking with the Viceroy in Phoenix Park, Dublin, on 6 May 1882.

In November 1885 after a brief Conservative interlude under Lord Salisbury, the Liberals won the majority in the election and Gladstone, now aged seventy-seven, was finally invited by a reluctant Queen back to office for the third time in February 1886. Eighty-five Home Rule candidates had

ABOVE 'Too Late!', the sheet music for a popular song in memory of General Gordon. Though the maverick General was besieged by the forces of the Mahdi at Khartoum, the decision to send a British force to relieve him was a delicate one for the Prime Minister Gladstone, concerning the complexities of Egyptian and Sudanese policy. To the Queen and the majority of the British people, it was simple: the imperialist adventurer was a hero who had been betrayed by vacillating and pusillanimous politicians.

been returned for Irish seats under the new franchise of the 1885 Reform Act. Gladstone announced that in his 'mission to pacify Ireland' he had concluded that Irish demands for Home Rule must be granted and as an old man, he was prepared to 'sacrifice himself for Ireland'. Within a month of returning to office he had drafted a comprehensive Home Rule Bill which would buy out the English landlords and give the Irish political self-determination. The Queen was horrified: it was another example of Gladstone's apparent death-wish to sunder her Empire. The Bill was introduced in the House of Commons on 8 April 1886 in a speech by the nearly octogenerian Prime Minister that lasted a little under three-and-a-half hours. 'The House listened with wonderful patience,' he observed, but 'like the house, he was a good deal exhausted …'

The battle for the Bill raged into the summer. Sir Henry Ponsonby replicated the Queen's views on the question: 'She is dead against Home Rule as calamitous for Ireland, hazardous for England and tending towards separation'.[43] She exhausted herself trying to resurrect the coalition of 'a Combination of Moderate & Patriotic men of both sides' (Conservatives and 'patriotic liberals' – that is non Radicals), which she had twice activated since 1884 in times of political crises, to save 'our dear great country' from falling into 'the reckless hands of Mr Gladstone …' that 'half crazy & really in many ways ridiculous old man'.

Now saddled with this 'old man in a hurry' the Queen was acting to frustrate his 'mission'. Throughout the crisis she sent the Conservative leader, Lord Salisbury, copies of all Gladstone's important letters to her – and often her replies to him. And on one occasion she asked Salisbury:

> pray how to protest ag[ain]st such a fearful danger and <u>possibility</u> and
> consult <u>together</u> HOW this contingency [that Gladstone might withdraw the
> Bill and re-present it the following year] can be stopped.[44]

Victoria was taking what she liked to imagine to be a non-party line on Home Rule appropriate for a monarch whose kingdom was in jeopardy; in fact she was acting to thwart the intentions of her elected government.

In his speech to the Commons on the second reading Gladstone pleaded:

> Ireland stands at your bar, expectant, hopeful, almost supplicant … think, I
> beseech you, think well, think wisely, think, not for the moment, but for all
> the years that are to come.[45]

In the event it was not the Queen who scuppered the bill. On 8 June 1886, a combination of Conservatives (Lord Randolph Churchill had played the orange card for the first time 'Ulster will fight and Ulster will be right') and those Whigs and Radicals who had defected from the the disparate groupings that made up the Liberal party, defeated the proposal of Home Rule for Ireland. Gladstone asked for a dissolution of Parliament.

Victoria and Gladstone met again in 1892; Victoria was seventy-three-years old and he was eighty-three and both leaned heavily on their walking sticks – when the G.O.M. returned to high office for the last time. He introduced a bill to grant Home Rule for Ireland again. It passed in the Commons by a narrow majority but fell in the Lords by 419 to 41 votes against in 1893. By this time the mood in the country had changed; Salisbury was cheered as he left the House of Commons after the vote by crowds singing 'Rule Britannia'; when Gladstone was opposed by his party it was because he was not sufficiently belligerent over national defence. He finally resigned on 3 March 1894 in a dispute over the naval budget. At his audience with the Queen she did not open the dispatch box which contained his resignation, and so she did not realise the moment of the occasion. When she did, she wrote wishing him a long retirement, but not offering a peerage since 'she knows that he would not accept it'.

Gladstone died on 19 May 1898. By 'entirely an oversight … no reference to Mr Gladstone's death was made in Court Circular the day after the event'.[46] The Queen wrote to her daughter Vicky, now the Dowager Empress Frederick of Germany:

> I cannot say that I think he was 'a great Englishman'. He was a clever
> man, full of talent, but he never tried to keep up the honour and prestige of
> G[rea]t Britain. He gave away the Transvaal & he abandoned Gordon, he
> destroyed the Irish church & tried to separate England from Ireland and he
> set class against class. The harm he did cannot be easily undone. But he
> was a good and very religious man.[47]

For his part Gladstone had likened the Queen's feelings for him to his when, as a young man, he had parted from a mule at the end of a holiday in Sicily:

> I had been on the back of the beast for many scores of hours. It had done
> me no wrong. It had rendered me much valuable service. But … I could
> not get up the smallest shred of feeling for the brute. I could neither love
> nor like it.[48]

When Gladstone resigned in 1894 he had served in Parliament for sixty-one years. The Queen had passed the half century of her reign seven years before.

BELOW *'The Last Hope.'*
Gladstone, portrayed as an ancient mariner adrift with a handful of Liberal supporters, waves a tattered 'Home Rule' banner in the hope of attracting the attention of the 'ship of state' as the galleon sails on impervious to Irish claims. The Second Home Rule Bill, introduced in February 1893, was passed by the Commons in September but rejected by the Lords the same month.

THE LAST HOPE.

CHAPTER EIGHT

A GLORIOUS REIGN

I T WILL BE VERY DIFFICULT TO describe it, but all went off admirably', wrote Queen Victoria in her journal for 21 June 1887. 'This day, fifty years ago, I had to go with a full Sovereign's escort to St James's, to appear at my proclamation …'

> The morning was beautiful and bright with a fresh air. Troops began passing early with bands playing and one heard constant cheering. Breakfasted … in the Chinese room. The scene outside was most colourful and reminded me of the Great Exhibition, which also took place on a fine day. Received many beautiful nosegays and presents … then dressed, wearing a dress and bonnet trimmed with white point d'Alençon, diamond ornaments in my bonnet, and pearls round my neck, with all my orders.

> At half-past eleven we left the Palace, I driving in a handsomely gilt landau drawn by six of the Creams, with dear Vicky and Alix, who sat in the back seat. Just in front of my carriage rode the 12 Indian officers and in front of them my 3 sons, 5 sons-in-law, 9 grandsons, and grandsons-in-law. Then came the carriage containing my 3 other daughters, 3 daughters-in-law, granddaughters, one granddaughter-in-law, and some of the suite. All other Royalties went in separate procession. George Cambridge rode the whole way next to my carriage, and the Master of Horse, Equerries etc., behind it with of course a Sovereign's escort. It really was a magnificent sight.[1]

Queen Victoria was sixty-eight and she had been Queen for fifty years; she had seven of her children still living. Leopold, a delicate haemophiliac, had died in France in 1884 but had surprised his mother, who rather presumed that his condition precluded paternity, by leaving two children from his marriage to Princess Helena of Waldeck-Pyrmont. Princess Alice was dead too as was her daughter Mary (May), both carried off by the same diphtheria epidemic. But Alice's surviving children had come to London for their grandmother's jubilee. There was Victoria, the eldest daughter, who was married to Louis of Battenberg. Her eldest daughter, Alice, who was two at the time of the Jubilee, was to become the mother of Prince Philip of Greece, who was to marry Victoria's great-great-granddaughter who was to ascend the throne in 1952 as Queen Elizabeth II. A son, Louis, born the year before his great-grandmother's death, was to become Earl Mountbatten of Burma, who was killed by an IRA bomb in 1979. Another of Princess Alice's daughters, the dazzlingly beautiful Alix (Alicky) who had rejected a proposal from her cousin the Duke of Clarence – if he had lived to inherit, he would have succeeded Bertie as King of England – became the wife of a Romanov, the doomed Nicholas II, Tsar of Russia. She was to perish with him and their family at the hands of the Bolsheviks in 1918.

Bertie, the Prince of Wales and his wife, Alix, who sat in the carriage with the Queen, had five children. Their oldest son, Albert Victor, Duke of Clarence, always known as Eddy, died of pneumonia five years after the

Jubilee and the heir apparent became George, Duke of York, who succeeded his father as King George V in 1910. Another daughter, Maud, married King Haakon of Norway.

Vicky, who was in the Queen's carriage too, was soon, on the death of her father-in-law, to be Empress of Germany. Alongside rode her husband Frederick. The Queen was particularly relieved to see that 'dear Fritz looked so handsome and well'; he had been suffering from a painful throat condition which turned out to be cancer and he died the next summer, having ruled as Emperor for only ninety-nine days. Their son Willy, was riding in the procession too, and his grandmother expressed herself enchanted with his son, also called Willy, who was two years old, 'a dear little boy'. Vicky had borne eight children, though two had died in infancy, Sigismund (Siggie) as a toddler in 1866 and Waldemar (Waldy) in 1879, at the age of eleven, from haemophilia. Princess Sophie, seventeen at the Jubilee, was soon to marry Prince Constantine, heir to the throne of Greece. Prince Alfred, a career sailor, and his wife, Princess Marie, were the parents of five children, though their eldest son 'young Alfred' died in 1899. A daughter, Marie, was to become Queen of Rumania.

ABOVE 'The Royal Oak' – the family tree of Victoria and Albert produced on the occasion of the Queen's Jubilee in 1887. From the sturdy trunk, the branches spread out across Europe to the great royal houses of Russia, Germany, Romania, Spain and Norway.

Victoria's third daughter, Helena, known as Lenchen, had married Prince Christian of Schleswig-Holstein and they had four children (the last, Harold, died in infancy), Victoria's fourth daughter, the only to marry a British subject, had no children: the marriage between Louise (Loosy) and the then Marquis of Lorne, who succeeded to his father's title as Duke of Argyll in 1900, was not successful. He was a Liberal MP who was appointed Governor General of Canada in 1878. The couple increasingly lived their lives separately, but there was no divorce in that generation of royals.

Special legislation had had to be enacted to bring Prince Arthur, Duke of Connaught, who had so distinguished himself in Egypt, home from India, where he was serving, to attend the celebrations. He and his wife, Princess

Louise of Prussia, had three young children in 1887. The eldest, Margaret, was to marry the man who became King Gustav IV of Sweden.

Beatrice had been the last to marry and her mother had been most reluctant for this to happen. Victoria felt every mother needed an unmarried daughter as a companion, and when Beatrice announced that she wished to marry Prince Henry of Battenberg, the Queen declared that she had the 'most violent dislike' of 'my precious Baby marrying at all' and insisted that 'Liko' as he was known, should do as *her* husband had done, and leave his native country to settle, without a proper job or defined role, in England. At the time of Victoria's jubilee Beatrice and Liko already had two of the four children they were to have. One, the infant Victoria Eugénie, was to become the Queen of Spain after her marriage to Alfonso XIII.

Queen Victoria had forty-two grandchildren, of whom thirty-two survived her. Her great-grandchildren multiplied exponentially to spread a dynastic web over the entire continent of Europe: it was estimated by 1990 that Victoria had 540 or so known living and legitimate descendants.[2]

Surrounded by her extended family, the Queen celebrated the most formal part of the Jubilee. On 20 June she had travelled by train up to London where 'all the Royalties were assembled' from the German states, Portugal, Austria, Belgium and, from further afield, Hawaii, Japan and Siam; they included a 'Persian Prince who speaks no English'. In the evening there was 'a large family dinner' round a horseshoe table 'with many lights on it'. The King of Denmark escorted the Queen into dinner and on her other side sat

ABOVE *A household name. In an age of growing mass production the Queen and her children are harnessed to advertise soap.*

BELOW *Four Generations of the British Monarchy: Victoria with her eldest son, Edward VII (standing right), her grandson, George V (standing left), and in the sailor suit his eldest son, Prince Edward of York, later Edward VIII.*

> Willy of Greece. The Princes were all in uniform, and the Princesses were beautifully dressed. Afterwards we went into the Ball-room, where my band played. I talked to as many as I could, and sat down with Marie of Belgium.

The next morning, 21 June 1887, the royal convoy processed to Westminster Abbey for a service of thanksgiving.

> The crowds were enormous … and there was such an extraordinary outburst of enthusiasm as I had hardly ever seen in London before; all the people seemed to be in such good humour. The old Chelsea Pensioners were in a stand near the Arch. The decorations along Piccadilly were quite beautiful, and there were most touching inscriptions. Seats and platforms were arranged up to the tops of the houses, and such waving of hands. Piccadilly, Regent Street and Pall Mall were all alike most festively decorated. Many schools were out, and many well-known faces were seen.[3]

As the Queen entered the Abbey

> God Save the Queen was played, and then changed to Handel's Occasional Overture, as I walked slowly up the Nave and Choir, which looked beautiful all filled with people. The House of

ABOVE *The Matriarch of Europe. The Royal family on the occasion of Queen Victoria's Jubilee, 1887, at Buckingham Palace, painted by L. Tuxen. 'I shall dread all this "Royal Mob" as Louis calls these tremendous royal assemblages than which I dislike nothing more', wrote Victoria to her eldest daughter. 'Do not worry yourself, dearest Mama about the guests and the fatigue, etc. The apprehension is worse than the reality', counselled Vicky, 'the fact that all want to shew their sympathy, affection and respect is gratifying and satisfying.'*

Commons was below us to the left, and I recognised several persons amongst them, but did not see Mr Gladstone though he was there ... I sat <u>alone</u> (oh! without my beloved husband, for whom this would have been such a proud day!) where I sat forty-nine years ago and received the homage of Princes and Peers, but in the old stone brought from Scotland, on which the old Kings of Scotland used to be crowned. My robes were beautifully draped on the chair. The service was very well done and arranged. The Te Deum, by my darling Albert, sounded beautiful, and the anthem ... was fine, especially the way in which the National Anthem and dear Albert's Chorale were worked in.

When they arrived back at the Palace the Queen took off the bonnet she habitually wore, on this day in preference to a crown – though it was a bonnet encrusted with diamonds – and handed out Jubilee brooches to her female kin and pins to the men. Present-giving to her followed in the small Ballroom: the royal children gave 'a very handsome piece of plate', whilst from the Queen of Hawaii, there was 'a present of very rare feathers, but very strangely arranged as a wreath round my monogram, also in feathers on a black ground, framed'. After this exertion the Queen was

quite exhausted and ready to faint, so I got in my rolling chair and was rolled back to my room. Here I lay down on the sofa and rested doing nothing but opening telegrams coming from every part of the country, so they could no longer be acknowledged and this will have to be done through the paper.[4]

Dinner was something of an ordeal, the Queen wearing a dress with the three emblems of her kingdom 'the rose, thistle, and shamrock embroidered on it, and my large diamonds' sat through endless speeches and loyal toasts though she was 'half dead with fatigue'. She tried to watch the magnificent fireworks display through the window without much success and rolled to her room, hearing as she went

> the noise of the crowd, which began yesterday, went on till late. Felt truly grateful that all had passed off so admirably, and this never-to-be-forgotten day will always leave the most gratifying and heart-stirring memories behind.[5]

The next day as the Queen breakfasted she heard reports of the 'splendid illuminations', and how 'thousands had thronged the streets ... and passed the Palace singing God Save the Queen and Rule Britannia.' Then there was more present-giving. Two 'magnificent silver-gilt flagons' from the Dukes and Duchesses of Cumberland and Cambridge, more plate, a 'beautiful pendant with a St George and the Dragon on a blue enamelled ground surrounded by two rows of large diamonds and a pearl drop' from Bertie's household, a painting that Lord Salisbury had done himself of 'old Richmond', a number of watercolours, and, brought by a

> Deputation 'from the 'Women of England' ... the signatures of the millions who have subscribed to a gift contained in a splendid gold coffer, of which Lady Strafford presented me with the key, and Lady Londonderry presented me with that of another very fine coffer, containing the signatures of the Women of Ireland.[6]

The Queen was invited to decide how the women's subscription appeal should be spent. There was no shortage of options: beds were being closed at Guy's hospital for want of funds and discontent over unemployment had led to rallies and protest meetings. The Queen herself had been distressed to hear 'booing and hooting, of perhaps only two or three, now and again all along the route [when she had been to Whitechapel to open the People's Palace in May] evidently sent there on purpose, and frequently the same people, probably Socialists and the worst Irish'.[7] The response of Lord Salisbury's Conservative government to these manifestations of discontent had been to close Trafalgar Square, a traditional theatre of free speech, to public meetings. This led to the 'Bloody Sunday' riot in November. A spoof Jubilee address, part drafted by Bernard Shaw, caught the current of this discontent:

> Owing to the operation of economic conditions which no operation of the existing laws can thwart, the vast wealth produced daily by the labour of my people is now distributed not only unequally, but so inequitably that the contrast between the luxury of idle and unprofitable persons, and the poverty of the industrious masses has become a scandal and a reproach to our civilisation, setting class against class, and causing among the helpless and blameless infants of my most hardworking subjects a mortality disgraceful to me as head of state, and unbearable to me as a woman and mother.[8]

In the event, the Queen decided that the money should be used to build an equestrian statue of Prince Albert to stand in Windsor Great Park, and when that did not begin to absorb the generous gift, the money went to establish Queen Victoria's Nursing Institute.

But more of the Queen's subjects were to share in the loyal celebrations and so after a short rest it was off to Hyde Park where

30,000 poor children, boys and girls with their schoolmasters and mistresses were assembled. Tents had been pitched for them to dine in, and all sorts of amusements had been provided for them. Each received an earthenware pot with my portrait on it. ... the children sang God Save the Queen somewhat out of tune, and then we drove to Paddington Station.[9]

When the Queen arrived in Windsor, it was the same story; cheering crowds lining the streets 'and every window and balcony full of people, Chinese lanterns and preparations for illuminations making a very pretty effect'.

The next day it was back to London for a garden party where Victoria was 'dreadfully done up by it and could not speak to, or see, all those I wished'. Her numerous family were beginning to have to return to their duties in their own countries or principalities, or like Alfred 'to rejoin his ship', but for the Queen herself the Jubilee celebrations continued with

a great reception of Indian Princes and Deputations to receive. She admired the handsome young Raj of Kutch, most beautifully dressed ... the Maharajah and Maharani of Kuch Behar ... also beautifully dressed and received yet more sumptuous gifts, 'a carved ruby set with fine diamonds ... beautiful silver ornaments for the table... an inlaid ivory writing and workbox in one ... a pearl ornament, which [Sir Partab Singh] had taken off his own puggaree, as a mark of fealty, saying everything he possessed was at my service.[10]

ABOVE 'The Munshi, Abdul Karim', a painting by Heinrich von Angeli. On 23 June 1887, the Queen recorded meeting 'my two Indian servants', the younger of whom, 'called Abdul Karim ... is tall, and with a fine, serious countenance ... they both kissed my feet'. They had come as part of the Jubilee celebrations. The Queen soon grew fond of Karim, whom she found 'a great comfort'. She called him her Munshi (teacher) and recommended that as well as teaching her Hindustani '... he is most handy in helping when she signs by drying the signatures. He learns with extraordinary assiduity'.

There was still the Spithead review of the Navy to come, and then the Indian Princes departed, leaving Victoria with two Indian servants of her own. One, Abdul Karim, was to play an important role in the Queen's last years. 'I am learning a few words of Hindustani to speak to my servants', wrote the Empress of India in her journal, 'It is a great interest to me for both the language and the people, I have naturally never come into real contact with before'. As her 'Munshi', teacher, Karim soon enjoyed an elevated – and envied – position. At first he had waited at table, but complained that as an educated man (he had been a clerk in Agra jail) he found that demeaning, and so he was promoted to help with the royal boxes – particularly when they contained correspondence relating to Indian matters. For her part the Queen had the Viennese artist von Angeli, who had painted her portrait a few years earlier, paint the Munshi, and fiercely defended him against racial prejudice and snobbery, commanding that he should sit among the gentry at the Braemar games, insisting that Indians were not be designated 'black men' at court. The Queen provided handsomely for his large, and rather irregular family, and in 1894 the Munshi was created the Queen's 'Indian Secretary' with the title of 'Hafiz' and a small staff of his own. All photographs showing him waiting at table were to be destroyed. Such was the jealousy of others in her household that the Queen was gleefully informed that Karim's social origins were not as he had represented, his 'Surgeon-General father' was in reality an apothecary at Agra jail. Victoria shamed their social snobbery as she had other's racism, reminding them that she had known '2 Archbishops who were sons respectively of a Butcher & a Grocer'.

Indeed she had become so enthralled with the subcontinent that she ruled but had never visited that she toyed with the idea of visiting Prince Arthur, who returned to serve in India after the Jubilee celebrations. 'I have such a g[rea]t longing for India ... you may think me crazy for saying this – but I can assure you I have been thinking of it – v[er]y much of late.'[11]

She took a great interest in Indian life – translating those interests close to her heart at home for the good of the Indian people. Hence she campaigned for safer and more painless childbirth. Meanwhile, at home, she tried to replicate what she would never see. Rudyard Kipling's father, a museum curator in Lahore, was consulted on the decoration of a magnificent white fretted-plaster Durbar Room that the Queen had built at Osborne.

Ten years after her Golden Jubilee, Emperor William of Germany wrote to his 'Dearest Grandmama' from Potsdam on 2 January 1897:

> as you are in the sixtieth year of your prosperous and glorious reign ... Have
> you any plans or wishes about our coming or not coming for your Jubilee,
> and whether some of our children are to come with us or not?[12]

In the ten years that had passed Victoria's family had suffered a number of deaths, and in foreign affairs relations between Britain and Germany had become somewhat strained. Less than a year after the 1887 celebrations Willy's father, Vicky's husband, had died and Victoria's grandson – 'that tiny, weeny little brat you often had in your arms and dear Grandpapa swung about in a napkin' – became Emperor of Germany.

Victoria still felt the loss of her oldest son-in-law keenly. 'What a calamity it was for the whole of Europe as well as for his own country!' she mused with prescience.[13] Another tragedy had been the death of Beatrice's husband, Prince Henry of Battenberg. His marriage to Beatrice had been at the price of living in extreme proximity to his mother-in-law, but he had sought action as a soldier when conflict arose between Britain and the Ashanti kingdom (now part of Ghana) in West Africa. 'To my astonishment and concern, Liko told me that he seriously wished to go on the Ashanti Expedition, and I told him it would never do,'[14] Victoria recorded, but Beatrice,

> hoped I would not oppose it, for he had set his heart on going. He smarted
> under his enforced inactivity ... he felt he was a soldier, brought up as such,
> and his brothers had all been on active service.[15]

So, despite the fact that in equatorial Africa 'the climate no doubt was bad, but with all care he might be able to avoid fever', she felt that 'she could not refuse, as long as darling Beatrice, with her strong sense of duty agrees'. On 5 December 1895 Liko set off.

At home at Osborne Beatrice and her mother waited, and Beatrice read the telegrams from the front to her mother. The Queen's sight was now so bad that her Private Secretary had 'developed a completely new handwriting, very large, with perfectly formed letters', which he practised in 'some copy-books issued for girl's schools' and when even this proved illegible he 'bought some special ink like boot varnish'. Frederick, the son of the Queen's former Private Secretary, Henry Ponsonby, invented a useful device involving a copper tray and a spirit lamp to 'dry my letters quickly, since blotting-paper was out of the question'. Increasingly, important messages had to be read to the Queen and those from her quavering hand were copied out by Ponsonby who 'thought these copies always looked so odd in my handwriting, especially sentences like "William is quite wrong: he should remember that as German Emperor, etc. etc." or "Bertie and Alix must not do this".'[16]

In the winter of 1895 the Queen was also preoccupied with news from another part of the continent: South Africa where, on 29 December, Jameson lead a raid from Bechuanaland (now Botswana) into the Boer-held Transvaal with the intention of uniting with the *Uitlanders* (mainly British immigrants who had gone to the Transvaal to mine gold) in an attempt to overthrow Stephanus Kruger's government. Intended to reclaim for the Empire the gold-rich lands occupied by the Dutch settlers, the abortive raid was to presage the Boer War. And when Emperor William sent a telegram, congratulating Kruger, it was an indication that Britain could not look to

RIGHT *Queen Victoria and Princess Beatrice with their retrievers, from a photograph, c.1875. The Queen was frequently painted or photographed with dogs. She had been so enchanted with Sir Edwin Landseer's portrait of her spaniel, Dash, that she commissioned another painting,* Queen Victoria's Favourite Pets, *showing Dash on a velvet stool, with a greyhound, Hector, and Nero, a deerhound. 'Nothing brutalises people more than cruelty to dumb animals,' she wrote, 'and to dogs, who are the companions of men, it is especially revolting.'*

Germany to stand aside from any imperialistic enterprise she might launch. As the Prime Minister, Lord Salisbury, was to write four years later:

> Both [France and Germany] have become Colonial Powers to a much greater extent than they were before, and the number of places where their paths cross the path of England is much larger than it used to be. Our relations with those two Powers will remain a subject of anxiety. Your Majesty's personal influence over the Emperor William is a powerful defence against danger in that direction ...[17]

On 10 January 1896 a telegram arrived from West Africa: 'Prince Henry is suffering from a fever, slight, but sufficient to prevent going on to the front'. It was an anxious time: 'Can think of nothing but dear Liko ... heard that dear Liko had been sent to a hospital ship ... We are dreadfully distressed and worried, and feel how keen the disappointment will be for him ...' He seemed to be recovering, but on 22 January:

> A terrible blow has fallen on us all, especially my poor darling Beatrice. Our dearly beloved Liko has been taken from us! ... he was so much better, and we were anxiously awaiting the news of his arrival at Madrid. What will become of my poor child? All she said in a trembling voice, apparently quite stunned, was, 'The life is gone out of me'.

What was to become of Beatrice was that she was to spend her widowhood as she had passed her girlhood: at her mother's side.

Victoria's reign was to be the triumph of age. The year 1897 was the sixtieth year of her reign – the longest ever tenancy of the throne of Great Britain: the 'Lady Ruler' had beaten the record of George III by nine months at this, her second, Jubilee – though *The Times* pointed out that this was a paltry span compared to the reign of the King of Persia who had reputedly sat on the Peacock throne for 500 years.

The celebrations were to be magnificent: but, what was the event to be called? And would the Queen, now aged seventy-eight, use the occasion to announce that she was abdicating in favour of the Prince of Wales? The question of a name was settled by Sir Arthur Bigge, Ponsonby's successor: the Golden Jubilee was to be followed by the Diamond. The Queen approved. She did not, however, entertain the possibility of standing down in favour of Bertie, now himself a grandfather.

The 1887 Jubilee had been a homage from the royal families of Europe. Ten years on it was to be different. 'No crowned heads' as Lord Salisbury described the decision to avoid over-exerting the Queen. And this proscription included the Emperor of Germany, despite his New Year hopes: 'there is not the slightest fear of the Queen giving way about the Emperor William's coming here in June. It would *never* do for many reasons ...' insisted Victoria: one, no doubt, being the Kruger telegram.[18]

It was largely the idea of the Colonial Secretary, Joseph Chamberlain, to invite to London the heads of the far flung British colonies. Victoria might be 'Grandmother of Europe', but she was also a diminutive figurehead at

BELOW *A* carte-de-visite *of Princess Beatrice. 'She is like a sunbeam in the house and also like a dove, an angel of peace who brings it wherever she goes and who is my greatest comfort,' wrote the Queen of her youngest daughter, who she called 'Baby' and kept close throughout her life.*

the pinnacle of a vast Empire and her Diamond Jubilee was to be an occasion to demonstrate and celebrate the extent of British dominion.

The actual day, 20 June, fell on a Sunday, and every church, chapel and synagogue throughout the land held a service of thanksgiving, whilst the Queen herself and members of her family attended a service in St George's Chapel, Windsor, at which Prince Albert's Te Deum was sung, a special Jubilee prayer was said and the choir sang a Jubilee hymn:

> Thou hast dower'd our queenly throne
> With sixty years of blessing

to music specially composed by Sir Arthur Sullivan of Gilbert and Sullivan operetta fame.

The Queen's age and slight infirmity had led to endless discussions about the form that the celebrations should take: at one time it had been mooted that the royal carriage should be pulled into St Paul's Cathedral, but it was considered that

> the idea of bringing horses into the building would shock people; why however, should they not be taken out and HM drawn in procession up the aisle? It would be a magnificent spectacle, and would afford the Queen the minimum of discomfort.[19]

ABOVE *Queen Victoria, 1887, the official Golden Jubilee portrait. The 'Widow of Windsor' was at last persuaded to participate in a great state pageant. The Prime Minister, Lord Salisbury, paid his respects on the achievement: 'He congratulates your Majesty very cordially and respectfully on the wonderful scenes of rejoicing of these last few days. He has heard on all sides of the impression it has made on our foreign visitors'.*

In the end the carnivalesque was rejected in favour of a stately three-hour procession which would wind from Buckingham Palace to the City and culminate in an open-air Te Deum in front of St Paul's.

On Jubilee day – 22 June 1897 – the Queen set out from Buckingham Palace at 11.15 a.m., a tiny figure dressed in black silk, trimmed with panels of grey satin and veiled with black net. she wore the habitual bonnet, on this occasion 'trimmed with creamy white flowers, and white aigrette and some black lace', and held aloft a black lace parasol, lined in white. Travelling in the state landau, drawn by eight cream horses, she was accompanied by the Princess of Wales 'very pretty in lilac' and Lenchen. The Prince of Wales and the seventy-eight-year-old Duke of Cambridge rode alongside, as he had done ten years earlier. She had 'an escort from the 2nd Life Guards and officers of the native Indian regiments, the latter riding immediately in front of my carriage'. The widowed Empress Frederick rode in a carriage alone, 'as her rank of Empress prevented her from sitting with her back to the horses'. Before she left the Palace Victoria had

> touched an electric button, by which I started a message which was telegraphed throughout the whole Empire. It was the following: 'From my heart I thank my beloved people, May God bless them!'[20]

According to *The Times*:

> Every city, town, village and remote settlement will celebrate the occasion ...
> the eyes of the whole Empire, and of millions of men beyond its pale will be
> fixed upon London, and upon the great and inspiring ceremony with which we
> celebrate the 60 years of the Queen's reign. They will be fixed upon the
> revered and beloved figure of the woman who for two full generations has
> represented to so large a faction of the human race the principles of order, of
> civilization, of rational progress. They will be fixed upon one who in a period
> of all-embracing change has offered during all these years an extraordinary
> instance of political and moral standards.

Troops from the colonies played a noticeable part in the procession. These
were the men whom Chamberlain stressed that

> since they represent the forces of the Empire ... it is most desirable that the
> Colonies should be encouraged to increase these forces and to identify them
> with the general defences of the Empire; and HM's Government are most
> anxious that their visit to this country at the expense of the Colonies should be
> recognised by the Home authorities as a most significant event which may
> have large consequences for the future.[21]

And the newspapers reported that when the Queen reviewed her Indian
troops she had addressed the officers in Hindustani, a report that the Queen,
who had been having difficulty in learning the language recently, admitted
was 'not true', though she added, 'I could have done so had I wished'. The
day of celebration was, the Queen wrote,

> a never-to-be-forgotten day. No one ever, I believe, has met with such an
> ovation as was given to me, passing through those six miles of
> streets, including Constitution Hill. The crowds were quite
> indescribable, and their enthusiasm truly marvellous and
> deeply touching. The cheering was quite deafening and
> every face seemed to be filled with real joy. I was much
> moved and gratified ...[22]

The Lord Mayor of the City of London presented the
Queen with the ceremonial sword and then

> immediately mounted his horse in his robes, and
> galloped past bare-headed [his hat having fallen off as
> he tussled, in full ceremonial dress to control his bolting
> mount] ... As we neared St Paul's the procession was often
> stopped, and the crowds broke out into singing God Save the
> Queen. In one house were assembled the survivors of the
> Charge of Balaclava. In front of the Cathedral the scene was
> most impressive. All the Colonial troops, on foot, were
> drawn up round the Square. My carriage, surrounded by
> all the Royal Princes, was drawn up close to the steps,
> where the Clergy were assembled, the Bishops in rich
> copes, with their croziers, the Archbishop of Canterbury

BELOW *'All Shall Celebrate',
a free meal for the elderly of
Lancaster on the occasion of the
Diamond Jubilee, 1897. The
celebrations took nine months to
organise and all over the country
there was an unprecedented number
of initiatives proposed to
commemorate the occasion – a
Jubilee convalescent home in
Bristol, a recreation ground in
Newcastle –* whilst Punch *mocked
the appeal for funds for 'self-
supporting orphans' and 'homes
for the affluent'.*

AT 12-0 O'CLOCK THERE WILL BE

A FREE DINNER
To 1,000 Aged People
IN THE MARKET.

and the Bishop of London each holding a very fine one. A Te Deum was sung
… the Lord's Prayer, most beautifully chanted, a special Jubilee prayer, and the
benediction concluded the short service, preceded by the singing of the <u>old 100th</u>
in which everyone joined. God Save the Queen was also sung … as I drove off,
the [Archbishop of Canterbury] gave out, 'Three cheers for the Queen.'

Then it was off to Mansion House, where the flustered Lord Mayor had
recovered his composure sufficiently to greet the Queen, standing with his
wife who presented her with

a beautiful silver basket full of orchids … we proceeded over London Bridge
where no spectators were allowed, only troops, and then along the Borough
Road, where there is a very poor population, but just as enthusiastic and
orderly as elsewhere.[23]

The procession snaked back over Westminster Bridge, past the Houses of
Parliament, up Whitehall and along the Mall, finally getting 'home at a
quarter to two' for 'a quiet luncheon with Vicky, Beatrice and her children.
Troops continually passing by …' That night Victoria attended a 'large
dinner in the Supper-room' and, wearing 'a black and silver dress with my
Jubilee necklace and the beautiful brooch given me by my household', the
Queen listened to 'Bertie who sat at my table, [give] out the health of the
Empress Frederick and my distinguished guests' and despite feeling 'very tired
… tried to speak to most of the Princes and Princesses'.

The Diamond Jubilee was more of a season than a day: the Queen had
progressed around the kingdom for loyal addresses before 22 June; afterwards
those from the Empire continued to flood in. The Viceroy of India, writing
from Simla, was able to assure

your Majesty that the loyalty, which is being witnessed in India, is the
spontaneous work of the people [and he was struck at the way in which from
remote districts, even from the hills of Hunza, messages have been pouring in
on him]. A full statement of these will be prepared and forwarded, as well as
the more formal addresses. Many of the latter are enclosed in caskets of
beautiful design and workmanship.[24]

The Prime Minister, Lord Salisbury, ventured

to take the opportunity to congratulate your Majesty respectfully, but most
heartily on the splendid success of [the] celebration. It will live in history as a
unique and unequalled demonstration of the attachment which has grown
more and more in intensity between the Sovereign of a vast Empire and her
subjects of every clime.[25]

Louise's father-in-law, the Duke of Argyll, thought the procession had been

a sight never equalled, and never to be forgotten. Although your Majesty's
Home Troops were far the finest, we were much interested in the Colonials.
Their uniform is dull-coloured. But we could not help remembering that no
Sovereign since the fall of Rome could muster subjects from so many and so
distant countries all over the world.[26]

The next day the Queen received loyal addresses from the Lords, Members of the House of Commons, the chairmen of County Councils and 400 English and Welsh mayors and Scottish Provosts in the 'Ball-room [at Buckingham Palace] where the heat was dreadful' and the House of Commons reception was disastrously and ineptly managed.

When she arrived in Slough which 'was very prettily decorated' there was another procession and more loyal addresses. At Eton, the Queen passed

> under an architectural arch, on which stood three boys dressed as heralds. Inside the arch stood four young Indian boys, in their native dress, sons of the Maharajah of Kuch, Behar, the Minister of Hydrebad, and the Prince of Gondal. The Eton volunteers [of whom one was a grandson of the Queen] formed a Guard of Honour.[27]

Over the following days there were still more loyal addresses from institutions and organisations from home and the Empire: the Queen recorded most days that she 'felt very tired' and the Prince of Wales frequently stepped in to receive the addresses. However, Victoria was very present at a large garden party at Buckingham Palace on 28 June at which the actress Ellen Terry and the actor-manager Henry Irving were presented and at another at Windsor, which had been arranged to conciliate the members of the House of Commons, whose loyal address had been so badly mismanaged that a compensatory invitation had to be extended to the disappointed and disaffected politicians.

One of the most significant moments of the Jubilee was on 2 July, when the Queen reviewed the Colonial troops at Windsor before their return home. Victoria noted in her journal:

BELOW *The Imperial troops on parade. The Diamond Jubilee celebrations were an occasion to hold together the complex and contradictory strands that made up the Empire. A Jubilee procession panorama was printed in aid of the 'Prince of Wales' Hospital Fund for London' in which this section showed 'detachments from the defences of the Far East, the Island of Hong Kong, and the Straits Settlements in the Malay Peninsula'.*

> It was a very interesting and curious sight, for there were men from every part
> of the world. The most notable among them were the Sikhs from India, the
> Hong-Kong Police from China, and the Houssas from West Africa, most of
> the latter having taken part in the Ashanti Expedition, and Beatrice had seen
> them before the Inspection. One of the English officers and a native had
> known Liko, and the latter was called up for me to speak to him. The Houssas
> are fine-looking men, but very black. On returning to the saluting point the
> troops marched past, reformed in line and gave a second royal salute.

The Jubilee had, indeed been an occasion not only to celebrate the Empire,
as Joseph Chamberlain had intended, but also to pronounce on it. The
reflections voiced in the press at the time seem united in their proselytising
of the benefits of the British civilising mission to those far-flung, primitive,
'empty lands' that lay beyond Europe.

A *Daily Mail* journalist watching the royal procession

> began to understand, as never before, what the Empire amounts to ... we send
> out a boy here and a boy there, and the boy takes hold of the savages. ... and
> teaches them to march and shoot ... and believe in him, and die for him and
> the Queen. A plain, stupid, uninspired people, they call us, and yet we are
> doing this with every kind of savage man there is.[28]

Whilst, for *The Times*, the rationale was rather more concerned with trade in
an age when the appeal of Empire for the mass of the British people needed
to be more than ceremonial:

> The surest foundation of the Imperial idea is that it should rest upon
> the necessity of the people. Within the limits of the Empire, under the
> protection of the British flag, we have a heritage of enormous wealth
> waiting to be realised by the efforts of our increasing population. There is
> enough to spare for many successive generations. Only labour is needed
> to put corn where thistles have hitherto grown. The poorest can contribute
> their labour and the value of the Empire to the poor is the best guarantee
> of its endurance.[29]

The next year was to see an imperial triumph when, in September 1898, the
Queen received a telegram from General Kitchener in the Sudan:

> This morning the British and Egyptian flags were hoisted on the walls of
> Gordon's Palace at Khartoum, upon which occasion enthusiastic cheers for her
> Majesty were given by both British and Egyptian troops; subsequently an
> impressive memorial service was held at the place where Gordon died.[30]

'Surely he is avenged', the Queen wrote in her diary of the reconquest of
Sudan as a result of the victory of Omdurman – the bones of the Mahdi had
been unearthed, and, it was rumoured, his skull discovered in use as an ink
well – and she telegraphed to Kitchener the offer of a peerage.

Another act of imperial conquest was to begin a year later, in 1899: if
Khartoum was to be avenged so must Majuba Hill and the Transvaal retaken
from the Boers. The intransigence of the Kruger government to the rights of

'British citizens resident in British South Africa', who had petitioned the Queen earlier that year that the civic and legal rights they thought they had enjoyed under the terms of the 1884 Convention were being transgressed, provided the *causus belli* that Joseph Chamberlain and Alfred Milner at home, and Cecil Rhodes in South Africa, had been seeking. The Queen was firm: 'I urged that whatever happened, we must not be humiliated in S Africa. We may have to send out a large force and call out the Reserves'.[31]

Troops were sent out from Britain and from India throughout the summer and by the beginning of October there were 70,000 British troops there under Sir Redvers Buller, ostensibly poised to thwart the Boer intention of 'setting up a South African republic consisting of the Transvaal, the Orange Free State and the Cape Colony'. Kruger issued what Chamberlain described as an 'ultimatum' to withdraw all troops that had arrived at the Cape since 1 June and all troops from the Transvaal-Natal border who had landed in order to forestall any Boer attack, and also to call back all ships intending on travelling to South Africa. Kruger required a reply by 5 p.m. on 11 October 1899. No reply would be constituted as a declaration of war. The reply came from Chamberlain: 'the conditions demanded by them [the South African Republic] are such as HM's Government deem it impossible to discuss.'[32]

Kruger's move had been to pre-empt a further build-up of troops and in the short term his tactics seemed to have been successful and British reverses mounted – as did the list of British casualties. Ladysmith, Kimberley and Mafeking were besieged and unease both at the morality and the mismanagement of the war began to be voiced at home. In the speech to be made by the Queen at the close of a session of Parliament at the end of October the phrase 'the splendid qualities of our soldiers' had to be substituted for 'the victories won', since there weren't any, and Sir Redvers became known as 'Sir Reverse'.

The Queen was concerned that the 'increased taxation, necessary to pay the expenses of the war, will not fall on the working classes; but [she] feared that they will be most affected by the extra sixpence on beer'.[33]

Lord Salisbury was dismisssive:

> It is not believed that the tax on beer will fall on the working classes so much as on the brewers. It would, not, however, be safe to lay down as a principle that the working class should bear no part of the cost of the war. It would not be fair on the richer classes, who at the elections are in a small minority. The policy of the country is decided by the working classes, and of course they don't pay income tax ...[34]

The working classes were to be participants in fighting for and paying for, if not always voting for, the great imperial adventure. Meanwhile, the press continued to snipe about the slowness of getting troops to South Africa and their less than successful military activity once they arrived.

So heavy were the losses of men for no advance in the early part of the war that 10 to 15 December 1899 was labelled 'Black Week'. The Queen, however, insisted that at Windsor 'no one is depressed in this house; we are not interested in the possibilities of defeat; they do not exist' and welcomed a fourteen-year-old bugler who had panicked and sounded an advance without orders. Too young to be court-martialled, he became a hero.

By the end of January 1900 Kitchener and Lord Roberts – whose only son was killed in the war – had arrived in the Transvaal to try to wrest the reverses, but Ladysmith, Kimberley and Mafeking were still unrelieved and Spion Kop had been abandoned with 200 dead and 'about 300 wounded, mostly badly'. At home the Queen sent telegrams of exhortation – and congratulations whenever possible – to her commanders in the field. (Colonel Robert Baden-Powell was by now in charge of the besieged troops at Mafeking.) She visited units about to set off to war and toured hospitals and convalescent homes in her wheelchair to talk to the wounded, she 'turned out khaki comforters [monogrammed VRI] as if her bread depended on it', and ordered the dispatch of slabs of chocolate to be given out to the soldiers. 'I like to think I am doing something for my soldiers', Victoria told one of her ladies-in-waiting, 'although it is so little'. She did not wish a repeat of what had happened in the last major war in which British troops had been involved when she 'had … made many things during the Crimea, but they <u>would</u> give them to the officers not at all what I intended'.[35]

In April, wearing a bonnet and clutching a parasol, both embroidered with silver shamrocks, the eighty-year-old Queen paid a rare visit to Ireland, to thank the Irish for their loyal support – and their fighting men – for the Boer War. She stayed for three weeks in Dublin, visiting hospitals, convents, schools, workplaces and the zoo. She 'made many purchases from local industries' and was gratified to believe that 'the Irish loved her'.

Victoria returned home from her exhausting visit on 26 April 1900 and

RIGHT *Colonel Robert Baden-Powell defending the British garrison at Mafeking during the Boer War; the siege, which lasted 217 days, was finally relieved on 19 May 1900. Though the Queen had sent telegrams of 'confidence and admiration' to Baden-Powell, she had not been amused to find out that during the siege, he had had stamps printed with his head replacing hers.*

less than a month later, on 19 May, came the news that Mafeking had been relieved. 'The people are quite mad with delight', the Queen wrote in her journal, 'and London is said to be indescribable'. But in South Africa, though Kruger had fled, many Boers fought on in a guerrilla war and were to be the first-ever victims of 'concentration camps' where disease and death were rife. In May 1902 the Peace of Vereeniging absorbed the Boer republics into the British Empire in return for a promise of self-government, honoured in 1907, and followed by a merger with Cape Colony and Natal in the Union of South Africa in 1910. In Britain, the ever more powerful Empire was balanced by an end to 'splendid isolation' and a search for European allies in the wake of German support for the Boers. And, just like the Crimean War some forty-five years earlier, the military inefficiencies and incompetencies of the Boer War led to army reforms, master-minded by Lord Haldane.

The Queen had not taken part in the Mafeking celebrations; she was eighty-one later that month and increasingly frail. Furthermore she was not sleeping well, her back gave her pain, her appetite was poor and she had been haunted by the deaths in the Boer War: 'she would often break down and cry at the long list of casualties – at least we thought them long in those days' recalled her Private Secretary Frederick Ponsonby.[36] Vicky was mortally ill with cancer of the spine and on 31 July 1900, Affie died of throat cancer. Writing to Vicky on the day of his death she lamented 'it is hard at eighty-one to lose a third grown-up child in the prime of life ...' At the end of October came news of another death, that of Lenchen's son, Christian, who

> had gone through the Indian campaign, Ashanti (where our beloved Liko was taken), the Soudan (going down in his ship), and now again in South Africa, had passed through endless hardships and dangers without being ill, or getting a scratch, just to fall a victim to this horrid fever (malaria), on the eve of his return home: oh! it is really too piteous.[37]

Then on Christmas Eve, Jane Churchill, who had been the Queen's lady-in-waiting for nearly fifty years died of a heart attack. Victoria continued with her constitutional duties, seeing Ministers, attending the Privy Council meetings, and welcoming contingents of troops home from the Boer War, but sometimes her mind wandered and her memory lapsed.

That December she made her usual pilgrimage of remembrance to the mausoleum at Frogmore on 14 December and then left for the Isle of Wight. At Osborne she was largely bedridden – and melancholy, 'because I see so badly' and partook of Christmas dinner alone in her room. But she could still take carriage rides and on New Year's day 1901, accompanied by her son Arthur, she paid a visit to a convalescent hospital to talk to the wounded soldiers. But her health was gradually deteriorating and her physician, Sir James Reid, detected signs of 'cerebral exhaustion', a series of minor strokes.

ABOVE *The Imperial troops at war: a fan celebrating the Boer War victories showing the Queen, with Colonel Robert Baden-Powell and Lord Roberts, with the Union Jack and Royal Standard crossed. The shamrock is represented in recognition of the part that Irish regiments played in the war. In Wolseley's view an initiative from the Queen permitting all Irish regiments to sport a 'national emblem' on St Patrick's Day in future years would have 'a magical effect upon that sentimental and imaginative race' – and might even subsume the nationalist cause in the imperial adventure.*

On 19 January 1901, the *Court Circular* announced that the Queen

> has not lately been in her usual health, and is unable at present to take her customary drives. The Queen during the past year has had a great strain upon her powers, which has rather told upon her Majesty's nervous system. It has, therefore, been thought advisable by her Majesty's physicians that the Queen should … abstain for the present from transacting business.[38]

On 18 January, Victoria's children had been summoned, though Bertie had a dinner engagement he felt he could not miss and travelled to Osborne the next morning. The Emperor of Germany arrived in London with Prince Arthur, who had been visiting Berlin, in the early morning of 20 January and set off for Osborne the next day.

At four o'clock in the afternoon of 22 January 1901, the royal physicians issued a bulletin 'The Queen is slowly sinking'. Two and a half hours later this was followed by another: 'The Queen died peacefully at 6.30'. Reporters in carriages and on bicycles were seen racing for the post office in East Cowes, and men were shouting as they ran, 'The Queen is dead'.

It had been so long – sixty-four years – since a reigning monarch had died, that 'no one was quite sure what the procedure was. We spent the evening looking up what had been done when George IV and William IV had died'.[39] But the Queen had left clear and strict instructions about her funeral and the next morning Bertie, now King Edward VII – since he had 'resolved to be known by the name of Edward, which has been borne by six of my ancestors. In so doing I do not undervalue the name of Albert, which I inherit from my ever-to-be-lamented, great and wise father' – crossed the Solent to attend the Privy Council meeting that would proclaim him King.

The dining room at Osborne was

turned into a mortuary chapel and hung around with curtains and draperies. The coffin was covered with crimson velvet and ermine with the crown in diamonds on a cushion, and the Order of the Garter, which the Queen had worn, was on a raised platform covered by the Royal Standard. The room was lighted by eight huge candles and there were palms round the room in addition to masses of wreaths.[40]

The 60th Rifles had arrived from Parkhurst barracks to mount guard but the 'very strong scent of the tuberoses and gardenias' banked around

BELOW *The Royal Mausoleum at Frogmore, a watercolour by A. Croft. Marble statues of Victoria and Albert, sculpted by Marochetti, lie side by side, the Queen's face is inclined slightly to that of her Prince Consort. The day Albert died, 14 December, was known in the royal household as 'Mausoleum Day'. Victoria not only made an annual pilgrimage to sit by the tomb of Albert; she found the mausoleum a frequent sanctuary. Thirty-six years later, she recorded: 'It gives me a strange feeling to contemplate what is to be our resting place. Oh! could I but be there soon!'*

the coffin was so overpowering that the guards had to be relieved every hour at first. The German Emperor was 'beyond praise ... he kept in the background', and then when all the royal children were assembled he had

> knelt down and supported the Queen with his arm [one arm being withered] ... The Emperor never moved for two and a half hours and remained quite still. His devotion to the Queen quite disarmed all the Royal family.[41]

On 1 February the coffin was placed aboard the royal yacht *Alberta* which sailed majestically through an avenue of towering warships to Portsmouth, where a special train with the blinds drawn conveyed it to Victoria station. The crowds stood silent in the streets and the drum beats rolled as the coffin 'of a soldier's daughter' was drawn in a gun-carriage to Paddington station.

When the gun-carriage was disembarked from the train at Windsor, it was found that the traces linking the horses had snapped. The hill from the station to the Castle was steep and the suggestion that two horses only should pull it seemed 'a most hazardous solution'. So, the horses were uncoupled and using the horse's traces as makeshift ropes, the gun-carriage was pulled by men of the naval guard of honour.

A brief ceremony was held at St George's Chapel and the little bigger than child-sized coffin lay in state there whilst a dress rehearsal was held for the final ceremony. It was just as well for under present plans the Queen would have gone to her resting place feet first and have been laid head to toe with the effigy of her late husband, which 'would never do'.[42]

On Monday 4 February the coffin was piped to the mausoleum at Frogmore where the inscription over the door read '*Vale desideratissime ...*' ('Farewell beloved'). The Queen's remains were laid alongside those of Prince Albert as snow fell softly outside. The marble figure of Victoria, sculpted at the time of her Prince's death, was finally located by the Ministry of Works, who had had it in storage for thirty-nine years, and it was placed alongside Albert's. It looked startlingly young.

'To write the life of Queen Victoria,' declared *The Times* on 23 January,

> is to relate the history of Great Britain during a period of great events, manifold changes and unexampled national prosperity. No reign in the annals of any country can compare with that of the late Sovereign, the throne is never vacant, and at the very moment of parting from our *Queen*, we have to proclaim our *King*.

BELOW '*The Queen is Dead. Long Live the King.*' *His friends were pleased that 'the Prince has succeeded to the throne before he is too old [Bertie was 60] and were confident that 'he will fill the throne admirably'. The Times was less sanguine, recalling that he had been 'importuned by temptation in its most seductive forms', and that he must often have 'prayed "lead us not into temptation" with a feeling akin to hopelessness'. Rudyard Kipling was even harsher, describing Edward VII as 'a corpulent voluptuary of no importance', but in fact his reign, though short, in no sense discredited the crown his mother had so carefully burnished.*

THE SUN, WEDNESDAY JANUARY 23, 1901.

THE QUEEN IS DEAD.
LONG LIVE THE KING'.
THE LAST SAD SCENE OF ALL.
PEACEFUL END OF A GLORIOUS REIGN.

THE QUEEN IS DEAD—LONG LIVE THE KING!

IT IS OUR SAD DUTY TO RECORD THE DEATH OF QUEEN VICTORIA, WHICH TOOK PLACE AT 6.30 p.m. YESTERDAY AT OSBORNE, IN THE BOSOM OF HER SORROWING FAMILY.

Her Gracious Majesty passed away in peace, after hovering between life and death for a period which, brief as it really

some colour seemed to be lent to the reports.

Official announcements on Friday night, however, allayed much anxiety

sad intimation with profound grief, which is shared by the citizens of London, who still pray that

ENDNOTES

Abbreviations
RA - Royal Archive
BE - Benson and Esher
QVJ - Queen Victoria's Journal

Introduction
1. George Buckle, ed., *The Letters of Queen Victoria*, 3rd series, London 1931, vol. III, pp. 124–25. Sir Matthew Ridley to Sir Arthur Bigge, 22 January 1897.
2. Ibid., vol. III, p. 179.
3. Walter Bagehot, *The English Constitution*, London 1867, p. 85.
4. Quoted in Dorothy Thompson, *Queen Victoria: Gender and Power*, London 1990, pp. 135–36.

Chapter One
1. Quoted in Richard Mullen and James Munson, *Victoria: Portrait of a Queen*, London 1987, p. 1.
2. Percy Bysshe Shelley, 'Sonnet in England in 1819', *Poetical Works*, Oxford 1970, pp. 574–75.
3. Baron E. von Stockmar, ed., *The Memoirs of Baron Stockmar*, 2 vols, London 1872, vol. I, p. 50.
4. A. Aspinall, ed., *Letters of Princess Charlotte*, London 1949, p. 31. Letter to Miss Mercer Elphinstone.
5. John Gore, ed., *A Selection of Letters and Papers of Thomas Creevey*, London 1949. The Duke of Wellington to Mr Creevy, 17 July 1818.
6. Gore 1949, pp. 162–64.
7. RA 45340. The Duke of Kent to Baron Mallet, 26 January 1819.
8. RA M2/25. Princess of Leiningen to the Duke of Kent, 25 January 1818.
9. *The Times*, 27 April 1818.
10. Quoted in Stanley Weintraub, *Victoria: Biography of a Queen*, London 1987, pp. 35–36.
11. Peter Quennell, ed., *The Private Letters of Princess Lieven to Prince Metternich 1820–1826*, London 1937, p. 200.
12. Viscount Esher, ed., *The Girlhood of Queen Victoria. A Selection from Her Majesty's Diaries between the Years 1832 and 1840*, 2 vols, London 1912, vol. I, pp. 5–7.
13. A.C. Benson and Viscount Esher, eds., *The Letters of Queen Victoria. A Selection from Her Majesty's Correspondence between the Years 1837 and 1861*, 3 vols, London 1907, vol. I, p. 10.
14. Hansard, 3 July 1820. Quoted in Monica Charlot, *Victoria, the Young Queen*, Oxford 1991, p. 39.
15. BE 1908, vol. I. The Duchess of Clarence to Princess Victoria, May 1821.
16. Ibid., vol. I, ch. II.

17. Ibid.
18. Rev. G. Davys 'Diary' in Marquis of Lorne *V.R.I. Her Life and Empire*, London n.d., pp. 56–62
19. Ibid., vol. I, ch. II.
20. Quoted in Mullen and Munson 1987, p. 11.
21. Ibid.
22. BE 1908, vol. I, ch. II.
23. Quennell 1937, p. 37.
24. BE 1908, vol. I, ch. II.
25. Ibid.
26. Hansard, 15 November 1830.
27. Esher 1912, vol. I, 8 November 1832.
28. Ibid., 1 August 1832.
29. RA MP 115/58. King William IV to Princess Victoria, 22 August 1835. Quoted in Charlot 1991, p. 65.
30. Ibid., RA M5/84. The Duchess of Kent to Princess Victoria, 2 September 1835.
31. RA, QVJ, 3 September 1835.
32. RA Y203/81. Baroness Lehzen to Queen Victoria, 2 December 1867, with Victoria's annotations in the margin. Quoted in Charlot 1991, p. 51.
33. Charles Greville, *The Greville Memoirs*, 8 vols, ed. H. Reeve, London 1875, vol. III, pp. 375–76.
34. Esher 1912, vol. I, p. 190.
35. BE 1908, vol. I. Princess Victoria to the King of the Belgians, 16 June 1837.
36. Ibid. Princess Victoria to the King of the Belgians, 19 June 1837.
37. Esher 1912, vol. I, pp. 195–96.

Chapter Two
1. BE 1908, vol. I. The King of the Belgians to Princess Victoria, 17 June 1837.
2. Esher 1912, vol. I, p. 197.
3. Henry Bulwer-Lytton, *St Stephen's*, London 1865. Quoted in Charlot 1991, p. 98.
4. Charles Greville, *The Greville Memoirs*, 3 vols, 1885, vol. I, pp. 22–23.
5. Ibid., vol. IV, p. 136.
6. RA MP 115/111. 30 June 1837.
7. Greville 1875, vol. IV, p. 416.
8. Ibid.
9. Stockmar 1872, vol. I, p. 373.
10. BE 1908, vol. I. The King of the Belgians to Queen Victoria, 23 June 1837.
11. Stockmar 1872, vol. I, pp. 373–74.
12. BE 1908, vol. I. The King of the Belgians to Queen Victoria, 30 June 1837.
13. Stockmar 1872, vol. I, p. 389.
14. RA M 7/46. The Duchess of Kent to Princess Victoria, 12 June 1837.
15. Greville 1875, vol. IV, p. 389.
16. RA M7/65. The Duchess of Kent to Queen Victoria, undated. Quoted in Charlot 1991, p. 91.

17. Esher 1912, vol. I, p. 211.
18. H. Maxwell, ed., *The Creevey Papers*, London 1903, p. 323.
19. Esher, 1912, p. 236.
20. Ibid., p. 206
21. Vera Watson, *A Queen at Home: An Intimate Account of the Social and Domestic Life of Queen Victoria's Court*, London 1952, p. 18.
22. Esher 1912, vol. I, pp. 356–57.
23. Greville 1875, vol. II, p. 105.
24. Harriet Georgiana, ed., *The Journal of Lady Mary Frampton*. Quoted in Charlot 1991, p. 117.
25. Esher 1912, vol. I, p. 359–60
26. Greville 1885, vol. I, p. 107.
27. RA, QVJ, 28 June 1838.
28. Greville 1885, vol. I, p. 109.
29. Esher 1912, vol. I, p. 363–64.
30. Quoted in Elizabeth Longford, *Victoria V.I.*, London 1964, p. 83.

Chapter Three
1. BE 1908, vol. I. The King of the Belgians to Queen Victoria, 16 January 1838.
2. RA, QVJ, 2 February 1839.
3. RA, Lady Portman's statement, 17 February 1839.
4. Lady Flora's statement, *Morning Post*, 14 September 1839.
5. Ibid.
6. RA, QVJ, 23 February 1839.
7. Greville 1885, vol. I, p. 172.
8. RA, QVJ, 27 June 1839.
9. Greville 1885, vol. IV, p.152.
10. BE 1908, vol. I. Lord Melbourne to Queen Victoria, 7 May 1839.
11. Ibid.
12. Ibid., vol. I, 8 May 1839
13. Ibid.
14. Ibid.
15. Esher 1912, vol. II, p. 180.
16. Charlot 1991, p.143.
17. BE 1908, vol. I, ch. VIII.
18. Ibid., vol. I, 8 May 1839.
19. Greville 1885, vol. I, p. 205, 10 May 1839.
20. BE 1908, vol. I, ch. VIII, Lord Melbourne to Queen Victoria, 9 May 1839.
21. Ibid., Sir Robert Peel to Queen Victoria, 10 May 1839.
22. BE 1908, ch. VIII, Queen Victoria to the King of the Belgians, 14 May 1839.
23. RA L17/58. Sir Arthur Bigge, 30 October 1897. Quoted in Longford 1964, p. 114.
24. Esher 1912, vol. II, p. 187, 27 May 1839.
25. Ibid., vol. II, p. 250.
26. Ibid., vol. II, pp. 189–90.

27. Ibid., vol. II, p. 226.
28. RA Y88/11. Princess Victoria to the King of the Belgians, 17 May 1836.
29. Esher 1912, vol. II, p. 188.
30. Stockmar 1872, vol. I, pp. 363–64.
31. Ibid., pp. 365–67.
32. Stockmar 1872, vol. I, pp. 371–72.
33. Esher 1912, vol. I, pp. 157–58, 18 May 1836.
34. Ibid., pp. 160–61, 10 June 1836.
35. Kurt Jagow, ed., *Letters of the Prince Consort, 1831–61*, London 1938, p. 13. Prince Albert to Duchess Marie of Saxe-Coburg and Gotha, 1 June 1836.
36. Stockmar 1872, vol. I, p. 372.
37. BE 1908, vol. I, Princess Victoria to the King of the Belgians, 7 June 1836.
38. RA LP. Queen Victoria to the King of the Belgians, 24 January 1838.
39. Esher 1912, vol. II, pp. 153–54.
40. BE 1908, vol. I. Queen Victoria to the King of the Belgians, 15 July 1839.
41. Stockmar 1872, vol. II, p. 3.
42. Esher 1912, vol. II, p. 262.
43. Ibid., p. 264.
44. Ibid., p. 265.
45. Ibid., p. 266.
46. Ibid., pp. 268–69.

Chapter Four
1. BE 1908, vol. I, Queen Victoria to Prince Albert, 31 January 1840.
2. Esher 1912, vol. II, p. 275.
3. Ibid., p. 270.
4. Jagow 1938, p. 27. Prince Albert to Queen Victoria, 17 November 1839.
5. BE 1908, vol. I. Queen Victoria to Prince Albert, 23 November 1839.
6. Ibid., Queen Victoria to Prince Albert, 27 November 1839.
7. BE 1908, Queen Victoria to Prince Albert, 17 January 1840.
8. Greville 1875, vol. IV, p. 226.
9. Ibid., pp. 253–54.
10. Ibid., ch. VIII. Queen Victoria to the King of the Belgians, 26 November 1839.
11. Stockmar 1872, vol. II, pp. 33–34.
12. Quoted in Charlot 1991, p. 174.
13. Greville 1875, vol. I, p. 258.
14. BE 1908, vol. I. The King of the Belgians to Queen Victoria, 31 January 1840.
15. Quoted in Thompson 1990, p. 36.
16. Jagow 1938, p. 37. Prince Albert to Queen Victoria, 10 December 1839.
17. Stockmar 1872, vol. II, p. 23.
18. BE 1908, vol. I. Queen Victoria to Prince Albert, 8 December 1839.
19. Jagow 1938, p. 55. Prince Albert to Queen Victoria, 18 December 1839.
20. Stockmar 1872, vol. II, p. 24.
21. RA QVJ, 8 January 1840.
22. Ibid., vol. II, pp. 318–20.
23. Quoted in Cecil Woodham-Smith, *Queen Victoria: Volume I, 1819–1861*, London 1972, p. 204.
24. Esher 1912, vol. II, pp. 320–21.

25. Ibid., p. 321.
25. *The Times*, 11 February 1840.
26. RA QVJ, 10–12 February 1840.
27. BE 1908, vol. I. Queen Victoria to Prince Albert, 8 December 1839.
28. Greville 1885, vol. I, 13 February 1840.
29. Quoted in Thompson 1990, p. 38.
30. Palmerston papers, Broadlands archive. Queen Victoria to Lord Palmerston, 5 June 1856. Quoted in Woodham-Smith 1972, p. 375.
31. Jagow 1938, p. 69.
32. RA Y54/8. Memorandum to Mr Anson, 15 August 1840. Quoted in Charlot 1991, p. 190.
33. BE 1908, vol. I. Memorandum by Mr Anson, detailing minutes of conversations with Lord Melbourne and Baron Stockmar, 28 May 1840.
34. RA LP. Queen Victoria to Marie of Württemberg, 4 June 1840.
35. Hector Bolitho, ed., *The Prince Consort and his Brother*, London 1933, p. 30.
36. Theodore Martin, *The Life of HRH the Prince Consort*, 6 vols, London 1880, vol. II, p. 297.
37. Bolitho 1933, p. 21.
38. Weintraub 1987, p. 145.
39. BE 1908, vol. I. Memorandum by Mr Anson, 15 January 1841.
40. BE 1908, vol. I. Queen Victoria to the King of the Belgians, 15 December 1840.
41. Queen Victoria to the King of the Belgians, Vol. 1, 5 January 1841.
42. Ibid.
43. Stockmar, 1872, vol. II, p. 100.
44. BE, vol. I, ch. IX. Memorandum by Mr Anson, 28 May 1840.
45. The Hon. Mrs Hugh Wyndham, ed., *The Correspondence of Sarah Spencer, Lady Lyttelton, 1787–1870*, p. 326. 3 February 1842. Quoted in Charlot 1991, p. 276.
46. Ibid.
47. BE 1908, vol. I. Queen Victoria to Lord Melbourne, 3 April 1845.
48. RA QVJ, 6 July 1849.
49. Martin 1880, vol. I, pp. 322–23.
50. David Duff, ed., 'Leaves from the Journal of Our Life in the Highlands', *Victoria in the Highlands*, London 1968, pp. 27–29.
51. Ibid., pp. 99–100.
52. Greville 1885, vol. III, pp. 302–303.

Chapter Five
1. BE 1908, vol. II. Queen Victoria to the King of the Belgians, 3 May 1851.
2. Ibid., vol. II. Queen Victoria to the King of the Belgians, 26 March 1850.
3. Hansard, vol. 112, p. 903.
4. Quoted in Robert Rhodes James, *Albert, Prince Consort*, London 1983.
5. BE 1908, vol. II. Queen Victoria to the King of the Belgians, 3 May 1851.
6. Rhodes James, 1983.
7. RA F25/1. Memorandum by Prince

Albert, 10 August 1851. Quoted in Woodham-Smith 1972, pp. 318–19.
8. BE 1908, vol. I. Memorandum by Lord Melbourne to Queen Victoria, 30 August 1841.
9. Martin 1880, vol. I, p. 113. Prince Albert to the Duchess of Kent, 18 June 1841.
10. BE 1908, vol. I. Queen Victoria to the King of the Belgians, 24 August 1841.
11. Ibid., memorandum by Mr Anson, 30 August 1841.
12. Ibid.
13. Greville 1885, vol. I. 6 September 1841.
14. Ibid., 17 September 1841.
15. RA Y54/100. Memorandum by Mr Anson, 26 December 1841.
16. BE 1908, vol. II. Queen Victoria to the King of the Belgians, 3 February 1852.
17. BE 1908, Queen Victoria to Sir Robert Peel, 23 January 1846.
18. Bolitho 1933, p. 82. 11 November 1845.
19. BE 1908, vol. II. Queen Victoria to Sir Robert Peel, 1 July 1846.
20. Ibid., Queen Victoria to the King of Prussia, 6 July 1850.
21. Ibid., Queen Victoria to the King of the Belgians, 9 July 1850.
22. BE 1908, vol. II. Queen Victoria to the King of the Belgians, 17 September 1852.
23. Quoted in Woodham-Smith 1972, p. 99.
24. BE 1908, vol. I. Queen Victoria to the King of the Belgians, 4 September 1843.
25. Ibid., Queen Victoria to the King of the Belgians, 11 June 1844.
26. Palmerston in the House of Commons, 4 February 1845. Quoted in Charlot 1991, pp. 303–304.
27. RA C9/46. Queen Victoria to Lord John Russell, 12 August 1850. Quoted in Woodham-Smith, 1972, p. 302.
28. The Hon. Evelyn Ashley, *The Life of Henry John Temple, Viscount Palmerston, 1846–1865*, 2 vols, 3rd ed, London 1877, vol. I, pp. 211–27.
29. Spencer Walpole, *The Life of Lord John Russell*, 2 vols, London 1889, vol. II, p. 133.
30. Ibid., Queen Victoria to the King of the Belgians, 13 October 1854.
31. RA QVJ, 12 November 1854. Quoted in Charlot 1991, p. 352.
32. Hector Bolitho, ed., *Further Letters of Queen Victoria*, London 1938, p. 51. Queen Victoria to Princess Augusta, 23 October 1854.
33. RA QVJ, 17 April 1855.
34. E.E.P. Tisdall, *Queen Victoria's Private Life*, London 1861, pp. 34–35.
35. RA QVJ., 3 March 1855.
36. BE 1908, vol. III. Queen Victoria to the King of the Belgians, 22 May 1855.
37. Ibid., vol. III. Queen Victoria to the King of Prussia, 17 March 1854.
38. Greville 1885, vol. IV, pp. 283–86.

Chapter Six
1. BE 1908, vol. III. Queen Victoria to the King of the Belgians, 22 September 1855.

2. Bolitho 1938, p. 59. Queen Victoria to Princess Augusta, 14 October 1854.

3. Duff 1968, p. 149.

4. RA QVJ, 29 September 1855.

5. BE 1908, vol. III. Queen Victoria to the King of the Belgians, 9 February 1858.

6. Roger Fulford, ed., *Dearest Child: Private Correspondence of Queen Victoria and the Crown Princess of Prussia*, London 1964, p. 94. 21 April 1858.

7. Egon Caesar, Count Cori, *The English Empress: A Study in the Relations between Queen Victoria and Her Eldest Daughter*, trans. E.M. Hodgson, London 1957, p. 50.

8. RA Z 172/17. General Bruce to Sir Charles Phipps, 14 October 1860. Quoted in Charlot 1991, p. 399.

9. RA Z461/92. Princess Victoria to Queen Victoria and Prince Albert, 26 September 1861. Quoted in Charlot 1991, p. 416.

10. RA Z141/94. Prince Albert to the Prince of Wales, 16 November 1861.

11. BE 1908, vol. III, Lord Palmerston to Queen Victoria, 29 November 1861.

12. Ibid., vol. III, Queen Victoria to the King of the Belgians, 12 December 1861.

13. It has been suggested by Daphne Bennett in *King Without a Crown* (London 1977), Appendix II, p. 381, that the diagnosis of typhoid fever does not appear to fit the facts. However, whilst Dr Jenner may have been slow to diagnose typhoid originally, he was very familiar with the later symptoms of the disease, and was entirely sure that Albert was suffering from typhoid.

14. RA Z140/62 undated. Queen Victoria to Lord Palmerston. Quoted in Charlot 1991, p. 420.

15. RA 172. 14 December 1861.

16. BE 1908, vol. III. Queen Victoria to the King of the Belgians, 20 December 1861.

17. RA Vic. Add Mss. A22/71 and 73. The Duchess of Atholl to Mrs Thomas Biddulph, 19 December 1861. Quoted in Longford 1964, p. 308.

18. Martin 1880, vol. V, p. 325.

19. Quoted in Weintraub 1987, p. 307.

20. RA Y203/78 and Z491. Queen Victoria's Reminiscences, January 1862. Quoted in Woodham-Smith 1987, p. 332.

21. A. L. Kennedy, ed., *Social and Political Letters to the Duchess of Manchester, 1858-1869*, London 1956.

22. Ibid.

23. Roger Fulford, ed., *Dearest Mama: Private Correspondence of Queen Victoria and the Crown Princess of Prussia, 1861-1864*, London 1968, p. 85, 2 July 1862.

24. BE 1908, vol. III.

25. George Earle Buckle, ed., *The Letters of Queen Victoria 1862-1878*, 2 vols, 2nd series, London 1926, vol. II. The Crown Princess of Prussia to Queen Victoria, 18 July 1870.

26. Ibid., Queen Victoria to Earl Granville, 20 July 1870.

27. Ibid., Queen Victoria to the Crown Princess of Prussia, 20 July 1870.

28. Ibid., memorandum by Queen Victoria, 9 September 1870.

29. Ibid., Queen Victoria to Earl Granville, 20 January 1871.

30. John Vincent, ed., *Disraeli, Derby and the Conservative Party: The Political Journals of Edward, Lord Stanley 1849-1869*, Hassocks, Sussex 1978, p. 210. Journal entry, 1 March 1864.

31. Ibid. p. 200

32. Ibid., p. 210.

33. Sidney Lee, *Queen Victoria: A Biography*, London 1902, p. 546.

34. Quoted in E.F. Benson, *An Illustrated Biography*, London 1987, p. 103.

35. Vincent 1978, pp. 198-99.

36. Buckle 1926, vol. II. The Prince of Wales to Queen Victoria, 5 June 1870.

37. Vincent 1978, p. 340.

38. Buckle 1926, vol. II, p. 159.

39. Ibid., vol. II. Queen Victoria to Earl Granville, 19 November 1871.

40. Ibid.

41. The Dean of Windsor and Hector Bolitho, eds, *Letters of Lady Augusta Stanley: A Young Lady at Court, 1849-1863*, London 1927, pp. 37-38.

42. Roger Fulford, ed., *Your Dear Letter: Private Correspondence of Queen Victoria and the Crown Princess of Prussia, 1865-1871*, London 1971, 5 April 1865.

43. Vincent 1978, pp. 247-48.

44. Ibid., p. 232.

45. Roger Fulford, ed., *Beloved Mama: Private Correspondence of Queen Victoria and the German Crown Princess 1878-1885*, London 1981, 4 April 1883.

Chapter Seven

1. Fulford 1971, 29 February 1868.

2. W.F. Monypenny and G.E. Buckle, *The Life of Benjamin Disraeli, Earl of Beaconsfield*, 6 vols., London 1910-20, Vol. III, pp. 290-91.

3. Fulford 1971, 3 March 1868.

4. G.W.E. Russell, *Collections and Recollections*, London 1898, p. 305.

5. Quoted in Sarah Bradford, *Disraeli*, London 1982.

6. Lady Augusta Stanley quoted in Sir H. Maxwell, *Life and Letters of George William Frederick, Fourth Earl of Clarendon*, 2 vols, London 1913.

7. Quoted in Longford 1964, p. 402.

8. Buckle 1926, vol. I, p. 559. Memorandum by General Grey, 4 December 1868.

9. Ibid., vol. II, p. 192. 19 February 1872.

10. Arthur Ponsonby, *Henry Ponsonby, Queen Victoria's Private Secretary: His Life from his Letters*, London 1943, pp. 192-93.

11. Ibid., p. 201-202.

12. Ibid., p. 103.

13. Ibid., pp. 214-17. Earl Spencer to Queen Victoria, 15 June 1872.

14. Roger Fulford, ed., *Darling Child: Private Correspondence of Queen Victoria and the Crown Princess of Prussia, 1871-1878*, London 1976, 13 March 1873.

15. Ibid., 10 February 1874.

16. Ponsonby 1943, p. 245.

17. Ibid., p. 141.

18. Buckle 1926, vol. II, Mr Disraeli to Queen Victoria, 11 January 1876.

19. Ibid., Queen Victoria to Mr Theodore Martin, 14 March 1876.

20. Fulford 1976, 12 September 1876

21. Ibid., p. 282, 15 February 1878.

22. Buckle 1926, vol. II, pp. 625-26. Queen Victoria to the Earl of Beaconsfield, 31 May 1878.

23. Ponsonby 1943, p. 184. Queen Victoria to Sir Henry Ponsonby, 4 April 1880.

24. Ibid., p. 187. Sir Henry Ponsonby to Queen Victoria, 15 April 1880.

25. Ibid. p. 188. Queen Victoria to Sir Henry Ponsonby, 16 April 1880.

26. Buckle 1926, vol. III. Queen Victoria to Sir Henry Ponsonby, 8 April 1880.

27. Ibid., vol. III. Queen Victoria to the Earl of Beaconsfield, 9 January 1881.

28. Ibid., vol. III. The Earl of Beaconsfield to Queen Victoria, 11 January 1881.

29. Ibid., vol. III. Queen Victoria to Earl Granville, 5 June 1880.

30. Quoted in Bradford 1982, pp. 749-50.

31. Buckle 1926., vol. III. Queen Victoria to Earl Granville, 8 August 1880.

32. Ibid., The Duke of Cambridge to Queen Victoria, 20 July 1882.

33. Ibid., QVJ, 13 September 1882.

34. Ibid., Queen Victoria to Mr Gladstone, 30 September 1882.

35. Ibid., Earl Granville to Queen Victoria, 4 January 1884.

36. Ibid., Queen Victoria to Earl Granville, 10 January 1884.

37. Ibid., Earl Granville to Queen Victoria (in cypher), 18 January 1884.

38. Ibid., Queen Victoria to Sir Evelyn Wood, 1 February 1884.

39. Ibid., p. 473, note.

40. Ibid., Queen Victoria to Mr Gladstone, 9 February 1884.

41. Ibid., QVJ, 5 February 1885.

42. Ibid., Mr Gladstone to Queen Victoria, 5 February 1885.

43. Ponsonby 1943, p. 210. Sir Henry Ponsonby to Edward Hamilton, 26 May 1886.

44. Quoted in Longford 1964, p. 489.

45. Ibid., p. 491.

46. George Earle Buckle, ed., *A Selection from Her Majesty's Correspondence and Journal Between the Years 1886-1901*, 3 vols, third series, London 1932, vol. III. Queen Victoria to Lord Salisbury, 27 May 1898.

47. Agatha Ramm, ed., *Beloved and Darling Child: Last Letters between Queen Victoria and her Eldest Daughter, 1886-1901*, Stroud 1990, 31 May 1898.

48. Philip Magnus, *Gladstone*, London 1954, p. 425.

Chapter Eight

1. Buckle 1932, vol. I, pp. 322–26.
2. Quoted in Marlene Eilers, *Queen Victoria's Descendants*, New York 1987.
3. Buckle 1932, vol. I. QVJ, 21 June 1887.
4. Ibid., vol. I, pp. 325–26.
5. Ibid., vol. I, p. 326.
6. Ibid., vol. I, p. 328. QVJ, 22 June 1887.
7. Ibid.
8. Quoted in Weintraub 1987, p. 22.
9. Buckle 1932, vol. I, pp. 328–29. QVJ, 22 June 1887.
10. Ibid., vol. I, p. 333. QVJ, 23 June 1887.
11. RA Victoria Add. Mss. A1/5153. Quoted in Longford 1964, p. 575.
12. Buckle 1932, vol. III, pp. 115–16. The German Emperor to Queen Victoria, 2 January 1897.
13. Ibid., vol. III, pp. 168–69. QVJ, 15 June 1897.
14. Ibid., vol. II, p. 575. QVJ, 17 November 1895.
15. Ibid., vol. II, pp. 575–76.
16. Sir Frederick Ponsonby, *Recollections of*

Three Reigns, London 1951, p. 57.
17. Buckle 1932, vol. III, pp. 392–93. Lord Salisbury to Queen Victoria, 12 August 1899.
18. Ibid., vol. III, p. 25. QVJ, 22 January 1896.
19. Ibid., vol. III, p. 127. Queen Victoria to Sir Arthur Bigge, 30 January 1897.
20. Ibid., vol. III, p. 175.
21. Buckle 1932, vol. III, pp. 165–66. Sir William Baillie-Hamilton (Chief Clerk to the Colonial Office) to Sir Arthur Bigge, 28 May 1897.
22. Buckle 1932, vol. III, QVJ, 22 June 1897.
23. Ibid.
24. Ibid., The Earl of Elgin to Queen Victoria, 22 June 1897.
25. Ibid., Lord Salisbury to Queen Victoria, 22 June 1897.
26. Ibid., The Duke of Argyll to Queen Victoria, 23 June 1897.
27. Ibid., vol. III, pp. 183–84. QVJ, 23 June 1897.
28. *Daily Mail*, 22 June 1897.

29. *The Times*, 22 June 1897.
30. Buckle 1932, vol. III, p. 274. General Kitchener to the Private Secretary, 5 September 1898.
31. Ibid., vol. III, p. 387. QVJ, 18 July 1899.
32. Ibid., vol. III, pp. 404–5. Telegram, Mr Chamberlain to Queen Victoria, 10 October 1899.
33. Ibid., vol. III, p. 409. Queen Victoria to Lord Salisbury, 20 October 1899.
34. Ibid., vol. III, pp. 409–10. Lord Salisbury to Queen Victoria, 21 October 1899.
35. Victor Mallet, ed., *Life with Queen Victoria: Marie Mallet's Letters from Court, 1887–1901*, London 1968, p. 184.
36. Ponsonby 1951, pp. 75–76.
37. Buckle 1932, vol. III, pp. 613–14. QVJ, 29 October 1900.
38. Quoted in Weintraub 1987, p. 634.
39. Ponsonby 1951, p. 83
40. Ibid., p. 84.
41. Ibid., pp. 82–83.
42. Ibid., pp. 91–92.

FURTHER READING

Queen Victoria's letters, journals and memoirs

Letters of Queen Victoria, 9 vols. ed. A.C. Benson and Viscount Esher (1st series) and George Earle Buckle (2nd & 3rd series) (London: John Murray, 1907-1931).

Victoria in the Highlands: The Personal Journal of Her Majesty Queen Victoria, (ed.) David Duff (London: Frederick Muller, 1971).

The Girlhood of Queen Victoria: A Selection from Her Majesty's Diaries Between the Years 1832 and 1840, (2 vols) ed. Viscount Esher (London: John Murray, 1912).

Dearest Child: Private Correspondence of Queen Victoria and the Crown Princess of Prussia, 1858–1861, (ed.) Roger Fulford (London: Evans, 1964).

Dearest Mama: Private Correspondence of Queen Victoria and the Crown Princess of Prussia, 1861–1864, (ed.) Roger Fulford (London, Evans, 1968).

Your Dear Letter: Private Correspondence of Queen Victoria and the Crown Princess of Prussia, 1865–1871, (ed.) Roger Fulford (London: Evans, 1971).

Darling Child: Private Correspondence of Queen Victoria and the German Crown Princess, 1871–1878, (ed.) Roger Fulford (London: Evans, 1976).

Beloved Mama: Private Correspondence of Queen Victoria and the German Crown Princess, 1878–1885, (ed.) Roger Fulford (London: Evans, 1976).

Beloved and Darling Child: Last Letters between Queen Victoria and her Eldest Daughter, 1886–1901, (ed.) Agatha Ramm (Stroud: Alan Sutton, 1990).

Advice to a Grand-daughter: Letters from Queen Victoria to Princess Victoria of Hesse, (ed.) Richard Hough (London: Heinemann, 1973).

Edith Sitwell, *Victoria of England*, (London: Faber and Faber, 1936).

Biographies and studies

Monica Charlot, *Victoria, the Young Queen*, (Oxford: Blackwell, 1991).

Elizabeth Longford, *Victoria R.I.*, (London: Weidenfeld & Nicolson, 1964).

Dorothy Marshall, *The Life and Times of Victoria*, (London: Weidenfeld & Nicolson, 1972).

Theodore Martin, *Life of the Prince Consort*, (6 vols. 7th ed. London: Smith & Elder, 1880).

Richard Mullen and James Munson, Victoria: *Portrait of a Queen*, (London: BBC Books, 1987).

Adrienne Munich, *Queen Victoria's Secrets*, (Columbia University Press, 1996).

Robert Rhodes James *Albert, Prince Consort: A Biography*, (London: Hamish Hamilton, 1983).

Lytton Strachey, *Queen Victoria*, (London: Chatto & Windus, 1921).

Dorothy Thompson, *Queen Victoria: Gender and Power*, (London: Virago, 1990).

E.E.P. Tisdall, *Queen Victoria's Private Life, 1837-1901* (London: Jarrolds, 1861).

Stanley Weintraub, *Victoria: Biography of a Queen*, (London: Unwin Hyman, 1987).

Cecil Woodham-Smith, *Queen Victoria: Her Life and Times. Volume one 1819–1861*, (London: Hamish Hamilton, 1972).

Other diaries, memoirs and collections of letters drawn upon are referenced in the endnotes.

INDEX

A

Aberdeen, Lord 93
Adelaide, Queen (*formerly*, Duchess of Clarence) 12, 15, 20, 23, 36
Afghanistan 127, 128
Albert Edward, Prince of Wales see Edward VII
Albert Memorial 108
Albert, Prince Consort 6, 8, 52-3, 69, 70, 71, 72, 73, 74-5, 76, 77, 84, 85, 86, 87, 88, 89, 91, 92, 93-4, 95, 96, 99
courtship and marriage 55, 59-68; Great Exhibition 79, 80, 81; illness and death 103, 104-7; memorials to 107-8, 109, 140; quarrels with Prince of Wales 102-3
Albert Victor, Prince, Duke of Clarence 110, 135-6
Alexandra, Princess of Wales 102, 109, 110, 111, 113, 115, 135, 144
Alfred, Prince, Duke of Edinburgh 72, 73, 75, 95, 105, 112, 122, 124, 136, 151
Alice, Princess 72, 73, 99, 101, 105, 109, 115, 126
American Civil War 104
Anglo-Boer War 128
Anglo-French alliance 93, 95, 97
Anson, George 64, 65, 68, 70, 85
Anti-Corn Law League 86
Argyll, Duke of 112, 136
Arthur, Prince, Duke of Connaught 6, 72, 75, 112, 129, 136-7, 141, 151, 152
Ashanti Expedition 141-2
assassination attempts 71, 121

B

Baden-Powell, Colonel Robert 150
Bagehot, Walter 8, 114, 115
Balmoral 76-7, 99
Battenberg, Prince Henry of 137, 141-2, 143
Beatrice, Princess 72, 99, 105, 107, 137, 141, 142, 143, 146
Bedchamber Crisis 48-50, 61

Biddulph, Sir Thomas 122
Bigge, Sir Arthur 143
Bismarck, Otto von 110, 125
Boer War 142, 148-51
Brougham, Lord 17, 32, 36, 62
Brown, John 115-17
Buckingham Palace 35, 73
Bulgaria 124, 126
Buller, Sir Redvers 149
Bulwer-Lytton, Henry 30

C

Cambridge, Adolphus, Duke of 12, 13, 52
Canrobert, General 94, 96
Carlyle, Thomas 30, 41
Caroline, Queen 11, 17-18
Castlereagh, Lord 20
Cavendish, Lord Frederick 131
Chamberlain, Joseph 7, 119, 143, 145, 149
Charlotte, Princess 11, 14, 15
Chartism 63-4, 83, 85
Christian, Prince 151
Churchill, Lord Randolph 119, 132
Clarence, Duchess of *see* Adelaide, Queen
Clarence, Duke of *see* William IV
Clarendon, Lord 71, 99, 107-8
Clark, Sir James 44, 76, 105
Clifden, Nellie 102, 103
Congress of Berlin 125, 127
Conroy, Sir John 24, 26, 34, 37, 44
Conservatives 120, 122, 126, 131
Conyngham, Lord 27, 51
Corn Laws 65, 86, 87, 119
Coronation of Queen Victoria 29, 37-41
Creevey, Thomas 14, 35-6
Crimean War 94-5, 96-7
Cruikshank, George 17, 49, 80
Crystal Palace 6, 79, 80, 81, 82
Cumberland, Ernest, Duke of 12, 13, 29, 31, 43, 62

D

Davys, Reverend George 21
Denmark 102, 110

Diamond Jubilee 6-8, 143-8
Dilke, Sir Charles 114, 115
Disraeli, Benjamin 106-7, 109, 117, 119-20, 121, 122, 123, 124, 125, 126, 127, 128
Don Pacifico incident 91
Dreikaiserbund 124

E

Eastern Question 89, 93, 124, 125
Edinburgh, Philip, Duke of 135
Edward, Prince of York (*later*, Edward VIII) 137
Edward VII (*formerly*, Albert Edward, Prince of Wales) 72, 73, 75, 82, 85, 95, 97, 101-3, 105, 108-9, 111, 112-13, 115, 116, 120-1, 124, 129, 135, 137, 144, 146, 147, 152, 153
Egypt 128-9, 130
Elizabeth II, Queen 8-9, 135
Ernest, Prince 52, 53, 54, 56, 57
Esher, Viscount 18-19
Eugénie, Empress 96, 97, 111

F

Fenton, Roger 96
Feodora, Princess 15, 21, 23, 24, 35
France 89-90
Franco-Prussian War 110
Frederick William, Emperor 99, 100, 101, 136, 141
Free Trade 83, 86, 87, 119

G

George III, King 11, 17, 34, 35
George IV, King (*formerly*, Prince Regent) 11, 12, 13, 16, 17, 17-18, 19, 23, 35, 39
George V, King 8, 136, 137
Germany 124, 125, 142-3
Gladstone, William 111, 113, 114-15, 119, 120, 121, 122, 124-5, 126-7, 128, 129, 131, 132-3, 138
Golden Jubilee 6, 7, 135-40, 144
Gordon, General 130, 131, 148
Granville, Earl 110
Great Exhibition 79-82, 99

Greville, Charles 15, 30-1, 34, 38, 40-1, 61, 63, 65, 67-8, 76-7, 85

H

Hastings, Lady Flora 44, 45, 49
Haynau, General 92
Helena, Princess 72, 105, 112, 136
Home Rule 121, 131-3

I

India 122, 123, 125, 141
Ireland 86-7, 121-2, 131, 150, 151

J

Jamaica Bill 46-7
Jenner, Dr William 105, 115-16

K

Karim, Abdul 140-1
Kensington Palace 11, 19, 26, 35
Kent, Edward, Duke of 11, 12, 13-14, 15-16, 17, 37
Kent, Victoire, Duchess of 11, 14, 15, 16, 19, 20, 21-2, 23, 24, 25-6, 33-4, 37, 45, 51, 70, 103, 105, 106
Kipling, Rudyard 153
Kitchener, General 148, 150
Kossuth, Louis 92, 93
Kruger, Stephanus 142, 149, 151

L

Lehzen, Fraülein 20, 21, 26, 32, 34, 36, 40, 72
Leopold, King of the Belgians 9, 11, 12, 17, 20, 29, 32-3, 35, 43-4, 50, 52, 53, 54, 55, 61, 62, 63, 64, 68, 71, 84, 90, 100, 101, 103, 105
Leopold, Prince 72, 75, 135
Liberals 120, 122, 131
Louis Philippe, King 89-90, 91
Louise, Princess 72, 105, 112, 115, 136
Lyttleton, Lady 72-3

M

Maud, Princess 136
Melbourne, Lord 29-31, 33, 34, 35, 36, 39, 41, 43, 44-5, 46-7, 48, 49, 50, 51, 52, 55, 56, 57, 60, 61, 62, 63, 64, 66, 67, 69, 70, 72, 74, 83, 84-5, 88
Mountbatten, Lord Louis 135

N

Napoleon III, Emperor 93, 94, 95, 110
Nicholas I, Tsar 52, 73, 90, 91, 93
Nicholas II, Tsar 52, 73, 135
Nightingale, Florence 66-7, 95, 112

O

official titles of Queen Victoria 7, 122-3
Osborne House 73-5
Ottoman Empire 89, 90
Oxford, Edward 71
Oxford Movement 60-1

P

Palmerston, Lord 36, 89, 90, 91, 92-3, 95, 99, 104, 105, 108, 109, 110
Paxton, Joseph 79, 80
Peel, Sir Robert 31, 32, 36, 47, 48-50, 61, 83, 84-5, 86, 87, 88, 119
Ponsonby, Frederick 142, 151
Ponsonby, Sir Henry 116, 120-1, 122, 126, 132
Poor Law Amendment Act 63
Proclamation of the Sovereign 29, 30, 31
Prussia 97, 100, 102, 110
Public Worship Bill 122

R

Reform Acts 25, 29, 120, 132
Reid, Sir James 151
republicanism 113-14, 116
Ridley, Sir Matthew 6-7
Roebuck, J.A. 95
royal household 36-7
Royal Mausoleum, Frogmore 108, 109, 151, 152, 153
royal prerogative 62, 84, 112
Royal Titles Bill 122-3
Russell, Lord John 62-3, 86, 91, 93
Russell, W.H. 94-5
Russia 93, 94, 97, 124, 125

S

Salisbury, Lord 8, 120, 131, 132, 133, 139, 143, 144, 146, 149
Schleswig-Holstein 91, 102, 109-10
Scotland 75-7
Shaw, George Bernard 139
Shelley, Percy Bysshe 11, 17, 18

Sibthorp, Colonel 63
Siebold, Frau 16, 52
Sinope, Massacre of 93
slavery 46, 70
Sophia, Princess 19
Sophie, Princess 136
South Africa 128, 142, 148-50, 151
Stanley, Lord 113, 116-17, 120
Stockmar, Baron 12, 17, 32, 33, 53, 54, 72, 85, 102
Sudan 130-1, 148
Suez Canal 123, 124, 125
Sullivan, Sir Arthur 9, 144
Sussex, Augustus Frederick, Duke of 13, 19, 29, 31

T

Tennyson, Alfred, Lord 107, 117
Tories 8, 48, 61, 84
see also Conservatives
Turkey 93, 94, 124, 125, 126

V

Victoria (Vicky), Princess Royal 70-1, 72, 73, 99-101, 102, 105, 110, 17, 119-20, 129, 133, 136, 138, 144, 151
Victoria and Albert Museum 82

W

Wellington, Arthur Wellesley, Duke of 6, 11, 13, 24, 31-2, 36, 40, 47, 48, 61, 62, 66, 70, 80, 88-9
Wharncliffe, Lady 22-3
Whigs 8, 46, 83, 84
William, Emperor 101, 109, 136, 141, 142, 143, 152, 153
William IV, King (formerly, Duke of Clarence) 12, 14, 15, 16, 17, 23, 24, 25, 26, 27, 35, 37, 40, 52, 106
Windsor Castle 17, 22, 27, 59, 67, 73, 100, 106, 123, 129

Y

York, Frederick, Duke of 12
Young England movement 119

ACKNOWLEDGEMENTS

AUTHOR'S ACKNOWLEDGEMENTS

I would like to thank the Royal Collection and the Royal Archive at Windsor Castle; the staff at the British Library and the London Library; Frank Prochaska for reading and commenting on the text; Stella Tillyard and John Brewer for their most generous hospitality; Janet Crowhurst for visits to Osborne. Philippa Lewis who did all the picture research; and Katie Bent, Helen Collins and Suzi Hedgecoe at Collins & Brown who were patient, encouraging and resourceful.

PUBLISHER'S ACKNOWLEDGEMENTS

The publisher would like to thank Emma Shackleton, Susan Martineau, Marie Lorimer and Debbie Marshall for their invaluable contributions, and the staff at Windsor Castle for their help.

The republication of material from the Royal Archives is granted by the gracious permission of Her Majesty The Queen.